Why Are Professors Liberal
and Why Do Conservatives Care?

Why Are
Professors Liberal

and
Why Do
Conservatives Care?

Neil Gross

HARVARD UNIVERSITY PRESS
Cambridge, Massachusetts
London, England
2013

Library of Congress Cataloging-in-Publication Data

Gross, Neil, 1971–
    Why are professors liberal and why do conservatives care? / Neil Gross.
        p.   cm.
    Includes bibliographical references and index.
    ISBN 978-0-674-05909-2 (hardcover : alk. paper)
    1. College teachers—United States—Political activity.
    2. Liberalism—United States.   I. Title.

    LB2331.72.G76   2013
    378.1'2—dc23   2012031469

Contents

Introduction

When one of my research assistants interviewed her back in 2007, Lorena, then thirty-five, was an assistant professor in a department of sociology at a college in the South.[1] A specialist in economic development who focuses on Latin America, Lorena told us that her research interests stem in part from her political commitments. She grew up in California, in an upper-middle-class Mexican American family. Although her mother, a school counselor, was more politically progressive than her father, an attorney, she recalled that in her "bilingual, bicultural household . . . issues of tolerance and justice were . . . big." In the 1980s, when she was in high school, Lorena underwent what she described as an "awakening experience." This, she noted, "was a time when there was so much conflict in Central America." Predisposed anyway to a liberal point of view, she soon came to realize "the role of the United States" in the region and how much better off people there would be if the U.S. government stopped trying to counter leftist insurgencies and prop up autocrats. A year abroad in Scandinavia convinced her that U.S. domestic policies were equally askew, tilted in favor of the rich. After college, she decided to undertake graduate work because she wanted to understand how and why American political power had come to be wielded to such ill effect.

Six years after completing her PhD, Lorena's political commitments had not wavered. Asked to describe her politics, she called herself "a liberal or a progressive," which, she said, means that she tends to "prioritize things like social, political, and economic justice." She told us that she supports redistributionist economic policies, such as steeply progressive tax rates; favors affirmative action for minorities in hiring and educational admissions; is committed to feminist ideals; and believes ardently in the need for immigration reform. She opposed the war in Iraq, then in its fourth year. Like many progressives, Lorena has mixed feelings about the Democratic Party. Still, she always votes Democratic. And she does more than vote. She belongs to "a progressive faculty group on campus," is active in community organizations on immigration issues, and is engaged politically through her research and teaching. Although she recognizes that social science and activism are different, and feels that no scholar should be indoctrinating students, she believes that in the final analysis all "knowledge is inherently political and subjective." Therefore, she told us, she allows her commitment to social justice to figure in her academic writing and lecturing. Her goal is to encourage students to be "more aware and active citizens" and to question social and political orthodoxies.

For many on the left, Lorena would seem to embody academic virtue. At a time when American colleges and universities are falling over themselves to lure students, tuition dollars, and corporate donors, remaking higher education so that courses can be offered on such heady and important subjects as fashion merchandising and video game programming, professors like Lorena might appear to be valiant figures, old-school intellectuals who push students to think critically and in their own writing speak truth to power. Yes, leftists would concede, it is important that researchers not subordinate scholarship to politics. But at a moment in history when not just the university but the media too have been massively corporatized, and with the conservative movement energized by opposition to President Barack Obama, is it not a good thing that Lorena and other professors like her are plying their trade, offering readers of academic works as well as students some critical counterweight to the usual insidious conservative fare? That Lorena is Hispanic and a woman might, from this perspective, make her even more virtuous. What a testament to the powerful ideal of social justice that a member of a minority group long excluded from the academic ranks would now use her position, a product of decades of collective struggle, to advocate for the rights of others.

So far, Lorena has flown under the radar of conservative activists and commentators like David Horowitz and Glenn Beck, who are much concerned with the politics of American professors. With more controversial figures to take on, such as former University of Colorado ethnic studies professor Ward Churchill and retired City University of New York sociologist Frances Fox Piven, conservative critics have had less to say about individual run-of-the-mill progressive or liberal academics. But it is not hard to imagine that a Horowitz or Beck would feel his blood boil on hearing Lorena describe her work. We all have our biases, a critic might admit. But in what universe is it acceptable for tax dollars to support research that is so unequivocally partisan? How does writing on Latin American development from the perspective of "social justice" even count as research? Furthermore, though Lorena may think she is not practicing indoctrination, is that not what she is doing, really? Stick an impressionable twenty-year-old in a classroom for fifteen weeks with a charismatic instructor who makes the case that conservatives are heartless or deluded and that the United States has evil designs, and the student is likely to veer left. While Lorena and her ilk may not pose the same threat to the country as radicals like Churchill or Piven, the fact that she is a typical figure in academe means there is something rotten with American higher education: it has become a bastion of liberal groupthink that squanders manpower on irrelevant research and fails to provide students with the education they need to make their way as proud American citizens in a complex, dangerous world.

This book is about professors more or less like Lorena and the conservatives who are angry at them. In one sense, anyway, conservative critics are right: Lorena *is* a typical figure, not demographically (there are few Hispanic female professors) but politically. Liberals, progressives, and those otherwise on the left are remarkably common in the American professoriate. In fact, academe contains a larger proportion of people who describe themselves as liberal than just about any other major occupation.[2] To be sure, many academic liberals work in fields like biology and chemistry, where there is not much room for their politics to affect either their teaching or their research. But in the social sciences and humanities, where the lines can more easily blur, there are plenty of Lorenas.

There is also no shortage of conservative critics. Horowitz and Beck may be two of the most visible current opponents of the liberal professoriate, yet standing behind them are dozens of advocacy organizations and scores of conservative commentators and reporters churning out a steady stream of op-eds, articles, books, blog posts, reports, and sound bites that characterize higher education as in a time of crisis owing to the pernicious influence of the academic left.[3] These complaints echo such classics of the culture wars as Allan Bloom's *The Closing of the American Mind* (1987), Roger Kimball's *Tenured Radicals* (1990), and Dinesh D'Souza's

Illiberal Education (1991).[4] Some Americans appear to be listening. Although confidence in colleges and universities remains relatively high, research shows that more than a third of the public believes political "bias" in higher education to be a "very serious" problem.[5] As Republican lawmakers in state after state put higher education budgets on the chopping block, it is hard not to believe that some are relishing the opportunity offered by the recent economic downturn to make sure that liberal academics get their comeuppance.[6]

But why do professors tend to be liberal? And what, besides opportunism, explains why conservatives are so eager to go after them? Much has been written on these questions by advocates, journalists, and scholars. Seven years of intensive social scientific research, however, have led me to believe that the most common explanations for "professorial liberalism" and the conservative uproar about it are either wrong or incomplete. This book explores both phenomena and attempts to provide a more satisfactory account. In doing so, it sheds new light not only on higher education but also on American society and politics more generally.

✦

Liberal professors and conservative critics of the academy do not agree on much. But you would think they could at least agree on the factual proposition that professors tend to sit on the left side of the political aisle. Our interviews with professors like Lorena, though, reveal that many dispute this basic point.[7] Probing faculty views of the liberal bias question, we asked Rick, a fifty-three-year-old associate professor of literature who also describes himself as a progressive, why there are not many conservatives in higher education. Rick was quick to correct us. Professors do often vote Democratic, he acknowledged. But he insisted that "the Democratic Party is quite conservative and . . . not left wing." "All you'd have to do to confirm that is look to Canada or any Northern European country," he explained. For example, he said, "you've got a lot of Democrats in this country who are not comfortable with the idea of same-sex marriage." He added, "I bet that if you check out [academic] administrators a lot of them are voting Republican."[8] And what about economists, engineers, and business professors? Factor all of them into your equation, Rick told us, and the university is going to start looking like a much less liberal place.

This line of thought is not illogical. It is true that by the measures political scientists use, the Democratic Party is to the right of left parties in many other nations.[9] And there are indeed pronounced differences in faculty political views across disciplines. Any adequate explanation of professorial politics has to account for this, but more relevant here is that some of the most conservative fields, such as business and the health sciences, have seen major gains in student enrollment in recent decades and, as a result, in faculty numbers. Business is now the most popular undergraduate major, and business professors make up 8% of the faculty.[10] Surely these changes push against whatever liberalism may be found elsewhere in the academy.

But people who advance this argument act a little like an ostrich with its head in the sand. Survey research shows that 51% of professors are Democrats, as compared to 35% of the voting-age American public.[11] Among Independents, who compose a third of the faculty, those leaning Democratic outnumber those leaning Republican by more than 2 to 1. That leaves the Republican Party only a 14% solid share of the professorial population, meaning that the professoriate is less than half as Republican as the country as a whole. True, you are not going to find many hammer-and-sickle flags at Democratic Party rallies. But professors are not just garden-variety Democrats; many are extremely liberal Democrats. Six out of ten Democratic professors would use the term *progressive* to describe themselves, and on a range of matters, from equalizing wealth to the death penalty, environmental protection to combating terrorism, most hold views that place them squarely to the left of most other Democrats nationally.[12] And these numbers take into account recent changes in the disciplinary makeup of the professoriate. By my calculations, between 50% and 60% of professors today can reasonably be described as leftist or liberal, at a time when only 17% of Americans fall into that category.[13] And while professors on the far left are often keen to distinguish themselves from their merely liberal peers, the fact is that a great many in the left/liberal camp would fit quite well in Canada's genuinely leftist New Democratic Party or among the Social Democrats in Sweden.

While some on the left are prone to denying that professors are a liberal lot, many on the right exhibit the opposite tendency: exaggerating professorial liberalism. This takes several forms. Some conservative social scientists, producing research on the academy that, like its counterpart on the left, involves as much advocacy as scholarship, have used questionable methodologies to suggest that nearly 75% of American professors are leftists or that the professoriate is growing vastly more liberal over time.[14] Still others write about the university as if it were an undifferentiated place politically, with professors of all disciplinary stripes marching in political lockstep.[15] Then there are over-the-top commentators like Ann Coulter, who depict academia as a breeding ground for radicalism. Writing about William Ayers, the controversial professor of education at the University of Illinois–Chicago who, in the 1960s, was one of the founders of the radical organization Weather Underground, which orchestrated a series of bombings to protest the Vietnam War and in support of an overthrow of the capitalist order, Coulter observed, "Ayers is such an imbecile, we ought to be amazed that he's teaching at a university . . . except all former violent radicals end up teaching. Roughly 80% of former Weathermen are full college professors—99% if you don't include the ones killed in shoot-outs with the police or in prison—i.e., not yet pardoned by a Democratic president. Any other profession would have banned a person like Ayers. Universities not only accept former domestic terrorists, but also move them to the front of the line."[16]

These claims are wrongheaded, too. For one thing, while conservative professors are a rarity, there are a significant number of academics on the center left or who have even more moderate views.[17] Half are Independents, although they do typically vote Democratic. Particularly when it comes to economic matters, however, center-left and moderate academics are quite different from their more progressive colleagues. To the extent that views of the economy affect professors' research, teaching, and public service work—which, again, may be more the case in some fields than in others—these are differences that matter.

On the question of change over time, academia *is* more liberal today than in the 1960s, but not dramatically so. And conservative commentators downplay the fact that professors my age, in their late thirties and early forties, are *less* likely than their predecessors to consider themselves radicals and are often critical of what they perceive to be the excesses of the 1960s-era academic left. Do professors in all disciplines agree politically? The answer is no. Invite some anthropologists and professors of engineering to lunch at the faculty club to talk politics and see what happens. As for Coulter's charge, it is hard to know whether to respond seriously or laugh. What the data here show are that self-identified radicals make up about 8% of the professoriate and are concentrated in a select number of social science and humanities fields.[18] Nearly all abhor violence.

*

If partisans cannot be trusted to offer accurate depictions of professors' politics, neither can they be relied on to explain why professors have the views they do. On the left, among those willing to acknowledge that the academic profession is more liberal than conservative, two explanations dominate. The first holds that liberals are smarter than conservatives. Is it therefore surprising that academia, which selects for smart people, contains a disproportionate number of progressives? If you want proof that liberals are smarter, this way of thinking goes, just compare President Obama to President George W. Bush and draw some inferences about the mental ability of the people who voted for each. Smart people gravitate toward the left, liberals like to assert, because a little clear thinking is enough to show just how foolish most conservative ideas are. The second argument concerns values. What do liberals value? Social justice and truth. What do conservatives value? Preserving their distorted vision of the American way of life and making money. So who is more likely to go into academia, where the quest for truth reigns supreme and salaries are lower than in the world of business?

On the right, a different argument is made, one that is equally self-serving. Many conservatives would like to get academic jobs, claim critics of the academy. They just cannot. Why? Because over time liberals have taken over higher education and refuse to hire people with dissenting views. Political bias and outright discrimination keep conservatives out of the academic fold.

None of these arguments holds much water. There is a statistical association between verbal intelligence and political liberalism.[19] But it is not as strong an association as liberals would like to believe, and quantitative research I will report shows that the higher than average cognitive ability of professors accounts for little of their liberal orientation. As for values, some of the liberal stereotypes are wrong: surveys find only minor differences between liberals and conservatives in the importance they place on making money.[20] In terms of a commitment to science and truth, it is correct, as surveys also show, that conservatives have less confidence in science than do liberals.[21] The primary reason is that about half of political conservatives in the United States are theologically conservative Protestants, many of whom are biblical literalists who do not believe in evolution.[22] A secondary reason is that many religious and secular conservatives—and among them, white men in particular—are skeptical about the science of climate change.[23] These facts should not be downplayed, but in other respects liberals and conservatives are fairly similar in their knowledge of and appreciation for science.[24] Views of evolution and global warming undoubtedly keep conservatives from flocking to fields like evolutionary biology and climatology, but there is no evidence that most conservatives have an intrinsically antiscientific worldview—and in any event this could not explain why conservatives are more underrepresented in the humanities than in the natural sciences.[25] On the bias and discrimination claim made by the right, while some liberal academics can be hostile to theories, methods, and ideas that they believe to be conservative in nature, a controversial experiment I conducted, which I will also describe in detail, suggests that in academia there is less discrimination against conservative scholars than critics charge.

It is not only partisans who have taken up the question of why professors tend to be liberal. Sociologists, for their part, have long been interested in explaining the left-leaning, democratic tendencies of academics and other intellectuals, including writers and journalists.[26] In recent years, the leading theoretical approach, associated with French sociologist Pierre Bourdieu, has argued that intellectuals' politics stem from their distinctive position in the class structure: intellectuals have only moderate levels of economic success, but their education and experience leave them in possession of a great deal of socially valued cultural knowledge and taste.[27] Ostensibly, this inclines them to the left for two reasons. First, the only way a group with more cultural than economic capital could acquire greater power and authority in society would be by convincing people that knowledge is more important than money. This means it is in the interests of intellectuals to attack the business class whenever possible, and what better way to do this than to be out front in supporting a program of economic redistribution and regulation?[28] Second, intellectuals have material interests: they would like to be paid more and have more financial support for their work. It is therefore natural that intellectuals would want to grow the state so that more money could be put into higher education budgets, research, funding for the arts, and so on—a liberal agenda.

Bourdieu's theory has much to commend it, but it does not suffice as an explanation. Americans who are better educated than they are paid do tend to be more liberal, but research shows that this explains only a modest share of the liberalism of professors.[29] What is more, evidence I will present indicates that most liberal professors formed their political views in the main well before they became academics—before they even developed the aspiration to step behind the lectern. To the extent that this is so, their politics are not really traceable to their social or economic interests as intellectuals. Nor can professorial liberalism be accounted for by focusing on the class backgrounds from which academics hail.

What, then, explains why professors are more liberal than other Americans? While cognitive ability, values, and factors related to social class have *some* role to play—alongside education and personality, as discussed in Chapter 2—my research suggests a more important factor is self-selection based on the political reputation of the academic profession. Professors are not just liberal in fact; they are also liberal in our stereotypes about them, and have been for a long time. Academic characters do not make frequent enough appearances in film or television for their portrayals to serve as reliable indicators of cultural views, but for the sake of illustration, think about some recent depictions: Jeff Daniels as novelist and literature professor Bernard Berkman in *The Squid and the Whale*; Mark Ruffalo and Peter Krause, also playing English professors, in *We Don't Live Here Anymore*; Janeane Garofalo as real-life women's studies professor (and then Democratic politician) Catherine Connolly in *The Laramie Project*; Maggie Gyllenhaal as the farcical, breastfeeding-obsessed professor LN in *Away We Go*; Dallas Roberts as math professor Owen Cavanaugh on the CBS drama *The Good Wife*. What do these characters have in common? Many are damaged goods psychologically, with inflated egos and philandering ways. Beyond that, they are also libertines, with several openly espousing leftist views to go along with their free-thinking lifestyles. Public opinion polls show that many Americans buy into the image of professors as a liberal, unconventional bunch.[30] This reputation itself has to be explained; I argue that it is not simply a reflection of the actual political views of professors but also a product of the historical circumstances in which the modern American academic profession was born and its subsequent history. Regardless, in terms of the day-to-day recruitment of academic personnel, the reputation has a significant effect: because of it—and also because of the left-supportive climate on many campuses—smart, liberal college students are apt to see becoming a professor as something that could fit perfectly well with their political identity, while smart, conservative students are inclined to think, "That's not for me," if the thought of an academic career crosses their minds at all. The parallel is with gender and occupational choice. Many women, but few men, go into nursing, for example, and this is mostly because nursing is perceived as a female occupation. In the same way, academic work is seen as a liberal pursuit, and this tends to pull liberals in and steer conservatives away, such that liberals are more inclined to go to graduate school and set their sights on academic jobs. A major goal of this book is to make a case that self-selection based on occupational reputation is the key to explaining professors' politics. But the argument could also have implications beyond the academy, with reputation-based political self-selection, and the occupational histories underlying it, helping to explain why not just professors but also journalists and social workers and artists, say, tend to be on the left, and why business executives, members of the clergy, military officers, law enforcement personnel, and engineers are often on the right.

✦

Since popular explanations for the liberalism of professors come up short, it is no shock that common accounts of conservative outrage do as well. On the left, the usual explanation for why conservatives are up in arms about liberal bias in higher education involves some combination of the following: conservative activists recognize that the academy is one of the few remaining strongholds of liberal belief, and they are going after it because they want to strike the final blow to the American left as they continue the march through the institutions that they began in the 1970s; this is a well-planned exercise, supported by the Republican Party and with massive funding from conservative philanthropies; conservatives are anti-intellectual and authoritarian, despising science and rational inquiry, and want to do whatever they can to snuff out real scholarship or any hint of dissent; conservative intolerance, for radical academics or anyone else, rises when the country is perceived to be under threat, as in the post-9/11 period. On the right, the story is more straightforward: in challenging professors whose views are out of step with the rest of the population, conservatives are not just taking on misguided thinkers; they are standing up to what amounts to corruption in higher education and upholding high professional standards for academic work.

Little social scientific research has been conducted on this topic, but a common view of the American conservative movement among sociologists fits with the more popular liberal narrative:

the movement is often seen as a carefully coordinated effort, spearheaded by a coalition of economic and religious elites, to counter progressive changes in American society since the 1960s.[31] From this point of view, taking aim at liberal professors who might influence students and shape the policy debate is just one component of a larger conservative plan for amassing power.

Again, none of these interpretations is entirely accurate. The best way to think about the contemporary American conservative movement is to see it as comprising a wide variety of groups and organizations, each representing a different constituency, each vying for a specific set of social and/or policy changes and for clout within the Republican Party. Sometimes the activities of these groups are well coordinated, but often they are not. Sometimes they represent reactions against changes initiated by the left, but just as often they involve clamoring for unprecedented reforms. To ask why there is sustained advocacy around an issue such as liberal bias in higher education is really to ask how and why the groups that have been pushing that issue have managed to position themselves favorably in the complex political ecology that is the movement, where they have to compete with other groups for scarce resources such as funding from donors, media attention, and influence with politicians.

In the case of the individuals and organizations fighting liberal dominance in academia, my research suggests they have been able to carve out a stable niche for themselves not simply because *some* conservative power players are invested in waging a war of ideas with the academic left but for a more subtle sociological reason as well: critics of the academy serve a rhetorical purpose for conservatism. In taking on liberal professors, they provide ammunition for a larger and ultimately far more important battle against "liberal elites." This battle has been crucial for the success of conservatism in the post–World War II era. During this time, conservative activists and politicians succeeded in attracting voters to the Republican Party and in pushing the GOP to the right partly by fashioning conservatism as a populist ideology—as a revolt of ordinary, God-fearing Americans fed up with wasteful and misguided spending by a bloated bureaucratic state. But populism, by its nature, requires a bashing of elites—some group with power said to be lording it over "the people"—and this has always presented a dilemma for conservatives, since conservatism, at least in its economic tenets, is congruent with the interests of the rich and often has their backing. The solution, advanced by the only sometimes populist William F. Buckley Jr. and others in his influential midcentury circle of conservative intellectuals and journalists, was to create a strong collective identity for modern American conservatism in some measure around the disparagement of liberal cultural elites and those in government said to be haughtily pushing the country in directions it did not wish to go. Criticism of the liberal professoriate was and remains a vital component of this effort, and commentators and organizations engaged in such criticism have usually been able to acquire sufficient resources to prosper. A side benefit is that in casting aspersions on liberal academics, conservatives have been able to bolster the authority of the many nonacademic intellectuals on whom the movement relies, especially those working in think tanks, who have been important in securing the movement's many electoral, legislative, judicial, and administrative gains. So far as I have been able to discover, there has never been a conspiratorial grand plan by the right to attack left-leaning professors in order to boost its populist credibility, and few conservative activists have understood their work in these terms. Nevertheless, the conservative movement lends support to such efforts. The second goal of my book is to argue for this set of causal claims.

✷

To advance these arguments, I draw on a considerable amount of research. I first became interested in the topic of professors and their politics in 2005. At that time I was an assistant professor at Harvard, watching in astonishment as the politics-laced controversy around then Harvard president Lawrence Summers—pilloried by liberals within the university for his comments on women and science, martyred by conservatives without—unfolded around me. This was the same period when David Horowitz's campaign for an "Academic Bill of Rights," designed to protect students against political indoctrination, was gaining momentum—to the surprise of those sociologists who assumed that nearly everyone in the United States saw colleges and universities as highly "legitimate" institutions and professors as beyond reproach.[32] It seemed to me, as I began reading the academic literature to gain a better understanding of these significant intrusions of politics into the life of the mind, that while theories and opinions about professorial politics abounded, rigorous studies were rare. So, with the help of a number of collaborators and research assistants, I set out to gather the data needed to answer the two questions that were piquing my interest: Why are professors liberal? and Why do conservatives care?

The first study I undertook, with sociologist Solon Simmons of George Mason University, was a public opinion survey. Conservative critics of the academy were in the midst of a major drive, but was anyone other than academics and journalists paying attention?

We posed questions about liberal bias in higher education to a representative sample of a thousand American adults.

With the opinion data in hand, Simmons and I thought the time was right to conduct a survey of professors to assess not simply whether they were feeling the heat from conservative efforts but what in fact their politics were. Was the professoriate really as liberal as conservatives were claiming? We randomly sampled more than 1,400 academics in all types of institutions—from community colleges to elite research universities—and in nearly all fields, asking questions about their social and political views.

Large-scale survey data are extremely important in social science, but they cannot provide the descriptive richness—access to the details and nuances of people's life experiences and ways of thinking—that more qualitative forms of inquiry can. After completing the two surveys, I therefore went back into the field to conduct more free-form interviews. To get a sense of why, beyond the simple fact of partisanship, many conservatives in the general public are worried about political bias in the academy while most liberals are not—one of the findings from the opinion poll—I commissioned interviews with sixty-nine residents of two states, Colorado and Wisconsin, that had seen major controversy around the issue (Colorado because of Ward Churchill; Wisconsin because of historical tensions between Madison and the rest of the state and because there had been a flap about a 9/11 denier, Kevin Barrett, who taught a course in UW's African Languages and Literature Department). My research assistants and I also conducted follow-up interviews with fifty-seven academics who had taken part in the professors survey, including Lorena and Rick. Focusing on scholars in a politically diverse array of departments—sociology, economics, literature, biology, and engineering—we explored more deeply than was possible in the survey their understanding of such terms as *liberal* and *conservative*, when and how their political views had formed, and their thoughts on the proper relationship between politics, teaching, and research.

These studies were enlightening but did not go very far in revealing the *causes* of professorial liberalism. To move forward in that direction, I needed data that would let me examine side by side the social characteristics of professors and people working outside of academe—for example, their respective ratios of cultural to economic capital—to determine how much of the political gap between the two groups was a function of factors flagged by different theories. Working with a Harvard graduate student, Ethan Fosse, I discovered that the General Social Survey (GSS), a survey of Americans carried out regularly since the early 1970s, had sampled over the course of its history 326 academics (alongside 43,703 nonacademics). Leveraging this fact, Fosse and I began using the GSS to assess major theories of professorial liberalism. Most did not stand up to scrutiny. It was this that led us to develop the theory of self-selection based on occupational reputation.

But was there factual support for our theory? The theory holds, again, that college-educated liberals are more likely than their conservative counterparts to go into academe and, as part of this, to pursue the advanced education—a doctoral degree—that is usually necessary for an academic job. To test this claim, Fosse and I, this time working with Jeremy Freese, a sociologist at Northwestern University, analyzed data from a large longitudinal study of adolescents begun in the mid-1990s. By the time of the most recent wave of data collection, in 2008, 534 study participants had enrolled in graduate school with the intention of completing a

PhD. We examined whether they were more likely to have been liberals in college, whether the graduate school experience had made them more liberal, and what role cognitive ability, values, personality, and other factors played in leading them to pursue doctorates.

While the study with Fosse and Freese showed that there are about as many liberals in graduate school as among young professors, lending credence to the self-selection argument, there was still one important hypothesis on which I did not have any data: the conservative argument that bias and discrimination against scholars on the right impede their entry into the academic profession. To fill this gap, I teamed up with Joseph Ma, an undergraduate at the University of British Columbia, where I moved after leaving Harvard, and again with Fosse. In the fall of 2010 we sent two emails from fake prospective students to each director of graduate study—the professor in graduate programs charged with overseeing admissions and graduate student progress—in the seventy-five leading American departments of sociology, political science, economics, history, and literature. The emails, which were matched on student qualifications and interest areas, asked about fit with the department. One, the control email, mentioned nothing about politics, whereas the other, the treatment, mentioned in passing that the student had worked on either the Obama or the McCain campaign. Ma, Fosse, and I then analyzed the responses received to determine whether, on average, responses to the liberal student were friendlier and more enthusiastic than those to the conservative student. As I will explain, we took a fair amount of flak after the study was released for having deceived our research subjects, despite the fact that the methodology we used is routine in research on other forms of discrimination.

What, though, explained conservative moves against the liberal professoriate? Interviews with members of the public were revealing, but it was also important to hear some answers from the horse's mouth, so I interviewed prominent conservative activists and journalists, including Horowitz. In addition, I amassed data on the many conservative organizations involved in the campaign against liberal bias in higher education and on the history of this line of conservative attack.

All of this research informs the chapters that follow. However, since I have had occasion to publish elsewhere the specialized articles that have come out of the research, I have tried to avoid any kind of technical presentation of my findings in this book, relegating most methodological issues to the endnotes and providing in the text an overview of my work and thinking in the area.

The claims of the book unfold over the course of seven chapters. In Chapter 1, I describe the politics of American professors today. In Chapter 2, I outline some of the leading theories of professorial liberalism and examine their strengths and weaknesses. In Chapter 3, I present the self-selection argument. In Chapter 4, I consider how that approach would explain political differences among professors. In Chapter 5, I tackle the "So what?" question, exploring professors' views of the connection between politics, teaching, and research, and some of the possible consequences for higher education and American society. Chapter 6 maps out the conservative campaign against liberal professors and evaluates two hypotheses that might explain it. Chapter 7 discusses an additional hypothesis before moving on to focus on the campaign's rhetorical function for conservative populism. In the conclusion, I summarize my findings, outline future lines of research, and consider broader implications. Because the structure of the book reflects to some extent the path down which my research led me as I was drawn into the topic, readers should not expect a traditional narrative arc. Instead, the book makes its way through a number of interrelated puzzles.

One final point should be added before getting the discussion under way. Some readers may wonder about my own politics and how, if at all, my political views have influenced the arguments I advance. Although I am now an expat living in Canada, I am a Democrat with very liberal social attitudes and more center-left views when it comes to issues like government regulation of the market and criminal justice policy. More important, however, is that I have worked hard, throughout the book and in all the research leading up to it, to abide by what the early twentieth-century German sociologist Max Weber called the "intrinsically simple demand that the investigator . . . should keep unconditionally separate the establishment of empirical facts . . . and his own practical evaluations, i.e., his evaluation of these facts as satisfactory or unsatisfactory."[33] Many of the professors studied for this project would doubt whether this demand can ever be met. But, like Weber, I see it as an ideal toward which social scientists should strive—perhaps more so now, in our intensely polarized political culture in which facts are often not recognized as such, than ever before. If my politics have influenced any of the analysis I offer in the pages that follow—and critics from both the left and the right will find ways to suggest they have—it is despite my best efforts at remaining impartial.

Chapter 1

The Politics of American Professors

Colleges and universities are linchpin institutions in American society. In the United States today there are more than 4,400 schools offering postsecondary instruction to nearly 20 million students.[1] Seventy percent of young adults take college courses of some kind, and nearly a third earn bachelor's degrees—three times the number that did so in the early 1970s.[2] Not just because of the large number of tuition-paying undergraduates but also because of the equally dramatic expansion of graduate and professional training, a growing emphasis within science and technology fields on producing research with commercial application, new expectations among student consumers that a multitude of services and products be made available to them on campus, and the increasing complexity of the university—which has required hiring legions of administrators as well as a massive support staff—higher education is now a multibillion-dollar industry. It provides direct or indirect employment to millions of Americans and is connected to most other sectors of the economy.[3]

Higher education institutions are no less important in noneconomic terms. While scholarship characterizing the United States as a "knowledge society" often highlights the role of advanced technical and scientific knowledge in providing a basis for economic growth, the flip side is that knowledge, as embedded in computers, new pharmaceuticals, complex financial instruments, or economic reports, now permeates everyday life.[4] Colleges and universities are key sites for the production, coordination, retention, and dissemination of knowledge. Beyond that, for many students where they went to school has become an essential marker of personal identity, while the social connections made there can affect opportunities, friendships, even marriage prospects for decades to come.[5]

Although at most schools professors have little to do with student life (as critics are quick to point out), in other respects they are at the heart of this enterprise, doing the research and imparting the knowledge that give higher education its reason for being. Altogether there are 1.4 million people who serve as professors or instructors in higher education, making up about 1% of the employed U.S. labor force.[6] About half are employed full time; the rest work in an adjunct capacity. The growth of the part-time faculty, which began in the 1970s but accelerated in the 1990s due to cost pressures, is one of several significant changes the American academic profession has undergone in recent decades—changes that have been thoroughly documented by higher education researchers.[7] But when it comes to knowing exactly how members of this important occupational group line up politically, scholars have not always had complete information.

The first step in explaining a social phenomenon is simply to get a grasp on it descriptively. That is what I aim to do in this chapter for the liberalism of the professoriate. To provide a bit of historical background, I begin by recounting two landmark studies on the topic from the mid-twentieth century. I then discuss the limited and sometimes problematic research on professorial politics carried out in the past fifteen years or so before painting my own portrait of the political landscape of contemporary academe.

＊

Higher education is much talked about today. But so has it been for a long while. In the 1950s and 1960s, when college enrollments began their meteoric rise, the size of the faculty expanded rapidly, and massive federal investment in research paved the way for American academic dominance, leading social scientists often turned their attention to higher education in the hopes of contributing to an emerging national conversation about the university. Two of the studies they produced put professorial politics front and center.

The first was by sociologist Paul Lazarsfeld.[8] The context was McCarthyism. Americans in government service were the main targets in Senator Joseph McCarthy's campaign to root out subversives, but academics also came in for close examination. Historian Ellen Schrecker estimates that "almost 20 percent of the witnesses called before congressional and state investigating committees were college teachers or graduate students."[9] In 1955 an arm of the Ford Foundation, led by former University of Chicago president Robert M. Hutchins, took up the cause of documenting the scope of these investigations and their consequences for academic freedom and civil discourse. Hutchins commissioned Lazarsfeld to conduct a study.

Lazarsfeld, a Jewish refugee from Vienna appropriately sensitive to threats to freedom, was also a pioneer in the use of social surveys, and he and his colleagues developed an extensive questionnaire to probe professors' experiences and perceptions of political scrutiny. He chose to limit his study to social scientists, since in his view this was the group most likely to "deal with controversial topics in their courses" and hence feel the heat from McCarthy and his allies.[10] A team of researchers fanned out across the country to administer the questionnaire to a random sample of 2,451 social scientists—historians, economists, sociologists, and political scientists, mostly—teaching at 182 colleges and universities. The data did not show that academia was being decimated by McCarthyism. Just over a fifth of respondents gave an affirmative answer to the question "In the past few years, have you felt that your own academic freedom has been threatened in any way?"[11] The majority detected little change from "6 or 7 years ago" in the willingness of their colleagues to express "unpopular political views in the classroom," "unpopular political views publicly in the community," or "unpopular political views privately among friends."[12] True, nearly half of respondents said that some faculty members at their institutions were more worried about political repression than before. But while there was agreement that "there is greater concern these days . . . on the part of the public and groups outside the college over teachers' political opinions," only half of the social scientists surveyed thought this concern harmful.[13] Summing up their findings, Lazarsfeld, writing with coauthor Wagner Thielens Jr. in 1958, observed, "There is indeed widespread apprehension among . . . social science teachers, but in general it is hardly of a paralyzing nature; the heads of these men and women are 'bloody but unbowed.' "[14]

Of equal significance was another set of findings. Savvy researcher that he was, Lazarsfeld thought to ask his respondents not just about academic freedom but also about their political views. He found that social scientists composed a remarkably liberal group. Well before the GOP's hard turn to the right in the 1970s and 1980s, just 16% of social scientists surveyed said they were Republicans.[15] Forty-seven percent said they were Democrats. Of those who reported voting in the 1952 presidential election, 65% voted for Democrat Adlai Stevenson, while in the country as a whole Stevenson got 44% of the vote.[16] Lazarsfeld did not ask his respondents to classify themselves as liberal or conservative, but he did ask whether they thought they were more or less liberal than the average person in the community where they worked. Sixty-seven percent responded "more liberal."[17] The professors in his sample also scored high on an index measuring "permissive" attitudes toward communism.[18]

Lazarsfeld's finding that social science leans left surely came as no surprise to conservatives like William F. Buckley Jr., whose 1951 book, *God and Man at Yale*, took special aim at economists, sociologists, and psychologists in New Haven said to be promoting a statist, redistributionist, secularizing agenda.[19] Indeed, it was the reputation of academia more generally as a hotbed for left/liberal views—a reputation already well established midcentury—that helped bring it to the attention of McCarthy. Still, the book by Lazarsfeld and Thielens was a major contribution. Earlier sociologists had written on the politics of intellectuals, but Lazarsfeld and Thielens were the first to document the political beliefs and orientations of the professoriate using empirical data so systematically collected. Their book also went beyond description by offering a preliminary theory of professorial politics—a theory of the "academic mind," discussed in Chapter 2.

The second major twentieth-century study of American professors' politics also relied on survey data, although the context for it was very different. The 1960s were obviously years of great social and political unrest, and colleges and universities were battlegrounds. Undergraduates were on the front lines of most of the major movements of the day, and protests and sit-ins became everyday occurrences on campuses across the country.[20] Needless to say, mass student protest was unsettling for higher education. The research enterprise hardly ceased, but many professors and administrators found the 1960s to be trying and wondered about the long-term ramifications. Would the disruption continue indefinitely? Would efforts to accommodate student demands do irreparable harm to the university? To what extent, though, were these concerns widely shared? For every stodgy old academic who denounced campus radicals as hoodlums, it seemed, could be found a younger scholar who appreciated what they were doing.

It was to shed light on this issue—on the question of whether the protests of the 1960s had produced a "divided academy"—that political scientist Everett Carll Ladd and sociologist Seymour Martin Lipset undertook a new study of professors and politics.[21] With funding from the Carnegie Commission on Higher Education, and working jointly with higher education scholar Martin Trow (who would soon publish a book about the politics of British academics), they fielded a survey in 1969 that dwarfed Lazarsfeld's in size.[22] It included more than 60,000 respondents drawn from 303 colleges and universities, ranging from junior colleges to prestigious Ivy League schools. Unlike Lazarsfeld, Ladd and Lipset surveyed professors in all disciplines. And because they wanted to determine if there was a relationship between being liberal on national issues and being liberal on matters of campus politics, they asked numerous questions about respondents' political beliefs.

Three key findings stand out from their research. First, echoing what Lazarsfeld had found looking only at social scientists, Ladd and Lipset reported that the professoriate as a whole was much more liberal and Democratic than the rest of the population. About 46% of professors in their survey identified themselves as left or liberal, 27% as middle of the road, and 28% as conservative.[23] By contrast, only 20% of the American public in 1970 was left or liberal. (The number among college students was 45%.) Professors also voted for Democratic presidential candidates at a substantially higher rate than the general electorate in every election since 1944, and especially since 1948.[24] The liberal self-identification and voting practices of the faculty, Ladd and Lipset found, carried through to their views on major issues of the day, such as the Vietnam War and school busing.

Second, Ladd and Lipset found significant differences by discipline, type of school, and age of the professor. On discipline they found a "rather neat progression from the most left-of-center subject to the most conservative, running from the social sciences to the humanities, law and the fine arts, through the physical and biological sciences, education, and medicine, on to business, engineering, the smaller applied professional schools such as nursing and home economics, and finally agriculture, the most conservative discipline group."[25] On type of school they found, as had Lazarsfeld, that professors tend to be further left the more professionally accomplished they are and the more elite the institutions where they work. On age their finding was that the youngest professors, products of the 1960s themselves, were the most left-leaning.

Third, Ladd and Lipset discovered that the relationship between views on national and campus politics was complex. All told, 57% of the faculty disapproved of student activism, while 43% approved. Faculty members with liberal politics were more likely to be in the approval camp, but few approved of activism "unreservedly." As the authors explained, "Many left-of-center academics gave at best half-hearted support to student activism because they found in it a threat to the independence and atmosphere of open inquiry necessary to nurture the various strains of the scholarly pursuit."[26]

The Divided Academy (1975), the book that reported these results, was rightly viewed at the time as a perceptive work of social science. Like Lazarsfeld's study, it marshaled high-quality quantitative data to validate for its day and age the "generalization" that "the political weight of American intellectuals, including leading academics, has been disproportionately on the progressive, liberal, and leftist side."[27] Although not without its flaws, the book brought sober and dispassionate analysis to a topic easily given to polemic. Lipset, an extraordinarily wide-ranging scholar, also sought to link his research to an emerging theoretical and historical literature on intellectuals, class, and social change.

With Lazarsfeld's and Ladd and Lipset's studies completed, the seeds were sown for the blossoming of a rich and sophisticated research literature on professorial politics. But the flowers never appeared. While a number of theoretical treatises were produced in the 1970s, 1980s, and 1990s, empirical work was slow to accumulate. The main reason was a lack of data. Researchers were forced to rely on three main data sources, all of them thin.

The first source was follow-up surveys to the 1969 Carnegie faculty survey. The 1975 Carnegie study contained a number of questions about politics, but in subsequent years the survey changed focus, becoming more concerned with academics' work responsibilities and views of university governance. What remained of the politics questions was a single item that asked professors to locate themselves on a five-point scale running from left to liberal to middle of the road to moderately conservative to conservative, with the wording of the question changing slightly over the years. Researchers analyzed data from this question to determine whether, compared to 1969, the professoriate was growing more or less liberal or remaining about the same politically. Data from 1984 suggested a slight move to the right, but the overall shift from 1969 to 1997—the date of the most recent survey—was to the left, and this during a period that saw more of a gain in conservative than liberal self-identification in the country as a whole.[28] Between the two time points, the number of academics identifying as left/liberal increased by 8 percentage points, while the number of conservatives declined by 1 percentage point. Movement left was observed in nearly all fields, although the extent of the change varied. Education, the fine arts, the health sciences, and the humanities saw particularly large gains in the left/liberal ranks, but more modest changes in the same direction could also be found in the natural sciences, the social sciences, engineering, even business. Looking across all disciplines, in 1997 about 57% of professors described themselves as left or liberal, 20% called themselves moderate, and 24% were conservatives. These are significant findings and provide clear evidence in support of the claim that at the end of the twentieth century the professoriate remained a solidly liberal bloc. But because the Carnegie surveys contained no other politics questions, it was impossible for researchers to get a sense from them for what professorial liberalism entailed in the way of attitudes or beliefs.

The second major data source consisted of supplementary research done by Ladd and Lipset. This includes a survey of professors they carried out in 1977 independent of the Carnegie Commission, as well as a 1979 survey of members of honorary societies, such as the National Academy of Sciences and the American Academy of Arts and Sciences, designed to shed light on the "academic mind at the top."[29] Unfortunately, this research failed to tell scholars much about academics and politics that they did not already know from *The Divided Academy*.

The third and final source of data was the survey of American college and university faculty carried out every few years since 1989 by the Higher Education Research Institute (HERI) at UCLA. Like the later Carnegie Commission surveys, the HERI surveys did not focus on politics and contained (and still contain today) just a single question about where professors fall on the political spectrum.[30] This question too was a self-identification item: faculty members were asked to classify themselves as "far left," "liberal," "middle of the road," conservative," or "far right." The data here showed almost no change from 1989 to 1998 in the proportion of full-time professors who described themselves as in the far left or liberal camp.[31] It is also interesting to note how much difference sampling strategies and question wording can make in survey results: according to the HERI data, in 1998 45% of professors described themselves as on the left side of the political continuum—12 percentage points less than the Carnegie data from just a year earlier. These points aside, once again it proved difficult for researchers to leverage major gains in understanding from a single survey question.

Perhaps sensing a void, in the late 1990s and early 2000s a new group of scholars appeared on the scene, conducting extensive research on professors and politics and gathering their own data. But there was a problem: these scholars undertook their research for explicitly political purposes. Outspoken conservative and libertarian intellectuals, their primary goal was to document how far left academia had veered in order to mount a more effective critique of it. From the standpoint of objectivity, social research undertaken to achieve political ends is not necessarily flawed. As Max Weber noted, motivations for undertaking research are one thing; methodological care is another.[32] But in this case the researchers appear to have made a number of poor methodological choices, as well as leaps of logic, because of their strong political commitments. They were also largely unconcerned with tying their research to social scientific theories that might provide meaningful explanations for the patterns they observed.

One example of work in this vein is sufficient to convey its character. In a study published in *Academic Questions,* the journal of the conservative National Association of Scholars, economist Daniel Klein and a student coauthor, Andrew Western, examined voter registration records in northern California to determine the proportion of faculty members at the University of California–Berkeley and Stanford who were Democrats or Republicans.[33] Klein described the study as part of an effort at "ascertaining the basic facts about ideological lopsidedness in academia" and noted that it was motivated by his desire, as a libertarian, "to understand why our political culture does not more readily and thoroughly embrace libertarian ideas."[34] Of the 1,497 faculty members investigated, party registration information was obtained for 67%. At Berkeley, 49% of faculty members were found to be registered Democrats, as compared to 5% registered Republicans, while at Stanford the numbers were 47% and 6%, respectively.[35] As economists Ethan Cohen-Cole and Steven Durlauf pointed out in response, the high proportion of faculty for whom no registration information could be obtained meant that Klein could claim no more than that "the percentage of Democrats at UC Berkeley lies between 49.0% and 82.3%, the percentage of Republicans lies between 5.0% and 37.3%, and the percentage of nonpartisan/declined to state lies between 10.5% and 42.8%," with comparable numbers for Stanford. In addition, Klein had chosen to study academics in one of the most liberal regions of the country. Yet despite these shortcomings, he nevertheless drew the conclusion that on the basis of his study it was now "established fact" that leading colleges and universities are "one-party campus[es]."[36] In fact, Klein was right: most leading colleges and universities *are* in essence one-party campuses (just as many leading corporations, law firms, and medical practices tilt heavily toward the GOP). But that conclusion could not be safely reached from his data.

When I first began working on professors and politics, this was the state of the research. There had been some standout studies in the past, but more recent work was not as in-depth or credible as one might hope. A new survey of American professors' politics was in order.

At the heart of the study that I carried out with Solon Simmons, the Politics of the American Professoriate survey (PAP), was a questionnaire containing more than 100 social and political attitudes items, with most taken verbatim from long-standing surveys of the general U.S. population such as the General Social Survey and the American National Election Study. Among the nonstandardized questions we included were several on political self-conception that probed the extent to which respondents thought of themselves using terms like *progressive* or *radical*. The survey was designed so that the sample would be representative of full-time professors teaching in all academic departments and programs nationwide in which students could earn either associate's or bachelor's degrees. (Simmons and I also surveyed a smaller number of part-time faculty, but I do not include part-time PAP respondents in most of the analyses I report in this book because they responded to the survey at a much lower rate than fulltimers, making estimates based on their responses less reliable.) Our final sample included 1,416 professors teaching in nearly every discipline and type of institution.[37] As described in the introduction, my research assistants and I later conducted interviews with select survey respondents.

Simmons and I have reported the raw numbers from the faculty survey elsewhere.[38] Although I repeat some of that information in this book, my strategy here is different, informed by a distinctive way of conceptualizing political orientation.

Three basic approaches to political orientation have been taken in political sociology and political science. The first focuses on opinions and preferences. In any democratic society, scholars assume, there will exist at any point a number of hotly debated issues to do with the proper scope and activity of government, such as the degree to which it should regulate banks, provide protections against unemployment, or legislate what happens in the bedroom or the conditions under which it should go to war. Most people do not have strong views on all the issues being debated around them, but, according to scholars who take this first approach, what opinions they do have combine with their interests and aims to form political preferences. To count as preferences in this scheme, views need not be arranged in a neat hierarchical order, with voters knowing exactly what their first, second, and third priorities are for government action under different kinds of constraints, as economists' preference models might require. Nevertheless, from this perspective, voting and other political behavior should be seen as efforts by individuals to put into office politicians who can be expected to enact policies congruent with their desires and beliefs.[39] On this account, a person is liberal if most of his or her opinions fall to the left in the general sense of favoring government intervention in the market to keep inequalities from growing too extreme and/or the preservation of liberty in personal life, moderate if those opinions fall to the middle of the political spectrum, and conservative if they fall to the right—although what this means specifically is seen to vary from place to place and time to time.[40]

A second approach highlights not opinions and preferences but values. Rooted in sociological and psychological research claiming that much of human behavior involves people's attempts to remain true to core principles that they have adopted, primarily as a result of socialization, the values approach to political orientation begins by identifying what are said to be universal dimensions along which people's values can vary. It then notes how different values and sets of values are associated with support for particular kinds of politicians, parties, and policies. For example, political scientists Marc Hetherington and Jonathan Weiler argue that a fundamental difference between contemporary Americans concerns how authoritarian they are: how much they prioritize authority, order, and discipline over self-expression and autonomy.[41] Hetherington and Weiler present evidence that this value difference, which they maintain shows up in different cognitive styles and in everyday activities such as parenting, lines up directly with support for Republican and Democratic candidates and with stances on issues ranging from military funding to abortion. Similarly, psychologist Shalom Schwartz argues that there are ten "universal values" to which people in any society may subscribe to varying degrees, such as hedonism, an emphasis on self-direction, and a desire for security or conformity.[42] Analyzing cross-national survey data, Schwartz finds a strong association between certain of these values and where individuals place themselves on a left-right political self-identification scale, although with differing patterns in different constellations of countries.[43] For scholars of values and politics, the point is not so much that values "cause" political opinions and preferences but that political orientation should be understood in terms of the values that undergird and organize it. From this point of view, the real difference between liberals and conservatives lies in the unique value profile of each group.[44]

A third approach is more historical. It assumes that when people figure out where they stand politically, they are not simply adopting this or that opinion or attitude or being faithful to an abstract value; they are also linking themselves to rich and long-standing traditions of political thought. For example, political scientist Alan Wolfe argues that American liberalism, even in its twenty-first-century variety, descends directly from the writings of John Locke, particularly as interpreted by founders of the republic like Thomas

Jefferson.[45] In the same way, historian George Nash traces an unbroken line in conservative thinking from Edmund Burke and Alexis de Tocqueville to American scholars in the post–World War II period who contributed to the growth of conservative ideology after decades of liberalism's dominance.[46] Seen in this light, liberalism and conservatism, as ideological traditions, might contain competing strands but are defined by a foundational set of beliefs and assumptions. Wolfe, for instance, claims that "liberals are impatient with arguments rooted in fear and self-protection. They tend to see the past's improvements in the human condition as reason for anticipating continued improvement in the future. . . . The fact that some societies lack liberalism's generosity of spirit is all the more reason for liberals to insist on reform, not only in the public and political sense, but in the private and human one."[47] Not everyone who holds liberal or conservative views will be aware of his or her debt to intellectual history, but for scholars like Wolfe and Nash, it would seem, a person does not qualify as liberal or conservative unless his or her worldview is consistent with the relatively complex ideological core of the respective tradition.

Each of these approaches wields analytical power, but all are limited by their failure to take seriously what the others offer—and by their disregard of identity as a key feature of political life.[48] A common response to the opinions approach is to point out that the average voter does not exhibit even the "thin" rationality that many of its exponents take for granted. Research by political scientists, sociologists, and others has long shown that most people's political views do not consist of opinions or beliefs that are fully integrated in a logical sense. Instead political views, especially for those without advanced levels of education, are often a confused, internally contradictory, shape-shifting jumble of ideas, assumptions, images, tropes, and slogans and are full of blind spots on topics about which people do not have much information or that they have never thought through.[49] At the same time, there is strong evidence that emotions and cognitive biases play major roles in political decision making.[50] These limitations, however, though real, do not justify the assertion made by scholars of values like psychologist Jonathan Haidt that for voters politics is mostly a matter of "moral intuition," with consciously held beliefs and opinions and the assessments of interest that may underlie them usually taking a backseat to more automatic cognitive and affective processes.[51] Were this the case, opinion more conventionally measured, which can shift much more rapidly than core values, would probably not account for political behavior as well as it does.[52] It is more reasonable to suppose that political orientation includes opinion- and value-based elements, which need not overlap perfectly, and to see the rationality of voters as varying across individuals and circumstances. As for the traditions approach, while it assumes implicitly that liberalism and conservatism are a matter of both opinions and values, it sets major restrictions on which opinions and values can be considered evidence of participation in a political tradition, rather than recognizing, as do the other two approaches, that it is normal for ideologies and political classifications to change and even be fundamentally reinvented over time.[53]

I draw on all three approaches in my political sketch of the American professoriate, attending to opinions, values, and participation in political traditions. Yet my sketch is also organized around a concept—political identity—that has been neglected in studies of political orientation. Citizens do not simply have opinions and values and connections with tradition. Partly by virtue of having those opinions, values, and connections, they often come to understand themselves as members of distinct social groups defined in political terms. And this group membership can be very important in their lives, becoming a major component of their identity, of the meanings they associate with themselves—so much so that their sense of political group membership can influence their behavior independent of opinions and values.[54] For example, in a study using nationally representative survey data, political scientist Donald Green and his colleagues found that whether people call themselves Democrats or Republicans and feel a sense of loyalty to their party is as important for their voting choices as their attitudes on social and economic issues.[55] Similarly, political psychologists Ariel Malka and Yphtach Lelkes discovered that people's thinking of themselves as liberal or conservative, and hence as members of groups that are even more fictive than those defined by party identification, affects their future evaluation of issues more than do the beliefs typically associated with a liberal or conservative orientation.[56]

I build on these insights by focusing my analysis on the major categories of political identity into which academics see themselves falling. Attitudes on issues certainly factor into identity, as do values. But an identity-based approach must be concerned with other things as well: with the everyday labels used for the political groups and factions to which professors view themselves as belonging; with what they take to be the defining features of those groups; with the cultural work they engage in to draw "symbolic boundaries" between themselves and others; and with the consequences for their behavior of the integration of all this into their narratives of political identity, the stories they tell themselves (and others) about who they are politically speaking.[57] My goal is to produce, within the restricted space of this chapter, a rough anthropological map of the politics of today's faculty, looking particularly at the left side of the political aisle—not assuming in advance that I will know which political tribes I will find there but allowing an understanding of this to emerge from my research.

To do so, I use the follow-up interviews with professors to construct a typology of political identity. Employing a statistical technique called latent class analysis, I then locate all PAP survey respondents in one of the identified categories and use the survey data to estimate the size of the groupings and how they are distributed across disciplines and types of institutions and vary with professors' demographic characteristics.[58]

✦

When conservative critics like Horowitz warn of "dangerous" American academics, they usually have in mind professors like Dave, an economist who was in his late 60s when we interviewed him. Dave exemplifies the first group of professors I want to highlight: Marxists and other self-described radicals in the academic ranks who, through their teaching, research, advocacy, and activism, hope to bring about fundamental changes to the economic structure of the United States and other capitalist societies—changes that would reduce private ownership of the means of production and force a significant redistribution of economic resources. Although radicals are a relatively small group within academia as a whole, in a number of social science and humanities disciplines—certainly not Dave's field of economics—they exert real intellectual influence. Because this is so, and because their political and intellectual views on several key issues place them at odds not just with conservatives but also with many liberal academics, radical professors are subjects of considerable controversy. Some, like Dave, revel in it.

Dave grew up in Beverly Hills. His father, who dropped out of school in the fourth grade, worked his way up and eventually ran a successful defense contracting business. Raised in a conservative household by nouveau riche parents—his father, he told us, "voted for Roosevelt first, and then after he got some money decided that Roosevelt wasn't the way to go"—Dave says he "went to college carrying all those conservative views and . . . racial prejudices." Then, he says, he "started learning": "I got to be more and more liberal and . . . involved with the possibilities that society could change and be better. . . . I was like everybody else in the 60s. I'm the same age as The Beatles and we rejected a whole bunch of things." Dave's college courses, he told us, as well as the many activists with whom he was becoming friends, convinced him not only that conservatism was wrongheaded but also that capitalism in any form was perverse, a system rigged to benefit the few at the expense of the many. While he thought the Soviet Union tyrannical, his opinion as a young man—and now—is that "what happened in the Soviet Union was not at all what Marx envisioned." Dave committed himself to doing whatever he could, within his limited sphere of influence, to push America in a more genuinely Marxist direction.

Deeply interested in economic matters, particularly of a comparative nature, Dave entered a doctoral program in economics but was criticized by his professors when he announced his plan to write a dissertation on how the war in Vietnam was little more than a neocolonialist debacle. Finding the neoclassical economics in which he was being trained to be "bullshit" anyway, he switched schools, eventually landing in a program where he could work not on Vietnam but on a topic nearly as close to his heart: student radicalization. With little chance of securing a position in a major economics department after graduation, Dave took a job at a community college, where, he says, the faculty is "so goddamned left you wouldn't believe it." There, for more than three decades, he has held forth in courses on Marx and radical political economy. Although his teaching has often gotten him into trouble—it is not uncommon, he told us, for parents to "come and say, 'You're brainwashing my child!' "—he makes no apologies for his behavior. "I think there is a place for getting out the liberal, radical type message," he said. "I think the place of the university is to expose people to different things—not what they're used to."

In some of his opinions, Dave, like the few other professors on the radical left our interviews netted, is virtually indistinguishable from the mass of other left-leaning academics: he told us that he supports women's rights, the rights of ethnic and racial minorities, gay rights, and environmental conservation and in 2007 was bitterly opposed to the war in Iraq, which he thought would "lead to absolute calamity, if it already hasn't." He consistently votes Democratic and campaigned for Kerry in 2004. But he identifies more with Bernie Sanders, the socialist senator from Vermont who forms part of the Democratic caucus but is an Independent, than with anyone in the party. At the end of the day, Dave believes that class inequality is the most significant ill affecting American society—and that nothing short of a radical reconfiguration of the economic order, which the Democratic

Party would never support, is going to change things much for the better. What he and other radicals have in common, he feels, is simply that they have had the clarity of vision to recognize the truth of this basic point—and the courage, unlike liberals, to not be afraid of utopian thinking.

How many professors like Dave are there? Eight percent of the college and university faculty surveyed by HERI in the 2004–2005 school year describe themselves as "far left."[59] Similarly, the PAP data show a radical grouping of 9% of professors. Not all of these academics are Marxists, but 43% say the term *Marxist* describes them at least moderately well (in academia as a whole that number is 5%), 77% say the term *radical* describes them moderately well or better, and 64% call themselves *activists*.[60] The political opinions of survey respondents in this group are consistent with Dave's: radicals are overwhelmingly supportive of same-sex relationships, abortion rights, and equality for women; believe strongly in the need for environmental regulation; are against the death penalty and pro-immigration; think the invasion of Iraq was a fiasco; and believe that diplomacy, not military intervention, is the best way to prevent terrorism. What separates them in attitudinal terms from "progressives"—the next group in the typology—is mostly their radicalism on matters of class. For example, one of the questions we asked on the survey, taken from the GSS, reads as follows:

> Some people think that the government in Washington ought
> to reduce the income differences between the rich and the
> poor, perhaps by raising the taxes of wealthy families or by
> giving income assistance to the poor. Others think that the
> government should not concern itself with reducing this

income difference between the rich and the poor. Where
would you place yourself in this debate? Think of a score of 1
as meaning that the government ought to reduce the income
differences between rich and poor, and a score of 7 meaning
that the government should not concern itself with reducing
income differences. What score between 1 and 7 comes closest to the way you feel?

Thirty-four percent of progressive professors—but 67% of
those in the radical grouping—gave a response of 1 to this question. And so it was with other, similar questions: about the need
for government help for needy Americans, about whether business corporations make too much profit, about whether government has a responsibility to provide people with jobs and a decent
standard of living, and so on. Had we asked still other class-related
questions—about the justness of capitalism versus socialism, say,
or the benefits of public ownership of industry (questions we did
not pose because of space constraints)—the radicals would have
stood out even more.

Like Dave, many survey respondents on the radical left are
ambivalent about the Democratic Party, which they believe is
beholden to corporate interests: more than a third describe themselves as Democratic-leaning Independents. What they would
really prefer is an altogether different political system. When push
comes to shove, however, they nearly all vote Democratic, at least
in presidential races.

What do we know about the demographics of radical academics? One thing of note is that they are underrepresented among
professors who were younger than thirty-six at the time of the

PAP study. Overall 7% of PAP respondents fell in this age range, but only 2% of radicals did. While the tradition of academic radicalism remains alive today, it is the ethos and experiences of the 1960s and 1970s that most shape the worldview of the group. Another important feature of the radical cluster is that it contains a disproportionately large number of women: 48% of radicals are female, as compared to 39% of all PAP respondents. Gays and lesbians are also overrepresented here. In racial and ethnic terms, the cluster is indistinguishable from most of the other ideological groupings. There are, however, differences in religious affiliation: 39% of those on the radical left say they are affiliated with no religion, as compared to 27% of professors overall.[61]

Where radical academics may differ most from their colleagues sociologically, though, is by institutional location and discipline. On institution the PAP data show that radicals are very much overrepresented at liberal arts colleges: 24% of radicals teach at liberal arts schools, as compared to 11% of the faculty overall. The differences are equally stark by field: professors on the radical left are far more likely than their peers to be located in the social sciences, the humanities, and interdisciplinary fields at the intersection of the two. According to the PAP data, 38% of sociologists, 18% of English professors, and 15% of political scientists, historians, and communications scholars belong to the radical left cluster. (However, the intersection of discipline with institutional location is such that one finds fewer radicals in these fields among professors teaching at elite doctoral-granting universities, which speaks to the restricted capacity of various strains of academic radicalism to reproduce themselves.) In natural science fields like biology and more applied fields like engineering, virtually no one is on the radical left.

✦

Similar to Dave in many respects, but different too, is Ben, a fifty-nine-year-old professor of English who teaches at an institution in the Midwest that grants bachelor's degrees. Ben does not object strenuously when people refer to his politics as liberal, but the term he prefers is *progressive*. In the 1990s, a number of liberal commentators and Democratic strategists suggested that those on the left begin rebranding themselves "progressives." The thinking was twofold. On the one hand, the word *liberal* had been so maligned by conservatives during political battles of the 1980s that new, uncontaminated language was felt necessary if the left was to have any hope of expanding its base of support and countering conservative gains. *Progressive* signaled the kind of forward thinking that strategists hoped would appeal. But it was not only forward thinking, for the term *progressive*, which harks back to a period in American history when solving social problems was at the forefront of the national agenda, was thought the perfect antidote to the right's charge that liberals are unpatriotic. True American patriotism, self-identified progressives could claim, requires fidelity not to a small town, theologically conservative vision of the American past or the doctrines of free market economics but to the ideals of those like "Fighting" Bob La Follette, the tough, reform-minded, early twentieth-century politician from Wisconsin who took on railroad monopolies and fought for the rights of labor.

As these arguments gained traction, many individuals and groups under the broad umbrella of the Democratic Party styled themselves progressives, including a number of centrist Democrats whose ideas would have been quite foreign to La Follette. Such widespread use of the term has led a number of pundits more recently to claim that *progressive* has become a "content-less label" and to argue that the time is once again at hand to embrace the moniker *liberal*.[62]

When we asked Ben to tell us what *progressive* meant to him, he said that a progressive is "someone who believes that we should actively work on social problems—both in and out of government; that we should address them and not just let them fester." But would not most liberals and moderates—and even a few conservatives—agree with this? Is progressivism as devoid of meaning in academia as elsewhere? Although interviewees like Ben might have had trouble coming up with a satisfactory definition on the fly, the way that they (and nonprogressives) used the term in passing suggests that they did mean something specific by it: in the eyes of many academics a progressive is someone with an across-the-board commitment to strongly liberal views who belongs neither to the radical left nor to the ranks of pro-business Democrats. Not yearning for socialism or communism—but not enthusiastic either about the high economic growth strategies and antiwelfare stances of so-called New Democrats—progressive academics would like to see the American state do whatever it can short of complete transformation of the economic system to achieve "social justice" in all areas, alongside environmental protection and stewardship. Progressive academics are readers of *The Nation* and Frank Rich, watchers of Rachel Maddow and (sometimes cringingly) Michael Moore, admirers of Scandinavia who would direct the tools of government toward reducing inequalities and improving the lives of the socially disadvantaged—through progressive taxation, vigorous enforcement of antidiscrimination laws, and strong social welfare and public education systems. Progressives form a sizable group: 31% of all professors.

Ben is typical. Although he has left-leaning views in all areas, he has been particularly concerned over the years with issues of racial justice. Ben grew up in Chicago, in a moderate Republican household. What converted him to the left and the Democratic Party, he says, was "Barry Goldwater in 1964." Why, we asked? "Well, I saw him as a racist. That was the height of the civil rights movement. I saw his unwillingness to address the civil rights issue as simply unconscionable. I thought his talk about 'Let's go drop nuclear bombs on North Vietnam to win the war' was crazed. And I found that's when we really began to detect what became Nixon's Southern Strategy—'Hey, we can win votes by being racist.'" "Given what now passes for conservatism," Ben added, "Goldwater looks pretty good to me." Ben says that he has spent a lot of time volunteering "inside ethnic neighborhoods and [on] racial identity issues." But it is to government that he looks for real advance in addressing racial disparities and to cure other social ills. Because he feels an allegiance to the Democratic Party— despite his feelings that it has been captured by special interests— and because he thinks the Democrats are light-years ahead of the Republicans on racial matters, Ben has been actively involved in Democratic political campaigns at the national and state levels, most recently working a "get out the vote" phone drive organized by MoveOn.org.

Why is Ben not classifiable as a radical? For one thing, his redistributionism has limits. Although he would prefer much less inequality, he does not favor a complete leveling of income or wealth differences, as some radicals might. "Equality of outcome," he told us, ". . . is unachievable and, perhaps, not even desirable." Beyond attitudinal differences, however, what distinguishes Ben's interview answers from Dave's is his failure to invoke any radical political-economic framework. For example, Marx or Marxism never came up in our discussions with him, and this is consistent with the survey data: only 3% of professors in the progressive group say that the term *Marxist* describes them at least moderately well. For Ben and most other progressives, being on the left means wanting to temper, not overturn, the capitalist order—and it entails as much of a focus on achieving social justice around race, immigration, sexuality, and gender as around class, as well as a belief that not all of these struggles are reducible to class.

Ben's doubts about radicalism also extend to political style. The one group of academics for which he has disdain is what he calls the "fascist left," who, in an effort to impose their views on others in what he thinks is a Stalinist fashion, would curtail free speech on campus through hate speech regulations and censorship of campus speakers. While not all progressive academics feel this way—more progressives favor hate speech regulations than oppose them—most of the progressives we interviewed said something to indicate their distance from radicalism. This was true of Howard, a forty-eight-year-old sociologist who insisted that since even U.S. Supreme Court Justice Louis Brandeis had argued that you cannot have a true democracy "with large levels of inequality," the need to reduce inequality "is not a radical idea." Yet progressives also see a major gap between themselves and other liberals who, as they understand it, are too uncritical of corporate capitalism and too willing to compromise with the right. Some progressives think that such liberals, epitomized by Bill Clinton, have undue influence with the Democratic Party, and they would prefer to vote for a more left-leaning third party than for the Democrats. Howard told us he agrees with Ralph Nader's assessment that instead of having two political parties in the United States we really have "a Democratic and a Republican wing of the business party." In 2000, before four years of George W. Bush wised them up, 5% of progressive academics cast their vote for Nader or other third-party candidates (radicals voted for Nader at a higher rate). Yet the vast majority (77%) are Democrats and vote as such.

Looking at demographics, while progressive academics do not differ much from their colleagues by race or gender, they have in common with radicals and center-lefters that a high proportion (41%) claim no religious affiliation. A disproportionately large number identify as gay or lesbian, and progressive academics have fewer children on average than most other professors.[63] Progressives are distributed fairly evenly across the institutional landscape of American higher education, except that they are somewhat overrepresented at elite, PhD-granting schools and somewhat underrepresented in community colleges. In addition, progressivism, unlike radicalism, is not the exclusive purview of the social sciences and the humanities. Although these disciplines do contain more progressives than average, progressives are also well represented in the natural sciences and "other" fields. In engineering and business they are scarcer.

✦

Progressives are keen to distinguish themselves from less liberal, more centrist Democrats. But does such a group really exist in academia? Consider the case of Sean, a fifty-three-year-old microbiologist who teaches at a four-year school in the Northeast. When we asked Sean to describe his politics, he responded in a curious way: "If you look at it from the outside, most people would probably describe me as a liberal." Indeed if one were to classify Sean solely according to his stated opinions on major issues, he would be squarely in the liberal camp. On inequality Sean told us, "Our economic policies are less progressive than they could be. . . . Growing inequality . . . is a serious issue." He "rejects . . . wholeheartedly" the value of a traditional division of labor between men and women. He disagrees with the idea that the use of military force is the best way to counter terrorism. And so on. He is a lifelong Democrat.

Beneath the surface lies greater complexity. Sean grew up in Pennsylvania. His mother and father were both clerical workers and on the left. One of Sean's most vivid political memories is of watching television coverage of the 1968 Democratic presidential convention with his father. As the television showed images of protesters being brutalized by police in the streets, his father muttered, "Gestapo, Gestapo," at the screen. Sean "had that background as a child," he told us. When he started college in the early 1970s, he naturally gravitated toward various left activist groups, becoming particularly involved with the Catholic left and its antinuclear campaigns. He remained an activist in the 1980s but soon noticed a shift in his perspective. Once more a single incident stands out in his memory. He and his wife attended a meeting of a community group in 1983 shortly after the Soviets shot down Korean Air Lines Flight 007. Community groups, he reminded my research assistant, "will think about issuing statements . . . whenever anything happens internationally." But the group could come to no consensus as to whether the Soviet action, which caused 269 civilian deaths, warranted condemnation. The Soviets were sworn enemies of America and of capitalism—did that not make them allies of the left? Sean found this attitude reprehensible. He started becoming "disillusioned" with what he called the "hard left" and came to see an element of truth in the conservative critique that leftists often and unjustifiably "blame America first." As he put it, "I became very troubled by the perspective that all of the enemies of the United States are good people, and everything that goes wrong is somehow our fault." Thus began what Sean described as his "political journey . . . rightward."

That Sean has moved into the center left becomes most evident in the explanations he offers for why he has the opinions he does. He would prefer less economic inequality, but mainly because he believes it creates "a basic social stability problem" for there to be "such a growing divide between the people who control the economic resources and the rest of the society." Pragmatic concerns about social functioning—not concerns about social justice—seem for him primary. Does he support affirmative action? In general he thinks it can make a positive contribution to "addressing historical inequality." But again his views are complicated. In fact he supports affirmative action only in college admissions, to create more of an opportunity society. In private- or public-sector hiring, he does not. Despite its potential benefits, he is "troubled" philosophically by affirmative action, which he said "runs against American values of treating people equally." On the war in Iraq, he told us that the "entire operation was a tragic mistake for the United States, and really for the world." But he initially supported the war effort, being "rather taken in by the claims of what was going to happen as sanctions were dissolved." And while he does think diplomacy better than military force for countering terrorism, he also said, "I do understand that certainly the threat of a military cost to harboring terrorists is a legitimate thing."

Where does this leave Sean? Is he a liberal? By most standards, yes. At the same time, he is clearly to the right of Ben and other progressives and thinks of his political commitments as standing in some tension with theirs.

The PAP survey data indicate that 14% of American academics are like Sean. How, in attitudinal terms, do professors in this center-left grouping differ from progressives? Ninety-six percent of progressives believe that poor people have a hard time because government benefits do not go very far, whereas this is true for 83% of those on the center left. While 61% of progressives say that business corporations make too much profit, this is so for 49% of center-lefters. Center-lefters are also less likely than progressives to support the right to abortion under any circumstance (71% versus 93%), more likely to oppose same-sex relationships (24% of center-lefters see such relationships as "wrong"), more likely to worry about immigration (20% of those on the center left agree that "the growing number of newcomers from other countries threatens traditional American customs and values"), and more likely to oppose affirmative action (almost half who answered a question about affirmative action in college admissions opposed it, as compared to a quarter of progressives.) Where just 13% of progressives favor the death penalty, 43% of academics like Sean do. Finally, to come back to the issue that originally drove Sean to the right, 38% of those on the center left say they are "very proud" to be Americans, as compared to 25% of progressive academics. (Forty-one percent of center-lefters say they are "somewhat proud.") Despite these differences, center-lefters in academe remain very much a part of the Democratic coalition: 55% are Democrats, while 36% are Democratic-leaning Independents. In 2004, 94% voted for Kerry.

At a conference I once attended, Lawrence Summers joked about belonging to the right wing of the Democratic Party. My point in calling attention to Sean is to show that there are other academics in the same position. How do center-lefters in American academe fall out in terms of demographics and disciplinary and institutional location? Demographically and institutionally they are hard to tell apart from other professors, except that the group contains somewhat more African Americans than average and more religious adherents than do the radical or progressive clusters. Center-lefters can be found in larger numbers in technical fields like business, finance, and mechanical engineering.

※

Together, radicals, progressives, and center-lefters make up the left/liberal flank of American academia. Looking at the numbers from the latent class analysis, this means that about 54% of American academics can be said to belong to the political left. A 1999 survey of the American college and university faculty conducted by Stanley Rothman, Robert Lichter, and Neil Nevitte yielded a not dissimilar 60% liberal figure—once a coding error responsible for a different finding widely disseminated in the press was corrected.[64] HERI data from 2004 to 2005 paint a broadly similar picture, showing that just over 50% of academics describe themselves as left or liberal. In conventional political opinion terms, some number of professors like Sean or Summers might be better described as left-leaning moderates than liberals per se.[65] Adjusting for this would reduce the proportion of professors classifiable as liberal, bridging the gap between the HERI data and other studies. Whether or not one accepts this, a reasonable conclusion is that between 50% and 60% of academics fall somewhere on the left side of the political spectrum.

How does the 50–60% left/liberal figure position academe in relation to other occupations, and professors to Americans in general? The PAP questions used to conduct the latent class analysis were drawn from a variety of surveys, so the analysis cannot be replicated exactly on data from the U.S. population as a whole.[66] If we use liberal–conservative self-identification as a rough index of political views, however, it becomes possible to say something meaningful. To elaborate on a point made in the introduction, here what one finds is that, depending on the scheme used to code the data (Are liberals those who say they are "extremely liberal" or "liberal"? Or should the "somewhat liberal" be included as well?), the professoriate either contains the highest proportion of liberals of any occupation in the United States for the period 1996–2010 or is right behind another famously liberal occupational group, authors and journalists. As compared to American adults overall, professors are about three times more liberal on average. (On the other side, members of the clergy—the most conservative occupation in American society—are about two and a half times more conservative than other Americans, while conservatives outnumber liberals in the medical profession, another right-leaning field, by a ratio of 2:1.)

Comparisons are also possible looking at party. Over the same period the professoriate was not the most Democratic occupation—

among the most Democratic workers, according to the GSS, were therapists, social workers, social scientists outside academe, telephone operators, attorneys, mail carriers, textile operatives, and precision metal workers—but it was near the top of the list. It was also not the case that the ratio of Democrats to Republicans on the faculty exceeded the ratio of Republicans to Democrats in conservative occupations. There may have been two Democratic professors for every one Republican, but the opposite was true, GSS data show, among farmers, religious workers, health administrators, real estate agents, and engineers, for example. Still, in 2004 a remarkable 77% of professors voted for John Kerry, whereas he received 48% of the popular vote.

Let us not exaggerate the leftism of American professors. The professoriate is obviously not bursting at the seams with revolutionaries. Nor are American professors as left-leaning as their counterparts in a number of other countries when judged by common metrics. Sociologist Clem Brooks has recently analyzed data from the International Social Survey Program with the goal of putting American professorial politics in comparative perspective.[67] He found that while professors in the United States are more liberal than academics in several other nations in their support for gender equality and a secular state, on most other issues they are near the middle of the pack, and on support for the welfare state they are near the bottom. In other words, it is American professors' social liberalism that is distinctive. Compared to the political views of most other Americans, though— which, outside liberal enclaves, are sufficiently conservative that British journalists John Micklethwait and Adrian Wooldridge could, with only some overstatement, characterize the United

States as a "right nation"—the politics of professors certainly stick out.[68]

⁘

The focus of this book is professorial liberalism. But a map of the political space of the university would be incomplete were it to say nothing about the other political factions located there. The interviews revealed three such groups: moderates, libertarians, and strong conservatives. Identifying these groups in the PAP data is challenging, for, among other reasons, Simmons and I did not, to our regret, ask respondents whether they considered themselves libertarians. A fair estimate based on the latent class analysis, however, is that, excluding those in the center left who might arguably form part of the political middle, 19% of professors can be considered moderates. As for the right, the data show two groups here: a small cluster of economic conservatives, composing 4% of the professoriate, and another conservative grouping representing 23% of professors, the standout characteristic of which is strongly conservative views on social and national security issues.[69] Libertarians are likely spread somewhere between these two clusters, with more of a presence in the former.[70] Given space constraints, brief examples of all three types will have to suffice.

Margene, fifty-four, is a typical academic moderate. A professor of biology at a community college, Margene told us that she is moderate in the sense that she "can go liberal on some issues and then conservative on others. It just depends." Where Sean, the center-lefter, was raised in a liberal family and later began moving right, Margene's parents, neither of whom finished college, were conservative Republicans who raised her in a strict Lutheran household. Margene told us that she had her parents' political voices in her head until she went to college, where she majored in political science and came to appreciate the liberal point of view. Later, after she switched to biology, she worked briefly for Bill Clinton while he was the governor of Arkansas, which also "swayed" her politically. Today she holds fairly liberal social attitudes. She is pro-choice and believes in an equal division of household labor between men and women, although she also supports the death penalty. When it comes to economic matters, her opinions are more mixed. She would prefer less inequality and thinks the poor should be given some basic level of income support. But she is not for taxing the rich and believes that the poor already get about as much government assistance as they deserve given that "many, many" poor people "don't choose to work." Over the years Margene has voted for both Democratic and Republican candidates, although she now feels somewhat closer to the Democratic side. The defining feature of her ideological stance, however, is her general discomfort with partisan labels and affiliations. Like most academic moderates, she would prefer that people stop defining themselves as Democrats or Republicans, liberals or conservatives, vote their conscience on issues, and attempt to find some kind of middle ground.

Like Margene, libertarians also tend to be liberal on social matters—at least when it comes to their views on government regulation of the private sphere—and conservative on economic ones. Yet for them, this is not a question of eclecticism but a self-conscious commitment to what they see as a consistent set of political and philosophical principles sometimes identified as "classic liberalism." Pride in consistency was plain to see in our interview with Brendan, a thirty-eight-year-old economist who teaches in the Northeast. Brendan described himself as a "libertarian conservative," which, he said, "means that I believe in minimal public involvement in economic and personal life." When we asked him to address some of the issues covered in the PAP survey, explaining his opinions to us, he took care to justify nearly every view in terms of "minimal public involvement," at one point saying nervously that he hoped all his answers lined up. Brendan recounted that he was first exposed to conservatism as a child, when his father, a banker turned real estate agent, took him inside the voting booth and told him to pull the lever for Ronald Reagan. Reagan remains a hero to him; pictures of Reagan and Margaret Thatcher hang in his office, he told us. It was while studying economics in college, however, that Brendan moved away from his parents' "moderate conservatism" and became a committed libertarian. He told us that in economics his "political beliefs are pretty common. The majority of theory that economists deal with suggests that . . . free market capitalism is the most efficient way to allocate resources, generate wealth, and improve living standards." Present him with a hot-button issue and he will deduce his opinion from these premises, citing economic research to back up his claims. Should the government reduce income differences between the rich and the poor by raising taxes on the wealthy? No, said Brendan. "We know that over time, tax incidence has some pretty powerful incentives on individual behavior, and taxing higher income individuals at higher rates may result in those individuals doing things like working less, hiring fewer people." What about his views on a traditional division of labor in the household? Brendan finds this "ridiculous." "It may be more efficient," he said, "for those sorts of homemaking and income-raising duties to be more evenly split, depending on circumstances, including education and professional opportunities." The value of diplomacy versus military strength for defeating terrorism? Brendan responded once again in terms not of moral right and wrong but of efficiency: "I think that using the military is part of defeating terrorism, but I'm not sure that it is the only tool that should be deployed." Brendan is nominally Republican, although he worried at the time of our interview that President Bush and the Republican Congress were leading the GOP away from what it was under Reagan that made it "great"—away from being what Brendan called "the low-tax, free enterprise party."

Proceeding from a very different set of assumptions is Julie, a forty-seven-year-old professor of engineering at a PhD-granting institution. Julie grew up in Pittsburgh in a Catholic household. Her father was a police officer, her mother a homemaker. Both her parents were conservative Republicans, and she imbibed their pro–free market, traditional family values, and belief in an immutable moral order. Her politics, she told us, are a direct reflection of her parents' and were influenced as well by her having married another Catholic—they now have three children—whose views reinforce her own. Julie opposes raising taxes on the rich in order to redistribute income because she "believe[s]"—morally, it would seem, and not simply on utilitarian grounds—"in a free, capitalistic society." While she thinks there is nothing wrong with women in the workforce—"I'm not quite that traditional," she said—she is pro-life, against gay marriage, and opposes affirmative action because "people should be hired based on their skills and abilities." She is hawkish on foreign policy and deeply patriotic. She is not much involved politically beyond keeping up with the news and voting, but she is a Republican and consistently votes the party line.

Where in academe can moderates, libertarians, and strong conservatives be found? Again, the PAP data are not very helpful in identifying libertarians, but something can be said about moderates and the two right-leaning groupings that the latent class analysis turned up. Table 1.1 shows how all six of the clusters are distributed across types of institutions and broad disciplinary areas. Economic and strong conservatives are underrepresented at elite, PhD-granting institutions and liberal arts colleges; strong conservatives are underrepresented as well at nonelite, PhD-granting schools and overrepresented in community colleges. In terms of disciplinary differences, economic and strong conservatives are overrepresented in business, and the former in engineering as well. A more fine-grained analysis shows that conservatives tend to cluster in fields like accounting, management information, marketing, and electrical engineering, while economics contains a higher proportion of strong conservatives than do social science fields such as sociology and psychology.

Demographically, the small economic conservative group skews young, with 47% of cluster members in the 36 to 49 age range, as compared to 33% in the professorial population overall. In both conservative groups one finds quite a few more men than women, while African Americans are overrepresented among moderates. These three groups of professors are also more religious than others. Twenty-two percent of moderates claim no religious affiliation; for those in the economic and strong conservative groupings only 7% and 8% do so, respectively, and here one finds an unusually large number of evangelical Protestants. Not surprisingly, in light of patterns in the general population, professors in the political center and on the right also have more children on average than other professors. Looking at party affiliation, the modal category

Table 1.1. Faculty political clusters by type of institution and academic field

	Political cluster						
	Radical left (9%)	Progressive (31%)	Center left (14%)	Moderate (19%)	Economic conservative (4%)	Strong conservative (23%)	Total
Institution type							
Community college	10	10	17	19	15	27	17
BA-granting	34	44	46	51	53	50	47
Liberal arts	24	15	9	7	5	5	11
Nonelite PhD	24	23	23	20	25	15	21
Elite PhD	8	8	4	3	2	2	5
Academic field							
Physical/biological sciences	3	9	10	10	5	7	8
Social sciences	46	27	19	19	7	16	23
Humanities	35	29	23	13	15	12	21
Engineering/computer science	2	8	11	14	22	13	11
Business	1	8	14	18	27	26	15
Other	13	19	22	26	25	26	22

Source: Politics of the American Professoriate survey, 2006, sample size 1,416.
Note: Numbers are column percentages and may not add to 100 because of rounding. Percentages in parentheses are cluster sizes.

among academic moderates is Democratic-leaning Independent (30%), while the two conservative clusters are decidedly Republican (for example, among strong conservatives 65% identify as Republican, and 23% are Republican-leaning).

While many of these differences are interesting and worthy of explanation, the first finding from the interviews and the PAP survey that must be accounted for is simply that there is in fact a concentration in the academic ranks of people broadly on the left. Chapter 2 considers some of the most common explanations that social scientists have offered for this phenomenon.

Chapter 2

Why Are They Liberal?
The Standard Explanations

Not long ago a story about some of my research ran on *Inside Higher Ed,* a higher education news website that is a competitor to the more established *Chronicle of Higher Education.* Like most web-based news sites, *Inside Higher Ed* allows readers to leave comments, and most readers who posted a comment that day offered their own views as to why professors tend to be on the left. "I always thought the reason for few conservative PhD holders was obvious," wrote Warren M. "Liberals are more intelligent." FK agreed: "The real answer . . . is simple, but not easy to accept. Most modern-day conservatives are not the intellectual heavy-weights of days past and are rather a group of ideologists or blind followers." Another perspective was advanced by Ossian-Sweet: "This is a no-brainer: Left-leaners want to make a good living, but they tend to detest capitalism and the business world in general, and may even want to undermine or actively attack it. Obvious career choice to pursue both of these goals is teaching." BeenThere, a conservative, had yet another opinion: "In many fields it looks like this. If you see yourself pursuing a leftist research paradigm your chances of having an easy and successful academic career are high. If you see yourself pursuing a counter-leftist research paradigm your chances of having an easy and successful academic career are low." "This isn't rocket science," BeenThere added. Mike G. was even more blunt. Liberals predominate in academe because "they select people just like themselves in the hiring process."[1]

Opinions such as these are commonplace; many find their counterparts in the claims of social scientists. But are they right? In this chapter I examine four hypotheses about the causes of professorial liberalism; these revolve around (1) academics' position in the class structure, (2) the effects of advanced education, (3) value differences between liberals and conservatives, and (4) cognitive and personality factors. Although all have some merit, none is close to fully satisfactory. Chapter 3 offers a better explanation, centered on the idea of occupational reputation-based political self-selection, and Chapter 4 shows how that approach can account for variation in political views among professors. Chapter 4 also considers the other major theory of professorial liberalism: that the left tilt in academe results from political bias and discrimination.

✦

The student unrest that roiled campuses in the 1960s and motivated Ladd and Lipset's *The Divided Academy* was hardly unique to the United States. Protests, sit-ins, and occasionally violent demonstrations by young people were common throughout North America, Europe, and beyond. Among European countries, few were more affected than France. In the first week of May 1968, thousands of university students began occupying the Sorbonne.

After a clash with police, millions of labor unionists marched to show their sympathies with the students, enacting a general strike. Although the disturbance began as a protest against the policies of university administrators and the French educational bureaucracy, as it escalated it transformed into a more general revolt against the capitalist order and the leadership of President Charles de Gaulle.[2]

May 1968 is well-known by humanists and those in the more humanistic social sciences not simply because it was a defining event in modern French history but also because several of the leading French philosophers and social theorists of the 1970s and 1980s were actively involved in the protests. Some have interpreted French poststructuralism that developed at the time as an expression of the themes of the revolt: anti-individualism, a questioning of established social hierarchies and conventions, attentiveness to subtle forms of power.[3] But the events were of no less interest to far-sighted scholars who recognized them even then as a turning point in French intellectual life.

One such scholar was Pierre Bourdieu. In 1967 Bourdieu began gathering data on faculty members teaching in Parisian institutions. His goal was to produce a sociological analysis of French academic life, one that would shed light on faculty and student involvement in the tumultuous events of those years. As part of this, Bourdieu sought to collect data on the political views of Parisian professors. So intensely conflictual were the late 1960s that many of the academics he contacted refused to answer questions about their politics, fearing that he was conducting some kind of political inquisition. He was forced to rely on public statements they had made. He proceeded not only to describe the politics of the faculty but also to offer a sophisticated explanation.

To do so Bourdieu employed ideas he was developing in his work on other sectors of French society. In the book that resulted from the research, *Homo Academicus* (1984), and elsewhere in his writings, particularly in a chapter of his 1979 book, *Distinction,* he argued that the political commitments of Parisian academics generally could be explained as a function of where the academic profession is located in the class structure of modern France—that is, as a function of academics' class position.[4] Rejecting the Marxian idea that social life is a struggle for power between two main economic classes, Bourdieu argued that individuals and families are actually positioned in a three-dimensional social space according to the levels of economic, cultural, and social capital at their disposal. For Bourdieu, economic capital refers primarily to income or wealth, cultural capital to high-status knowledge or taste, and social capital to connections to powerful individuals. All three, in his view, are vital and scarce resources that people seek to accumulate. Bourdieu thought that the real collective struggles in society are not between broadly defined classes but between more fine-grained groupings of individuals with similar combinations and endowments of these resources. On the one hand, he argued, those with similar mixes of economic, cultural, and social capital will tend to have similar styles of life. This creates a sense of commonality, providing a basis for collective action. On the other hand, the groups thus created, which he sometimes called "class fractions," have strong interests in improving or at least maintaining their social standing relative to other groups by working in any way possible to augment the amount of capital at their disposal or to increase its value.

Politics was one of the means of augmentation Bourdieu identified. Generally speaking, he proposed, people with similar profiles of economic, cultural, and social capital will have similar political orientations: they will latch onto political positions consistent with their lifestyle and worldview and, as important, will support state action that would benefit them and others like them in the competition with other groups and class fractions. For Bourdieu, as for many other sociologists writing on politics, in the final analysis political beliefs and commitments come down to people's "class interests"—to voters lining up behind positions and politicians that it makes sense for them to support given where they stand in the socioeconomic order.

The defining sociological characteristic of intellectuals, Bourdieu continued—not just academics but all intellectuals—is that they have high levels of cultural capital (advanced educational credentials, knowledge of high-status topics like literature, avant-garde art, and philosophy, and sophisticated tastes) but only middling levels of economic capital (most receive middle-class salaries). The maintenance or improvement of their position in social space would best be served, he suggested, by state policies that downgrade the importance of economic capital and put a premium on educational and cultural pursuits. Left-leaning governments often do just that, reining in the power of the business classes, giving prominent roles to intellectuals to carry out state planning, empowering the educational bureaucracy. But, according to Bourdieu, this is not the only reason intellectuals gravitate left. They also come to realize that although in some ways they may belong to the dominant stratum in society, in that they are accorded high levels of respect and prestige, they are in fact "dominated" members of that stratum: under typical conditions they have far less power than businessmen and politicians. This makes intellectuals naturally sympathetic toward other groups that are socially dominated and further solidifies their commitment to progressivism.

In his research on Parisian academics, Bourdieu confirmed the obvious: most were on the left. But not all fit this mold. In some disciplines, such as law and medicine, professors could be found who were more supportive of the existing regime. Bourdieu argued that the explanation lay once again in professors' profiles of economic, cultural, and social capital—and in their relationship to power. As a group, professors have more cultural than economic capital. But not all professors are alike. Professors of law and medicine, his research showed, were more likely than other academics to come from upper-class families, to have attended prestigious schools, and more generally to have upper-class lifestyles, including social connections to businesspeople. What is more, professors of law and medicine were pressed into government service at higher rates than their colleagues in the social sciences, the humanities, and the natural sciences. Was it therefore surprising that they were more supportive of the political and economic status quo?

Bourdieu's argument that academics' politics are rooted in their position in the class structure—and that political variation among them is also so rooted—may be the dominant explanation for the liberalism of professors among sociologists today.[5] And not without reason: it synthesizes a great deal of information, is nonobvious, and appears plausible. But it does not explain the politics of American professors very well.

This is not because Bourdieu's more general theory of society is necessarily wrong or inapplicable to American political dynamics. Some problems with explanatory overreach aside, it is a powerful framework indeed, and if anything may be underappreciated for making sense of American politics. A common criticism of Bourdieu by American scholars has been that his focus on cultural capital does not travel: in the contemporary United States, critics contend, those in higher social class positions obviously command greater economic resources than others, but it is not clear that they have, and distinguish themselves on the basis of, greater cultural resources in the sense of having refined tastes when it comes to art, literature, film, and so on.[6] Many American economic elites, the argument goes—particularly outside the Northeast—are cultural philistines who prefer Godiva to Godard and spend their leisure time on the golf course, not in museums, as their French equivalents might. Yet champions of Bourdieu retort that this dismissal is too hasty. Texas oilmen may not be aficionados of avant-garde art, but research shows that Americans in higher socioeconomic positions do tend to consume more sophisticated forms of culture.[7] At the same time, they are more likely to be cultural "omnivores," appreciating a great variety of cultural forms, highbrow and lowbrow, whereas those in the lower middle class and working class often have more restricted cultural palates.[8] A considerable amount of research has gone into analyzing the consequences of this for American class relations, taking up questions like whether omnivorism has become a new marker of class status that is used as a basis for social exclusion.[9] But there could be important political consequences as well. One of the more remarkable sociopolitical developments of recent decades has been a shift of educated professionals, once stalwart Republicans, into the Democratic Party.[10] Several explanations have been proposed, including the Republican Party's move to the right on social issues. But another possible explanation is that professionals (as opposed to the superrich) are among the groups most heavily invested in cultural omnivorism and related practices and are throwing their weight behind the Democrats because they perceive an affinity with their strategies for maintaining social distinction. Republicans, who prioritize heartland values over eclecticism and multiculturalism and who insist on standardized testing for students rather than promoting the free creative expression that professionals often encourage in their children, typically enact policies that interfere with professionals' efforts at using culture to give themselves and their kids a leg up in the competition for social resources (however much Republicans might be "good" for professionals in other ways, such as in their support for more regressive tax structures).[11]

Professors are among the highly educated professionals invested in cultural omnivorism, and it is possible that *some* of their support for the Democratic Party derives from this same source. But professors have been liberals and Democrats for decades, long before other professionals began trending in that direction and long before current practices of upper-middle-class distinction arose.

What about Bourdieu's original theory, though—that professors are liberal because liberalism is the fate of those who have more cultural than economic capital? This is not the full story either, at least not in the United States. If Bourdieu were correct, much of the political gap between professors and other Americans would be explained by the disparity between professors' level of education (a good overall indicator of their cultural capital) and their income. Quite apart from liberal insistence on market regulation, most should also hold negative views of business, born of hostility toward the "dominant fraction of the dominant class" and a desire to distance themselves from it culturally. When Ethan Fosse and

I examined the first of these factors using data from the GSS, however, assessing statistically how much of the political gap between professors and nonprofessors was a function of it, we found that the education-income disparity accounted for 13%.[12] Thirteen percent of a social phenomenon accounted for is not bad for social science theory, given the complexity of the social world, but clearly the bulk of professorial liberalism is explained by something else. Beyond that, the 13% figure is ambiguous. Is it evidence that people with high levels of education but comparatively modest incomes lean left because it is in their class interests to do so? Is it, as the research of sociologist Stephen Vaisey might suggest, because—for reasons only indirectly tied to class interests—people experience a sense of psychological strain when not all of their "status characteristics" line up, leading some to protest against the status quo?[13] Or could it be that liberals are simply more likely than conservatives to enter knowledge work and related fields in which workers are typically better educated than they are paid, not because they necessarily value cultural more than economic capital but because such fields seem to them a good fit with who they are politically?[14]

Nor does Bourdieu's theory fit the PAP data as well as one might like, or data derived from follow-up interviews to the survey. Bear in mind the findings from Chapter 1. Most professors vote Democratic and hold liberal views on social issues. But only radicals and two-thirds of progressives are hostile to the business class in the sense of believing that American businesses and corporations are greedy and make too much profit. The rest—a small majority—appear to begrudge the world of commerce little. Professors' liberalism on social issues might be understood in terms of cultural differentiation from social conservatives, but given that social conservatives tend to come from lower social class origins in the contemporary American context, it is hard to see how such differentiation could help professors in their competition for social power with economic elites, as Bourdieu's account would have it.

On the point about professors being part of the dominated fraction of the dominant class, while in the interviews we conducted radical and progressive faculty members, especially, could often be found expressing sympathy for dispossessed minorities, only interviewees who were themselves members of minority groups talked about this in relationship to a realization of their own subordinate status within the field of power. One group of academics that most observers would agree *is* socially dominated, and perceives itself as such, consists of scholars who teach on a part-time basis, usually for a meager salary. If Bourdieu's theory were right, we would expect adjunct faculty to be much more to the left than full-timers. But the PAP data show that on average part-time professors are actually slightly *less* liberal than others.[15]

Bourdieu's account of professorial politics based on class position is also in tension with what we know about when in professors' lives their political views form. A working assumption in his theory, as in many sociological theories of class politics, is that some feature of the work situation—in the case of professors, the fact that they have more cultural knowledge than remuneration—sets up objective social and economic interests that structure political choices and commitments. If this assumption were true for academics, we might expect their political views to change upon becoming professors or when they start down the path toward becoming professors, for it is then that they would begin to realize where their true class interests lie. But such changes do not appear to be common. For example, Ladd and Lipset asked their respondents to characterize their political views when they were seniors in college. Although findings from survey items that ask people to reach far back into their memories must be regarded with particular caution, of professors who reported that they had been leftists as college seniors, 90% were still leftists or liberals at the time of the survey.[16] Of those who had been liberals in college, 73% remained leftists or liberals as professors. Similarly, graduate student Catherine Cheng and I examined transcripts from the follow-up interviews to the PAP survey to determine when in their lives interviewees said their politics took shape.[17] In 80% of the cases involving liberal interviewees—and 70% in the interview sample overall—professors reported that their political views were well established by the time they were in their early twenties. Could this be because, at this point in their lives, they had already set their sights on academic careers and could anticipate that they would be "investing" most heavily in cultural and intellectual capital? Maybe. However, the same pattern obtained whether or not interviewees reported having known then that they were going to go into academe. A majority (66%) said their political views had actually been formed during their high school years, when, for most people, any number of occupational possibilities remain on the table.

Two additional findings bear on this same point. One of the things Fosse, Jeremy Freese, and I looked at in our longitudinal study of graduate school attendance was whether students become more liberal during graduate school. Although graduate school liberalization could reflect the general effects of education or learning about the academic role—two possibilities discussed later in this chapter—it might also reflect a growing awareness of the interests associated with one's future class position. We found that young Americans enrolled in graduate programs in 2007–2008 *had* become more liberal since their college days—but so had other young, college-educated Americans who did not go to graduate school. The liberalizing effect of enrollment in a PhD program was modest.[18]

Yet another way into this issue is to look at the voting histories of professors in the PAP survey who are young enough that they would not yet have been professors during some of the elections we asked about. Of the professors in our sample, 30% received their highest degrees after 1996. Among professors in this group who reported that they voted for Kerry in 2004, 83% who voted in 1996 said that they did so for Bill Clinton, while 90% voted for Clinton in 1992. Most, it would seem, already knew as young adults where their political sympathies lay. And this squares with what we know from other research on political socialization. Political attitudes, particularly on policy issues, can and do shift over a lifetime, but the majority of Americans who form strong partisan attachments and ideological commitments do so in adolescence or young adulthood and retain them over the years.[19] Switching party or ideology is quite rare, which is why the Democrats and the GOP focus so much attention on uncommitted swing voters. To date, scholars of class politics have not done as much as they should to incorporate research on political socialization into their theories, but the point here is simply that the life histories of most academics do not match up well with a theoretical account that sees their class position as workers as underlying their political choices.

But what about that aspect of Bourdieu's theory that focuses not on the class position of the professoriate but on the class *backgrounds* of professors? Perhaps class shapes professors' politics not in the sense that their jobs establish interests to which their political preferences are a response but instead in that they take on as young people the political attitudes that their parents held because of *their* class position, leaning left as a group because academics have common origins in a particular corner of the class structure? While Bourdieu's approach makes much of people's current class situations, it also attends closely to the development, in childhood and adolescence, of class-based attitudes and lifeways, including political dispositions and educational and occupational aspirations.

It is true that class background affects the odds that one will become a professor. Professors tend to come from better educated, higher income families than other Americans. As part of this, academic work runs in families: if one of your parents is a professor, the chances increase that you will become one too. But according to statistical models, these factors do not explain professors' politics. The fact that 18% of professors during the period 1974–2008 had fathers with advanced degrees, as compared to 5% of other Americans, does nothing in statistical terms to explain the liberalism of the occupation, while their higher than average parental incomes should, if anything, make them more conservative than other workers given general patterns in the American population.[20] People whose parents are professors might be expected to be liberals and Democrats, but there are not enough academics from academic families—only about 9% of professors have fathers or mothers with PhDs, according to the PAP data—that this could account for the politics of the professoriate overall, while a smaller proportion of professors have parents who worked in other fields associated with high cultural capital than Bourdieu's theory would lead us to expect.[21]

Beyond Bourdieu, however, there are two other class-related possibilities worth considering. Could it be, as sociologist Michèle Lamont has speculated, that professors and other members of the so-called New Class—knowledge workers broadly construed whom some sociologists, writing in the 1970s and 1980s, believed to be on the road to forming a coherent class as opposed to merely a class fraction—lean left not just out of an interest in cultural differentiation, but for more directly material reasons?[22] Perhaps in the United States knowledge workers vote Democratic and are liberals because they know on which side their bread is buttered—that the Democrats put money into higher education, research, and the arts, whereas Republicans do not. To test this theory, Fosse and I looked to see how much of the political gap between professors and other Americans could be explained by the fact that a much higher proportion of the former are public-sector employees with material interests in increased state spending. The answer was almost none.[23] Other scholars of class, conceiving of the class structure differently than Bourdieu, have noted that small business owners and the self-employed often have conservative economic views since their economic interests are best served by state policies that impose few regulations on business and allow them to easily pass on wealth to their children.[24] There are no self-employed professors. Could this explain their relative liberalism? It does not, Fosse and I found.[25]

✦

What about a more straightforward theory? In the 1980s and 1990s there was much debate among sociologists about the New Class concept—about whether it made sense theoretically and empirically to conceive of knowledge workers as on their way to forming a class.[26] One of the skeptics was sociologist Steven Brint. In a series of papers, he argued that the idea of the New Class was overblown.[27] Although white-collar workers did seem to be becoming more liberal, Brint noted that there were major political differences between professors, engineers, software programmers, and others. So what reason was there for believing they were coming to cohere as a group and would soon lead a major political realignment? Using survey data, Brint also demonstrated that one of the main factors distinguishing those knowledge workers who did lean left, such as professors, from those who did not was simply that the former had undergone more years of formal education. It was well established in the research literature, Brint pointed out, that education has a liberalizing effect on social and political attitudes, leading people to be more concerned with the plight of the socially disadvantaged, more open to diversity, more tolerant of political dissent, and less religious.[28] Perhaps the main cause of the liberalism of professors is simply that academics have to spend an extraordinarily long time in school before they can begin their careers?[29]

In the research from the 1960s and 1970s to which Brint was referring, the finding that higher education is linked with more liberal attitudes and politics was explained in a number of ways.[30] Having established the association using cross-sectional survey data or with longitudinal data following students at a select number of schools over the course of their undergraduate education, researchers argued that college makes people more liberal and tolerant by increasing their level of cognitive sophistication, exposing them to Enlightenment ideas of rationality and rights, increasing the distance between them and their sometimes conservative parents, and, not least, exposing them to diverse peers. The classic piece of research in this vein was Theodore Newcomb's longitudinal study of undergraduates at Bennington College in the 1930s, which was then a women's college.[31] Many of the women Newcomb followed veered left during their college days under the tutelage of their New Deal–supportive professors and remained there for the rest of their lives. If undergraduate education could produce such effects, surely they would only be magnified by the more intense experience of graduate school.

This is another plausible theory. In its favor it is simple and parsimonious and does not rest on hard-to-prove claims about the nature of the class structure or people's interests. To test it, Fosse and I looked to see how much of the political gap between professors and nonprofessors in the GSS data could be explained by the fact that a very large proportion of academics possess advanced degrees, a mark of their having spent so many years in the educational system.[32] This factor turned out to be consequential. It accounted for nearly 20% of the difference in political orientation between professors and other Americans and was the most statistically powerful variable in our analysis. Brint appeared to be right: college makes people more liberal and tolerant, and graduate school all the more so.

In point of fact, there are overlaps between Brint's claim and claims put forth by previous generations of researchers like Lazarsfeld and Ladd and Lipset, as well as some unexpected overlaps with Bourdieu. Lazarsfeld and Ladd and Lipset made their contributions to the study of professorial politics during a time when sociologists commonly assumed that society should be understood in terms of people playing out well-defined social roles, distinct positions in the social structure, each revolving around a set of behavioral rules and scripts enshrined in social norms. Building on this assumption, Lazarsfeld and Ladd and Lipset highlighted what they saw as distinctive features of the academic role. At its core, they claimed, the academic role involves "intellectualism"—a tendency to see the world through the lens bequeathed by scholars and writers of generations past and by one's contemporaries and to write and teach on the basis of such a vision.[33] As they saw it, this entails, among other things, a thoroughgoing commitment to reason, unrelenting skepticism toward claims not backed up by evidence and logic, a prioritization of ideas over material concerns, and a creative orientation—an abiding concern to move the intellectual tradition forward. Not all academics are intellectual in this sense and show evidence of what Lazarsfeld and Thielens called the "academic mind," but, these researchers claimed, in traditional liberal arts fields most are and do.[34] Wherever academics can be found acting as intellectuals, these researchers suggested, leftists and liberals could also be found. This was so because, in their view, conservatism, particularly in its modern American form, is the antithesis of intellectualism, as it involves a rejection of rationality and Enlightenment values in favor of an emphasis on dogmatism and religion. (With this claim the sociologists arguably gave themselves over to their own politics.) It is no surprise, then, that there are few conservative professors and that professors tend to be more liberal the closer they are to the liberal arts core of the university and to its institutional center—doctoral-granting universities—where commitments to intellectualism run deep.

Lazarsfeld and Ladd and Lipset recognized three mechanisms by which intellectualism could influence professorial politics. They believed the professoriate tends to draw into it people with the disposition and personality characteristics necessary to become intellectuals and that such people would tend to be on the left because of both the intrinsic nature of intellectualism and the fact that in the West intellectualism as a cultural tradition has historically had a left-critical bearing. Ladd and Lipset, for their part, also held that intellectualism is unevenly distributed across demographic groups. To the extent that groups that encourage intellectualism in their young might lean left for other reasons as well, this could draw even more liberals into academe. The main group Ladd and Lipset had in mind was Jews, and they traced some of the liberalism of American higher education to the overrepresentation of Jews in the professoriate after World War II, particularly in elite institutions.[35] Finally, and most relevant here, the researchers recognized that future academics learn a great deal during the course of their graduate training, including the norms and values of the academic profession. As they learn how to act like intellectuals and scientists, graduate students could be expected to move even further left, not because of leftist indoctrination but simply as a consequence of becoming more complex thinkers.

Although Bourdieu was suspicious of the notion of social roles, in one respect his theory is similar. One interpretation has him claiming that for French academics reared in a national intellectual tradition that stretches from Émile Zola to Jean-Paul Sartre and beyond, intellectual work and leftism had become so closely associated that as young scholars were apprenticed under their advisors many would begin to take on a leftist orientation in an almost mimetic fashion, in the same way that they learned other aspects of what Bourdieu called the "academic habitus," such as distinctive ways of talking and writing about ideas. Recently Louis Menand, in *The Marketplace of Ideas* (2010), put forth a similar explanation for the left/liberal tendencies of humanities professors.[36] Humanists have to endure extremely long PhD programs, Menand observed, and are under strong pressure while in graduate school to think and act like their mentors—politically as well as intellectually—if they are to have any hope of landing a coveted tenure-track job.

Whether the focus is on the general liberalizing effect of higher education or the specific effects of graduate training, this explanation for the politics of professors is a powerful one—at first glance. Empirically it has several things going for it. First, educational differences between professors and other Americans do go a fair way toward accounting statistically for the political gap between the two groups. Second, the theory helps us make sense not only of professorial liberalism but of the left-leaning tendencies of other occupational groups as well. As Brint was correct to note, many of the other liberal occupations in American society— such as social worker, therapist, writer, and journalist—are also populated by workers who often have advanced degrees. Third, the finding that education produces more liberal attitudes has long been viewed as one of the most stable and solid findings in social science—a veritable social scientific truism.[37] Fourth, the theory is consistent with certain patterns in the PAP data. As Chapter 1 showed, conservatives are particularly underrepresented in more "intellectual" liberal arts fields and in institutions that take intellectualism seriously, such as doctoral-granting universities and liberal arts colleges. What is more, in line especially with Ladd and Lipset's take on the matter, there is something of an association between political views and the tendency of academics to identify themselves as intellectuals. In the PAP survey, 97% of radicals and 85% of progressives said that the term *intellectual* described them moderately well or better, as compared to 67% of strong conservatives, say. When Fosse and I used the GSS to try to quantify levels of intellectualism among professors and other Americans by measuring their tolerance for controversial ideas, on the grounds that intellectualism entails a commitment to rational deliberation and free speech, we found that this variable accounted for a not insignificant 12% of the politics gap between the two groups.[38]

On further reflection, however, problems begin to appear with the hypothesis that professors are liberal because of their advanced education. The main one is that, as noted earlier, people do *not* become substantially more liberal as a result of their graduate school experiences. My study with Fosse and Freese found that 36% of doctoral seekers had become more liberal since college (with most of this reflecting a minor shift in political position rather than an about-face), as compared to 29% of people who stopped going to school after receiving their bachelor's degree—a relatively minor difference offset by the fact that a higher proportion of doctoral seekers had also become more conservative.[39] While graduate school is a time of intense learning and professional development, it does not appear to result in a major reconstruction of most attendees' political worldviews. Consistent with these quantitative findings, in the PAP follow-up interviews few professors recalled graduate school as a key time in their political development, except in the sense that some sociologists and English professors remembered being exposed then to theories and ideas that provided them with what they saw as stronger justifications for their preexisting political commitments.

Beyond this, there is growing reason to question the truism that higher education produces dramatically more liberal attitudes. To be sure, college students and new college graduates compose, on the whole, a liberal and tolerant group, and this is true not just in the United States but in many other countries as well.[40] However, recent social science research, revisiting the findings of Newcomb and his colleagues, has discovered that much of this is explained not by the liberalizing effects of higher education but by the fact that adolescents who are more liberal and tolerant—and who are on a path toward becoming even more so in their early twenties—are simply more likely to attend college and graduate from it.[41] For example, Fosse and I, working with sociologist Jeremy Uecker, have recently been analyzing longitudinal data to determine how much of the greater liberalism of college graduates today might be a function of some of the characteristics that lead people to select into college in the first place and do well there, such as having educated parents or growing up in a knowledge work–intensive area. We find that selection factors such as these account for the bulk of the observed ideological difference between college graduates and others.[42] One possible explanation for the disparity between these findings and older research might be historical variation in the nature of the college experience. Menand, among others, has argued that the 1950s and 1960s were unusual for American higher education in every respect, and it is possible that students then were so engaged with college life that it did have a transformative political effect on them, as it did earlier for the Bennington women, whereas for today's students it does not.[43] In *Academically Adrift* (2011), sociologists Richard Arum and Josipa Roksa have shown that college students now spend much less time studying than in decades past and that they are, in other ways as well, less academically serious.[44] To the extent that academic engagement and the cognitive growth associated with it is one causal pathway toward liberalization, this change could be consequential for politics. Yet this interpretation will not stand, for political scientists Laura Stoker and M. Kent Jennings have found, examining longitudinal data on people who went to college in the 1960s, that once selection variables are attended to, much of the heralded collegiate liberalization effect of that era vanishes as well.[45] Although we should not dismiss college liberalization claims entirely—the evidence that attending college produces greater tolerance for diversity is stronger than the evidence for other aspects of liberalization, while research also shows college to be a time when some young people can be radicalized and drawn into social movement activity—the latest wave of studies provides additional reason to doubt whether the liberalism of professors results primarily from their having spent many years in school.[46] Chapter 3 develops another interpretation of the finding that much of the politics gap between professors and other Americans is a function of education: liberals are more inclined than conservatives to pursue the advanced education necessary to become professors.

✦

In Chapter 1 I briefly considered the work of social scientists who argue that the most fundamental differences separating those on the left and those on the right are differences in values: different understandings of the good and of morality and of what is important in life. Values, these researchers claim, are what give rise to political worldviews, knit the like-minded together in "value communities," and anchor opinions on policy matters.[47] Several researchers proceeding from these assumptions—although from preference-based, not psychological versions of them—have sought to make sense of professorial liberalism, and the explanation they have formulated is the third theory that bears consideration.

Political scientists Matthew Woessner and April Kelly-Woessner are the leading figures here. They too argue that the proximate cause of there being few conservative professors is that not very many conservatives pursue PhDs, restricting the number of conservatives in what they called the "academic pipeline."[48] In their view, two factors are at work. First, liberals are overrepresented among college students and recent college graduates. Since this is the pool from which nearly all graduate students are drawn, it is hardly a surprise that there are more liberal than conservative graduate students. Second, among college-educated young adults, liberals are especially likely to go to graduate school, and this, they claimed, is because some of the things that liberals value that make them liberal lead naturally toward the pursuit of higher learning, while conservative values lead away from it. More specifically, they argued that liberal college students are more likely to value intellectual, artistic, and scientific achievement, whereas conservatives are more likely to value financial success and getting married and having children at an early age. Valuing intellectual, artistic, and scientific achievement—very much like the disposition to intellectualism discussed by Ladd and Lipset—is conducive to the pursuit of academic careers for obvious reasons, said Woessner and Kelly-Woessner, while young people prioritizing financial success or early family formation recognize that academe would be a poor choice for them, given the reality of academic salaries and the intense pressures of graduate school and tenure. Analyzing HERI college student data, Woessner and Kelly-Woessner found that self-described liberals were more likely than conservatives to say they intended to pursue doctorates and that variables measuring the values highlighted by their theory were associated with such an intention.

Although not linked to it explicitly, Woessner and Kelly-Woessner's argument ties in with work by sociologists and economists on "job values."[49] How do people entering the labor market make decisions about what lines of work to pursue? Where some would argue that the overriding factor is how much money people can expect to make given their skills and credentials, in most sociological and economic models of occupational choice the preferences that people have for different kinds of labor and for working under different kinds of employment conditions are also given their due. These preferences, scholars argue, are shaped by more general job values, things that people look for above all else in their work lives. It is not hard to imagine how this line of thinking could be developed into an explanation of professorial politics that goes even beyond the claims of Woessner and Kelly-Woessner. For example, while tenure-track jobs are increasingly hard to get, once professors have tenure their jobs are secure. They can be fired only for gross misconduct, and they can be laid off only if the institutions for which they work are in true financial distress. While everyone values job security, some people may value it more than others. The civil servant may take great comfort in the predictability of his paycheck, while the entrepreneur may be willing to risk financial catastrophe for the chance at striking it rich. Perhaps people who are smart and deeply desirous of job security are more likely to seek out academic careers. Since this might reflect discomfort with the vicissitudes of the market, it is not unreasonable to suppose that those who are risk-averse when it comes to employment might also tend to be political liberals. Alternatively, perhaps the major value difference between conservatives and liberals is not that conservatives want to get rich but simply that they are more oriented toward monetary concerns, while liberals are free spirits more committed to what sociologist Ronald Inglehart calls "postmaterialist values"—those to do with the care, feeding, and development of the self.[50] Post-materialists might think that the most important feature of a job is its capacity to provide a sense of meaning and purpose, as academic careers do in spades. Yet another take on the matter, linked to the research of sociologist Melvin Kohn, focuses on work autonomy.[51] Professors set their own hours, have great discretion in how they organize their teaching and research, and do not really have a boss. The academic life might thus appeal especially to people who value autonomy highly—and those same people would tend to oppose social conservatism, seeing state-imposed restrictions on people's private lives and choices as violations.

Is the job values explanation for professorial liberalism right? One problem is the set of assumptions that underlies it. Most scholarship on values and job choice assumes that young adults have clear and relatively stable preferences for certain kinds of employment, as well as good information about what different occupations entail. They then compare their preferences, along with assessments of their skills and credentials and the state of the labor market, to this information and choose a career path that maximizes on their values. Most work on jobs and values, in other words, assumes a high degree of rationality on the part of young people. Such an assumption can lead to elegant theories, but if there is one social group not known for being highly informed and rational, it is the young. Interview-based research on young adults shows that for many, job values are protean and subject to rapid change with new experience, that many pay surprisingly little attention to the process of choosing a career, and that the amount of knowledge young people have about different career options is limited, often a function of what they have seen on television or what they have been able to glean from people in their immediate social networks.[52] On this last point, while young, college-educated adults know *something* about what it means to be a professor—from the media, from interactions they may have had with academics in the classroom or in office hours, from elsewhere—there is reason to suspect that for most, this information does not amount to much. For example, I teach at a research university, and most of what my colleagues and I are evaluated on administratively is our research output. Yet our undergraduate students—even those who say they might be interested in academic careers—routinely assume that most of our energy is put into teaching. Less anecdotally, among college students whom Simmons and I reached as part of our poll measuring public attitudes toward liberal bias in higher education, 50% said they had never heard of tenure, an indication of considerable ignorance about the academic profession. Along the same lines, about a fifth of students said "Don't know" in response to a question about whether college and university professors are paid too much, too little, or just the right amount—likely because they did not know how much professors are paid. True, one would not need terribly much information about an academic career to conclude that one is not going to get rich as an academic or that the job might provide one with a sense of meaning or with some work autonomy. But how many students—aside from the most savvy ones at Chicago, Harvard, or Berkeley, or whose parents are professors—would have the foresight to realize that it is challenging to have children while on the tenure track, or know how exactly a professorial salary at various levels compares to salaries in other occupations, or understand fully what the chances are of landing a good academic job after graduate school, or even be completely clear as to what it is that professors spend their time doing? If this information is murky, how could calculations of fit with job values—themselves unclear for most young people—be the main thing responsible for the decision to start down an academic career path, except in the general sense that obviously one is not going to become an academic unless one appreciates intellectual pursuits?[53]

Second, there are direct empirical reasons to be wary of the values hypothesis. For one thing, there is more value heterogeneity within political camps than stereotypes would have it. As *New York Times* columnist David Brooks reminded us, for every liberal do-gooder willing to give up everything to make a better world there is a bourgeois bohemian equally desirous of social justice and a Wolf range.[54] Many conservatives dream of careers as CEOs; many want to give back to their community by becoming police officers or ministers. Surveys find only small differences between liberals and conservatives in how much importance they say they place on monetary success. Among the college students in Woessner and Kelly-Woessner's study, it was moderates, not conservatives, who said they valued moneymaking the most, although conservatives were somewhat more likely than liberals to state that financial success was important to them.[55]

Furthermore, whenever my colleagues and I have tried to test the job values hypothesis, it has come up short. In our paper using GSS data, Fosse and I examined how much of the politics gap between professors and nonprofessors could be explained by the fact that professors care more about the meaningfulness of work than other Americans and less about other features of the employment situation, such as high income potential. The difference, we found, accounted for just 4% of the political gap between professors and nonprofessors. Likewise Fosse, Freese, and I found that the somewhat greater value that conservative college students place on material success or starting a family early, relative to liberals, does little to account for their diminished tendency to enroll in PhD programs.[56] And that professors report higher levels of autonomy on the job than other workers does not seem to be related to their liberal politics.[57]

Finally, what about the idea that conservatives value science less than liberals? Survey data from the GSS do show that conservatives have lower levels of confidence in the scientific community. According to the GSS, 45% of conservatives, compared to 19% of liberals, also believe that "we trust too much in science." Does this help to explain why more liberals than conservatives become professors? No doubt it plays some role, but how large? As indicated previously, the main factor accounting for these differences is religion: as a group, conservatives trust science less mostly because they are more religious. Some commentators have sought to portray theologically conservative Protestants in particular as inhabiting an alternative epistemological universe, one in which the natural world is seen as operating according to principles totally foreign to science.[58] There are indeed fundamentalists and evangelicals—and devout Catholics and Mormons and Orthodox Jews and others—for whom this is the case, and we would not expect very many of them to become academics. But sociologist

John Evans has shown that while conservative Protestants have major beefs with the idea of evolution, those who go to college do not take fewer science courses than others, suggesting that claims of a complete devaluation of science may be overstated.[59] Unfortunately, GSS data do not permit a strong test of whether and to what degree attitudes toward science contribute to professorial liberalism.[60] But it is possible to make an indirect test: if differing values with respect to science were a key driver of the liberalism of professors, we would expect to find religious differences between professors and other Americans accounting for much of the distinctive politics of the former group. Yet Fosse and I found that such differences account for only about 10% of the political gap between professors and others.[61]

This finding is in line with two other points. First, if different orientations toward science explained professors' politics, we might expect liberal views to be most common among professors in the natural sciences. But humanists and social scientists are the most left-leaning disciplinary groups. In the PAP data, there is a weak *negative* association between the liberalism of respondents and the extent to which they identify themselves as scientists.[62] Second, two of the occupational categories in American society since 1996 with the highest proportion of self-identified conservatives are intrinsically scientific: natural scientists working outside academe (34% conservative) and physicians and dentists (30% conservative).[63] While economic interests are probably at play here (natural scientists outside academe often work in conservative industries like oil and pharmaceuticals; doctors and dentists tend to be very well paid), if conservatives' antiscience stance automatically kept them from going into knowledge work jobs it is unlikely we would see as many conservatives working in these fields as we do.

⁕

My research with Freese and Fosse, as well as the study by Woessner and Kelly-Woessner, establishes that an important part of the explanation for the liberalism of professors is that liberals are more inclined than conservatives to go to graduate school. But what if the main reason for this is not differences in values, but differences in even more deep-seated characteristics?

Over the past two decades the interdisciplinary field of political psychology has been expanding rapidly. An important area of research is the effect of cognitive and personality factors on ideology, partisanship, and political participation.[64] Two findings here bear on professorial politics.

The first concerns the connection between intelligence, social liberalism, and religiosity. Research suggests that greater cognitive ability—in particular, greater verbal intelligence—tends to be associated with a more liberal, tolerant worldview on matters such as homosexuality, abortion, and political dissent and disobedience. It is also linked with religious skepticism. Since right-leaning parties often embrace more authoritarian, religiously inspired agendas, these associations may influence political preferences. In a series of longitudinal studies carried out in the United Kingdom psychologist Ian Deary has shown that "bright children become Enlightened adults"; that is, cognitive ability measured in the elementary school years is linked with more tolerant attitudes and a left political orientation in adulthood.[65] Some of this, Deary argues, is a result of education: smarter people go further in school, and education (in his view) liberalizes. But there is also, he argues, a direct effect of intelligence on attitudes. Political psychologists have offered various explanations for these correlations, including the alleged complexity of liberal ideology and the natural tension between heightened intelligence and beliefs about the supernatural. Regardless of the underlying mechanisms, it is not hard to infer the implications for explanations of professorial politics. Academic work, whether in the sciences, the humanities, or elsewhere, requires brain power. Could not this fact alone explain the greater tendency of professors, as well as of other highly intelligent knowledge workers, to be on the left?

The findings of political psychologists on personality are also relevant. Most psychologists conceive of personality as comprising cognitive, affective, and behavioral tendencies that endure over the course of people's lives and play themselves out in a wide variety of situations and circumstances.[66] Psychologists recognize that personality may be affected by individual and social experiences, such as trauma, but the early appearance of personality traits in childhood, along with evidence from twin studies, suggests that the roots of personality lie in genetic inheritance and random variation in the population.

The dimensions along which personality can vary are subject to some debate, but most psychologists operate with a five-dimensional model: people may be more or less conscientious, open to new experience, extraverted, agreeable, and neurotic. Political psychologists have shown that certain of these personality traits, along with other personality-related characteristics, are associated with support for liberal or conservative political ideologies and political attitudes. For example, John Jost, one of the most prolific researchers in the area, reports, using multiple sources of data, that liberals tend to rate higher than conservatives on openness to new experience and lower on conscientiousness and that conservatives also exhibit other psychological characteristics, such as "fear of death" and hostility toward social outgroups.[67] In Jost's view, liberalism, as an ideology, is about embracing social change and progress and protecting the vulnerable in society, where conservatism is about resisting change and prioritizing the welfare of people in one's own social group. Those whose personalities lead them to embrace change and universalism typically become liberals, he argues, while those made nervous by change become conservatives.[68] According to political psychologists, shared personality characteristics between parents and their offspring go some way toward accounting for the long-standing finding from the political socialization literature that political orientation and partisan affiliation are often passed down within families.

The connection to professorial politics is this: among psychologists, another term for openness to new experience is intellectualism, and among the questions sometimes asked in personality inventories to measure openness to new experience are those pertaining to interest in abstract ideas, art, and imagination. Thinking complex thoughts that may lead one to see the world in a new way and opening oneself up to aesthetic experiences are taken by psychologists to be signs of a general willingness and eagerness to embrace the new. Academic work, some have argued (including Ladd and Lipset), demands precisely such an embrace, for scientific and intellectual pursuits often push in unanticipated directions, while also requiring more directly an interest in and facility with abstraction. Vocational psychologists have long theorized that personality factors are important, along with job values and financial considerations, in shaping people's career choices, so it makes sense to think that people who are more open to new experience and interested in abstract ideas might be more apt to go into academic work.[69] This could explain the greater prevalence of leftists in academe, as well as the greater concentration of leftists in nonapplied disciplines that require more abstract thinking. To the extent that intellectualism—here understood as a feature of personality rather than as a cultural disposition—is at a premium in other knowledge work fields as well, personality might also explain the leftism of intellectuals in general.

But it is not only intellectualism that may be at play. Although intellectual and scientific work requires a great deal of discipline, again the work environment of academe is different from what one finds in other organizational settings: much less structured and rigid. While the sheer fact of autonomy in academic life might not matter for explaining professorial politics, it is possible that a relatively unstructured work environment might appeal to people who, in personality terms, are low in conscientiousness, as in the stereotype of the disorganized, absentminded professor. This could further account for academic hostility toward conservative ideologies stressing order and rigidity.

Yet another version of the personality argument highlights one of the many differences between liberals and conservatives flagged in Jost's studies. An active research paradigm in social psychology, led by Jim Sidanius, revolves around the concept of "social dominance orientation."[70] The idea here, pushing in a new direction claims first made in a classic work of social science from the 1950s, *The Authoritarian Personality,* is that people vary in how comfortable they are with social hierarchies in general and in how much they want their in-group specifically to "dominate and be superior to out-groups."[71] Analyzing data mostly from student samples, Sidanius and his colleagues have found that, on average, conservatives score higher than liberals on measures of social dominance orientation. Sidanius views these associations in causal terms: genetic inheritance and random variation explain why people have given levels of comfort with social hierarchy, and this then shapes their politics. Importantly, he argues that social dominance orientation also influences occupational choices. With respect to social dominance orientation, Sidanius claims—following in the footsteps of other researchers in social psychology—that people seek "person-organization congruence," meaning in this case that, depending on their predilections, they look for work in organizations and fields that are either "hierarchy attenuating" or "hierarchy enhancing."[72] Again using data on college students, Sidanius and his colleagues have shown that people who score high on social dominance measures are more likely to want to go into occupations like law enforcement, while those who score low gravitate toward fields like civil rights law and charitable work.[73] Given that Sidanius sees higher education as a hierarchy-attenuating institution, his approach might explain the liberalism of the professoriate by noting the draw of academic work for those with a low social dominance orientation, who, for that same reason, would tend to be liberals.[74]

It would be foolish to deny that cognitive factors, personality, and politics may be linked—especially in light of growing evidence of a genetic basis for political belief, with personality characteristics a likely mediating mechanism.[75] But a slam-dunk empirical case has not yet been made for psychological theories of professorial politics. The research that currently exists suggests that cognitive and personality differences explain no more than a fraction of the liberalism of American professors. The GSS has no personality measures, but it does contain a simple vocabulary test often used to gauge cognitive ability. Professors score higher on this test than do other Americans. But Fosse and I found that by itself the difference explains little of the political gap between professors and others.[76] As for the low levels of religious belief among academics that are tied to their politics, the evidence is not strong that this association is a function of higher cognitive ability.[77]

The survey that Fosse, Freese, and I analyzed in our study of graduate school attendance contained a more sophisticated vocabulary test.[78] We found that higher cognitive ability increased the odds that a student would enroll in a doctoral program rather than stop with a bachelor's degree. But this fact did not do much to explain why the liberals in our sample were more likely than the conservatives to go to graduate school.[79] I obtained a similar result when looking at data from the HERI College Senior Survey (CSS) from 1994 to 1999, which asks students about their probable careers. About 2% of the 156,573 respondents to the survey during those years indicated that they planned to become college teachers. Not surprisingly, college seniors who said they planned to become professors had higher SAT scores than others. There was also a modest relationship in the CSS data between SAT scores and political orientation: liberal students scored 14 points higher on average than their conservative counterparts on the verbal portion—although 9 points lower on the math portion.[80] But in a statistical model predicting the likelihood of aspiring to be a professor, the effect of political liberalism was little changed when students' SAT scores were factored in.[81]

What about personality? The PAP survey did not contain any personality measures, but we were able to look at personality in our study of who goes to graduate school. While the stereotype of the disorganized professor may have some basis in reality, we found no significant relationship between conscientiousness and graduate school attendance. On openness to new experience, the survey we analyzed measured this by asking respondents two questions, one about their level of interest in abstract ideas and the other about how imaginative they were. Although one might think imaginativeness a key marker of openness to new ideas, we found it had no effect on the odds of going to graduate school. Being interested in abstract ideas did. This turns out to be a strong predictor of graduate school attendance and helps to account for differences between liberals and conservatives: about a third of the greater propensity of liberals to go to graduate school rather than stop with a bachelor's degree is a function of this single variable.

What does this mean, though? At a basic level, it simply tells us that conservative young people are less likely than their liberal counterparts to say they are interested in abstraction and that being interested in abstraction correlates with going to graduate school. Does the former reflect intrinsic personality differences? It certainly might. But it could also reflect differences in the ideological strategies of the left and the right as these have been filtered down to shape individual worldviews, self-conceptions, and patterns of everyday behavior. For much of the past fifty years the American conservative movement has presented itself as a commonsense alternative to the frivolities and utopianism of liberal thinking. This could reflect a strategic effort at winning the support of that segment of the American population that, for psychological reasons, privileges common sense over complexity. Yet one would also expect, holding in-born psychological differences constant, that young conservatives brought up on this rhetoric would be very likely to say that, no, they are not interested in abstract ideas leading nowhere; they are interested in concrete ideas, including concrete ideas about how to make the country run better. To the extent that this is so, however, asking survey questions about interest in abstraction would simply be another way of measuring immersion in conservatism as it is currently practiced.[82] A similar problem plagues a great deal of research by political psychologists on personality and ideology: too often personality is inferred from people's self-descriptions or from behavioral patterns that could just as easily reflect divergent ways of being in the world that are normative in liberal and conservative communities—ways of being that may have become normative for sociological reasons having little to do with personality. Of course, there need not be a complete trade-off between psychological and sociological accounts of politics; in fact the best work in the area highlights brain-society interactions. But rarely is the sociological effectively bracketed out before proclamations are made about the strength of the personality-politics relationship.

As for social dominance orientation, it is reasonable enough to suppose that people may vary in their comfort levels with social hierarchy. But to render such a claim useful for the social scientific analysis of politics, one would have to find a way to measure social dominance orientation that is not a measure of people's political attitudes (a problem slightly different from tapping into the norms and practices of liberal and conservative communities). None of the measures developed by Sidanius meet this standard. Although these have evolved, nearly all query people about their views of optimum levels of social and economic equality and what should be done to achieve it, when such views clearly compose a crucial axis along which liberal and conservative political ideologies differ.[83] What a surprise, then, to find that social dominance orientation and conservatism are related! On the notion of person-organization congruence, again this is sensible in principle, but the problem here is that Sidanius and his colleagues have proceeded by coding organizations, jobs, even college majors as hierarchy-enhancing or hierarchy-attenuating as they see fit, with little attention to their research subjects' subjective perceptions, when subjective perceptions are what should matter in the occupational choice process (at least in the aspirations stage).[84] This leads to unanswered questions. For example, do people who go into police work really think of it as an occupation in which they will have an opportunity to dominate others or to help one group dominate another? Or is it the case, as ethnographic research suggests, that police recruits often view the job more idealistically, seeing criminal law as designed to *prevent* one group of people (criminals) from exerting dominance over others (victims)?[85] These objections do not mean that social dominance orientation plays no role in explaining the liberalism or conservatism of workers in different fields. But there is no real evidence at present that it contributes to the liberalism of the professoriate. And besides, even if students were drawn into academic work feeling that they would find in higher education a hierarchy-attenuating environment, what would they discover there? While professors like to describe themselves as having an egalitarian and universalistic bent, from the standpoint of the sociology of science and knowledge academia looks like a fairly hierarchical place, with well-established social roles and power differentials between professors of different ranks and between professors and students and with equally well-established status hierarchies among professors in different types of institutions.

But if the evidence is far from conclusive that cognitive or personality differences explain why professors are liberal—and if the evidence on class, education, and values is equally underwhelming—where does the explanation lie? The answer may be in political self-selection based on occupational reputation.

Chapter 3

Political Self-Selection and the Academic Profession

Chapter 2 discussed several studies showing that liberals are more likely than conservatives to attend graduate school, pursuing the doctoral degrees that are the stepping-stones to academic careers. But how large is this difference? In their study of college student aspirations, Woessner and Kelly-Woessner found that twice as many liberals as conservatives say they plan to pursue doctorates.[1] More dramatically, Ethan Fosse, Jeremy Freese, and I discovered that in the sample of young American adults with which we were working, 49% of those currently enrolled in graduate programs with the aim of completing a PhD identified as liberal and just 18% as conservative. If you compare these numbers to findings from the PAP survey, concentrating for the sake of comparability on the youngest cohort of professors (those thirty-five and under), the results are striking. In this group of academics, 60% describe themselves as any shade of liberal and 25% as any shade of conservative. In other words, among college students who want to go to graduate school and among graduate students, liberals outnumber conservatives by roughly the same proportion that liberals outnumber conservatives among those who have recently entered the academic profession. This fact, combined with the finding from the study Fosse and I carried out showing that advanced degree holding is the single most important statistical factor accounting for the politics gap between professors and other Americans, strongly suggests that most of professorial liberalism is a function of who decides to go to graduate school.

And yet most of the "usual suspects" explanations for this do not pan out. Liberals do not attend graduate school in greater numbers because of differences from conservatives in social class background. For example, while the sons and daughters of educated professionals are more likely to seek PhDs, this does not account for liberals' greater affinity for graduate work, Fosse, Freese, and I found. It does not seem to be because liberals and conservatives have different values; it is not because liberals are smarter than conservatives; and personality factors may not get us far down the road toward an explanation either.

In this chapter, I develop an alternative account: for historical reasons the professoriate has developed such a strong reputation for liberalism that smart young liberals today are apt to think of academic work as something that might be appropriate and suitable for them to pursue, whereas smart young conservatives see academe as foreign territory and embark on other career paths. After laying out the foundations of this theory, I present empirical evidence that supports it and discuss the historical conditions that led academe to have the reputation it does.

✳

To understand why professors are liberal you have to start by thinking about . . . gender inequality. Among scholars concerned with inequities of gender in the United States, a major interest has been in explaining the gender wage gap. In the 1960s female workers earned an average of 60 cents for every dollar earned by a man. In the 1980s the gap narrowed. Although progress toward wage equality has been marked by fits and starts, today the number stands at around 80 cents.[2] Bias and discrimination in the setting of pay levels contribute to this disparity, research shows, but so do differences in the composition of the male and female workforces.[3] Historically female workers have tended to have less education, do more part-time work, and spend more time out of the labor force caring for their families—factors that have kept their wages in check. Also important is occupational sex segregation: across the various tiers of the labor market, men tend to predominate in jobs for which pay (and benefit) levels are higher.[4] As every first-year sociology student learns, more than 90% of auto mechanics, truck drivers, firefighters, airline pilots, and mechanical engineers are male, while more than 90% of child care workers, receptionists, preschool teachers, and secretaries are female.[5]

What explains occupational sex segregation? Some claim that intrinsic differences between men and women in aptitude and ability are part of the story, while others cite evidence suggesting that managers and employees in male-dominated fields block the entry of female workers. A different line of research in sociology focuses on the "sex typing" of jobs.[6] In part because some jobs have been male-dominated for so long, the argument goes, and other jobs female-dominated, young people making decisions about what they want to do for a living have fuzzy images in their heads, the product of cultural experience, about whether any particular occupation seems to be more masculine or feminine in nature—in terms of the quality of the work, the work environment, or the typical features and characteristics of workers. Wanting to do work that will bring desired material rewards and be meaningful, but also accord with their sense of who they are as men and women, workers then self-select into occupations that they perceive to be gender appropriate, helping to reproduce the gender gap in wages year after year.

In one of the many excellent empirical studies built on these insights, sociologist Shelley Correll used longitudinal data to help figure out why more men than women in college major in science, technology, engineering, and mathematics (STEM) fields, gateways to lucrative careers in today's knowledge economy.[7] Correll discovered that a key factor predicting whether someone majors in a STEM field is how confident that person is in her or his math skills. High school boys, she found, encouraged by their parents and teachers and implicitly viewing math as a boy thing, have more self-confidence than girls—even when their actual levels of mathematical ability are equivalent. These self-assessments lead to different educational trajectories: girls become less likely to tough it out through challenging high school math classes. By the time they get to college, Correll argued, many women are scared of math, view majoring in a STEM field as outside their areas of interest and expertise, and find that well-paid STEM occupations such as engineering hold little appeal.

As Fosse and I thought about it after completing our analysis of the GSS data, it dawned on us that a similar set of dynamics, substituting politics (and to a lesser extent religion) for gender, might well account for the greater tendency of liberals than conservatives to pursue academic careers. What if, over the years, academe had become "politically typed" as a liberal, secular occupation, just as other occupations had become typed as conservative? Would it not then be the case that young liberals with high academic aptitude—and their parents and friends and teachers—would view it as one of several perfectly reasonable career options, where conservatives would tend to see it as a bad fit?[8]

The work that sociologists of gender have done on sex typing and occupational sex segregation builds on a number of sociological concepts and assumptions. Spelling these out is the best way to explain the theory of political typing.

The first building block is the concept of educational and occupational aspirations. Young people making plans for their future work usually lack full information about the many career paths they could follow. Yet sociologists have long recognized (along with parents and high school guidance counselors) that there is a great deal of variation among the young in how much detailed planning they do for their future and in how high they set their educational and occupational sights. Holding ability and class background constant, researchers in the 1960s found that teens who aspired to attend and complete college and who organized their high school experiences with this goal in mind were more likely to go to college and, as a result, to wind up with good-paying jobs.[9] But such aspirations *do* vary by class: while many working-class kids are eager to make better lives for themselves financially, on average kids from working-class backgrounds are less likely than their middle-class peers to aspire to college completion in a serious way—an important factor explaining why there is not more upward mobility. Subsequent research has turned up fewer class-based differences in educational aspirations than were observed in the 1960s; today nearly 60% of high school seniors say they expect to complete a bachelor's degree.[10] Still, studies continue to show that young people from different backgrounds differ in how much effort they put into planning for their future and in what kind of future they imagine, and those aspirational differences (alongside resource constraints) influence educational and life outcomes.[11] Work on the sex typing of jobs and occupational sex segregation builds on the notion of aspirations by arguing that, while career goals and specific educational plans may be unclear for many young people, these goals are nevertheless shaped by the mental images they have about the gendered nature of different kinds of employment.[12] With different ambitions and visions for their future, young men and women are set up right from the start to have different life experiences.

A second building block is a general understanding of how human beings make consequential life decisions. Against the idea that people are normally rational and calculative, many scholars of gender inequality who work on sex typing assume that processes to do with "self-concept congruence" loom large in human life.[13] Drawing on a rich body of research by social psychologists, they argue that people often make choices or follow certain paths without fully recognizing that by doing so they *are* making choices out of a social-psychological interest—reinforced by feedback from the people to whom they are closest—in remaining true to understandings they have of who they are or who they would like to become: understandings of the groups and/or social categories to which they belong, as well as understandings of who they are as individuals. Social psychologists and other scholars of identity have argued not simply that the motive of self-concept congruence is powerful—so powerful that in some circumstances it can override and displace rational calculations of utility—but also that, to a certain extent, utility maximization follows selfhood: what one would like to maximize depends on the kind of person one understands oneself to be. Scholars of gender inequality draw on these ideas when they assume that understandings of oneself as a gendered being influence occupational choices. It is not that men are intrinsically interested in x and women y and pick their jobs accordingly. Rather it is people's sense of themselves as men or women, given prevailing "gender ideologies," that lead them to be interested in x or y in the first place. That same sense operates independently to make some jobs "thinkable"—because they are seen as consistent with understandings of the gendered self—and others not. The view in much of the literature on sex typing is that, except where people set out to push established boundaries, these processes usually operate in the background, without much conscious thought being given to the gender appropriateness of ambitions.

The final concept is the self-reproducing social pattern. As a discipline, sociology is very much interested in accounting for social stability: in explaining how and why social structures may remain intact over the long haul despite people's efforts to change them or the random fluctuations of history. Broadly speaking, sociologists have distinguished between two types of social stability. The first occurs when the external, or "exogenous," circumstances responsible for bringing about some social outcome remain unchanged. For example, a rich nation situated in close proximity to a poor one is destined to receive a relatively steady flow of migrants over the course of its history. In the second type of stability, the external circumstances contributing to an outcome may or may not change, but the outcome also comes to have a self-reproducing quality: its previous existence helps to ensure its continuity. For instance, sociologists of organizations have shown that once firms have survived beyond the initial risky start-up phase, the odds of their long-term survival rise.[14] This is so because by then they have honed organizational routines and practices that give them an edge over competitors; because age allows them to accumulate capital; and because, over time, they become part of the cultural landscape, ensuring brand loyalty and continued market share. When social patterns have this kind of stable, self-reproducing quality, they are "endogenously" driven.[15] As the organizational survival example suggests, sociologists view endogenously driven social patterns are anchored partly in cultural understandings: people come to see the world in such and such a way ("A is a major player in the industry, too big to fail") and, seeing the world in that way, act so as to reproduce the pattern. These assumptions enter into work on the sex typing of occupations. Research here is often concerned to explain long-term patterns of inequality in wages and conceives of the underlying processes as having a self-reproducing character: a major part of the explanation for why there is occupational sex segregation at time T_2 is simply that there was also occupational sex segregation at time T_1, with people repeating the historical pattern via the assumptions it sets up about the gendered nature of different forms of employment. It is here that cultural understandings of gender and work enter in.

The theory that academe is politically typed builds on all three of these foundations. Aspirations are central. Unlike some occupations, but in common with all other modern professions, academic work is not something one stumbles into. Except in the rare case when a former politician, political pundit, or business person golden-parachutes into an academic post, launching a career as a professor takes years of study, hard work, and preparation and requires foresight and planning. Doctoral students may sometimes be confused and unsure of themselves, as any dissertation advisor can attest, but they would never have made it into graduate school were they not able, starting as undergraduates, to project themselves forward in time, envisioning themselves as PhD recipients and working in a systematic manner to bring about this outcome. While many young people entering doctoral programs are uncertain about what kind of work they will do if and when they graduate, a safe assumption is that, for most, particularly in fields in which industry work is not an option, their educational aspirations come bundled with at least some interest in academic employment.

What kind of young person is likely to form the ambition to become an academic? Prior research suggests that the odds of deciding as an undergraduate that one might like to become a professor increase if (1) one comes from an academic family or otherwise has highly educated, intellectual parents (as discussed in Chapter 2), (2) one does extremely well in school and thoroughly enjoys being in an academic environment, (3) one has fallen in love with an academic field, and (4) one attends a college or university in which entry into academe is strongly encouraged by the faculty or by student peer cultures.[16] To these observations the theory of political typing adds that the odds also increase if one stands on the left side of the political aisle.

In sociology, research that takes self-concept congruence seriously usually focuses on aspects of the self thought to be highly relevant across many kinds of social situations, such as gender or race. But, as mentioned in Chapter 1, there is reason to think that political identity may also be a key feature of the self, at least for a subset of the population. Its effects on entry into the professoriate could come about directly or indirectly.

In a direct effect, a young person invested politically would come to think of an academic career as being on the menu of occupations from which she or he might choose—or not—based on perceptions of the political tilt of academic work. Since academia is liberal not just in fact but also in people's stereotypes about it—no matter how limited their knowledge of the realities of academic life may be—young, academically talented leftists and progressives are apt to view an academic career as congruent with their self-concepts, whereas they might not feel that way about a corporate job, say. Conservatives should tend to feel the opposite.

In an indirect effect, political identity would affect the aspiration to become a professor by influencing one of the factors leading to a desire for an academic career. For example, as many conservative critics have noted, liberal politics are very much in evidence on American college campuses, from multicultural reading requirements to student conduct rules about tolerance and diversity, from the iconography one sees on posters in the hallway to the speakers typically brought in by student organizations. At most schools there is no shortage of "safe spaces" for conservatives: business programs, religious organizations, Republican political clubs. But few conservative students are likely to feel completely at home and comfortable in the contemporary American academic environment, restricting the number who will form the aspiration to spend their lives there. Equally significant, as I discuss in more detail in Chapter 4, is that some of the most prominent social science and humanities fields are, on the whole, more liberal than conservative in terms of intellectual content: in the kinds of questions that scholars pose, in the theories used to address them, and so on. In light of these leanings, how many young conservatives are going to fall in love with sociology or anthropology or literature in their current academic incarnations? Not many, judging from research showing that politics influences students' choice of college major.[17]

Finally, politics might affect the aspiration to become a professor through the composition of social networks. Especially for students whose parents are not professors or other knowledge workers, forming the aspiration to do academic work might depend on establishing a close relationship with a professor who can act as a mentor, pointing out the joys and benefits of an academic life and providing critical advice and letters of recommendation for graduate school. As Woessner and Kelly-Woessner have noted, given evidence that liberals are often more comfortable forming relationships with other liberals, and conservatives with other conservatives, the paucity of conservative academics should tend to restrict the availability of mentors for conservative students, placing an even tighter lid on the formation of their professorial ambitions.[18] At the same time, if conservative students were hesitant to attend undergraduate institutions like Harvard or Berkeley, known for both their liberalism and for funneling students into academic careers, this would also reduce their flow into the academy.[19] While both direct and indirect effects of political identity on the ambition to become a professor might in some cases be based on explicit calculations on the part of individuals, Fosse and I assumed—in line with the claims of scholars writing on sex typing—that more commonly the effects would come about without much conscious consideration. Students generally have the sense that academe leans left, but typically they do not form ambitions about professorial employment by carefully thinking through the extent of their political fit; political fit would instead be perceived as a vague sense of comfort (or discomfort) with the aspiration to become a professor, an ambition that would also have to square with other aspects of one's identity in order to take hold. (Of course, some number of people contemplating careers in the social sciences or humanities do consciously attend to fit, thinking that as professors they might somehow make a contribution to progressive social change.) Conservative students toying with the idea of becoming a professor might give questions of political fit a great deal of consideration, but our theory was that most conservative students would never toy with the idea in the first place.[20]

Religion should matter as well. A majority of American professors believe in God, but the occupation has a strong reputation for secularism, if not irreligiosity, and this should reduce the number of people with strong religious views who aspire to become academics.[21] This might be because there is an intrinsic conflict between a religious worldview and a scientific or rational one, but it could also be because religious believers wish to stay out of the lion's den of secularism and not risk compromising their social identity as a person of faith. Given the typical associations between traditional religiosity and political conservatism, a reputation for secularism should further reduce the number of conservatives entering academe.

When Fosse and I first presented our theory, some critics accused it of being circular.[22] The theory seems to explain the politics of professors in terms of the politics of professors: academics are liberal because academics have a reputation for liberalism. This objection is valid insofar as it highlights the need to account for the historical origins of the academic profession's liberal reputation—I offer such an account below—but invalid if it imagines that it has identified some logical flaw with the theory: the whole point is to flag the significant endogenous component to professorial liberalism. Professors tend to be liberal year after year not primarily for exogenous reasons: not because their relatively unchanging class position makes them liberal or because the demands of academic work continually call forth new entrants to the field with specific bundles of psychological characteristics. Instead, Fosse and I argued, events occurring around the time the American academic profession was first founded, in the late nineteenth century and early twentieth, "imprinted" it in a liberal mold. That imprinting, combined with later historical developments, has given academe a reputation for liberalism that, in any given year, draws in many more liberals than conservatives in a process that further reinforces its liberal reputation.[23] (Our claim was not that students know this history but that it has shaped the reputation of the academic profession.) It makes no more sense to charge such an account with circularity than it does to object when someone says, in response to a question about why the United States does not have a monarch, that the main reason is the American Revolution and the institutional and cultural structures that have kept the resulting system of democratic governance in place since that time.[24]

How does the theory of political self-selection on the basis of occupational reputation stand up empirically? No one has yet followed a large random sample of high-achieving liberal and conservative students from their last years of high school all the way through and then beyond their graduation from college, watching their educational and occupational aspirations take shape, grow, and change over time, and looking for direct evidence that liberals are drawn to graduate school and academic work because they sense a fit with their politics, while conservatives are led away. But there is circumstantial evidence of such a process.

To begin, while most Americans do not know much about professors, the perception that academe leans left *is* widely shared. Depictions of professors in the movies and on television are not the only evidence of this. In the public opinion poll Simmons and I carried out examining attitudes toward political bias in higher education, we asked respondents to estimate how liberal or conservative they thought the average college or university professor was on various issues. Fifty-two percent guessed that the average professor was liberal on economic issues (with 30% guessing moderate and just 19% guessing conservative), 54% guessed liberal on national security issues, and 59% guessed liberal on social issues. We also asked respondents how well they thought the term *radical* described the typical professor. A remarkable 62% said it described professors very well or somewhat well. Finally, when we asked respondents whether they thought colleges and universities favor professors who hold liberal social and political views, the majority responded affirmatively. These numbers suggest that the professoriate is politically typed in public perceptions.[25] It also appears to be religiously typed. While most respondents to the poll (81%) believed that American colleges and university are welcoming to students of faith, 69% told us that the average professor is only somewhat religious, while 27% described the average professor as not religious at all.

But do such perceptions affect the ambitions of liberals or conservatives to become academics? Without data tracking ambition formation we cannot be sure. Consider the following, however. We know not simply that liberals attend graduate school at a higher rate than conservatives, but also that differences in their aspiration to do so are evident early on. To Woessner and Kelly-Woessner's finding that liberal college students are twice as likely as their conservative peers to state their intention to complete a doctorate can be added a finding from an analysis that Fosse ran on college freshmen data. Surveys done by HERI during freshman orientation week every year since 1971 (the first year of the data to which Fosse had access; the survey started in 1966) show that on average about 50% of those students who say they aspire to become professors are liberal, and only about 20% are conservative. In the most recent year for which data were available, 2007, the numbers were 53% and 17%, respectively—again, about the same ratio as can be found among current graduate students and young professors. (Not everyone who becomes a professor knows as a college freshman that she or he will do so, but early aspirations do predict entry into the academic profession.[26]) Since these differences are evident before most students ever set foot in a college classroom, it is unlikely—although not impossible—that they reflect a rational calculation on the part of young conservatives intimately familiar with the ins and outs of academic life who have concluded that they have little chance of succeeding in academia. A more plausible explanation is that the differences are explained by only half-conscious perceptions of identity fit, likely influenced by how different educational pathways and lines of work are seen by the people closest to high schoolers: their friends and family. On this point, another finding from the public opinion poll Simmons and I conducted is telling: liberals and conservatives differ considerably in their estimations of the prestige of academic employment. For example, we found that 43% of Republicans as compared to 59% of Democrats are of the view that being a professor is a "very prestigious" job. Given that the most common pattern is for young Democrats to be raised in Democratic households and young Republicans in Republican ones, it is reasonable to think that aspirational differences concerning academic employment may be grounded in implicit assessments of what would be seen as appropriate, suitable, and laudable given the political identities that prevail in one's immediate social surroundings.[27]

Also relevant are the answers that professors gave during interviews to a question we posed asking why *they* thought liberals predominate in academe. These ran the gamut. The most common explanations offered, however, were that (1) liberals tend to be more open-minded than conservatives, with open-mindedness a requirement for academic work (mentioned by 41% of interviewees), and that (2) conservatives are too interested in making money to want jobs as professors (mentioned by 30%).[28] While both claims can be questioned, they speak to strongly held stereotypes about liberals and conservatives. For example, when we asked a thirty-seven-year-old engineering professor at an institution in the South why there are few conservative professors, he said, "I think the idea of conservatism flies in the face of what we all value as academic freedom. We don't want to be told how to do or how not to do [our work] or have any restriction put on how to think, whether from government or neighbors or spouse." "That's a pretty typical faculty mind-set," he added, so in his view it was hardly surprising that few conservatives choose to become professors. A different version of this argument was offered by a fifty-six-year-old sociologist teaching in the Northeast. "The . . . enterprise in which we're engaged in terms of teaching . . . lends itself more to an inquisitive, questioning approach," she said, "which I don't think conservatives are very tolerant of." These interviewees were both liberal. But even some academics who described themselves as having conservative tendencies gave a similar explanation, as in the case of a thirty-five-year-old biologist who grew up in a Republican family. His explanation for the predominance of liberals in academe? "Thinking is dangerous. A lot of conservative views end up being a bit simplistic. . . . I think when you're trained to think as an academic, there's an openness to ideas that goes along with that, and I think that resonates a little more with being a liberal." Not all conservative academics we interviewed felt this way, of course, but even those who offered alternative accounts stressed that their liberal colleagues tended to see them and other conservatives as closed-minded, something they found galling in light of their view of academe as a liberal echo chamber. These data thus suggest that among academics there is widespread belief in a natural affinity between liberalism and academic employment—in much the same way that among construction workers (and the general public) there is a widespread belief that construction is an intrinsically male job.[29] I address in Chapter 4 the question of whether this belief might lead to discrimination against conservatives hoping to enter the academic profession. The point here is that, to the extent that such views are also held by talented undergraduates and their friends and family members, they should tend to increase the appeal of academic work for liberals and decrease it for conservatives.

In a related vein, there is evidence that, in large part because they perceive the contemporary academic environment to be a bastion of liberalism, young conservatives do not feel altogether comfortable there (unless they are located in one of a relatively small number of conservative academic enclaves). Woessner and Kelly-Woessner report that conservative college students are some-what *more* satisfied with their college experience overall than liberal students, and Rothman, Kelly-Woessner, and Woessner, analyzing data on faculty attitudes, find that Republican professors are no less satisfied with their careers than Democratic ones and would still choose to become professors if they had to do it all over again.[30] Yet sociologists Amy Binder and Kate Wood, writing about conservative college students, show that many deeply resent the courses they take in which, the students believe, they are asked to toe the liberal line, as when breadth requirements force them to endure English classes stressing the value of multiculturalism. Particularly at nonelite schools, Binder and Wood show (elite students being more genteel), conservative undergraduates also express dismay about the general liberal climate that prevails on campus, protesting it with actions designed to affront liberal sensibilities. They write:

> Even those . . . conservative . . . [students] who do not personally think provocative action is a good idea understand it to be necessary on . . . campus, which they describe as absurdly liberal. As one conservative student explained, ". . . the College Republicans are really important . . . because they provide, in my opinion, really the only contrast to the professors. They're the other side." . . . Thus, he elaborated, even if he disliked the combative tactics of events like the Affirmative Action Bake Sale—or Catch an Illegal Alien Day (where students marked as illegal immigrants are mock-

> imprisoned by citizen students), the Global Warming Beach
> Party (where environmental concerns are ridiculed with sun-
> tan oil and beer), or the Conservative Coming Out Day (a
> twist on LGBT coming out celebrations, where conservatives
> make their presence on liberal campuses known)—he partici-
> pated in the . . . College Republicans . . . in order to coun-
> teract the effects of a liberal professoriate and to spread the
> conservative message.[31]

Few students who feel this way are going to entertain the possibility of becoming academics.

Finally, the theory of self-selection on the basis of academe's
political reputation, and to a lesser extent its religious one, ac-
cords with the findings from my quantitative research with Fosse.
With other hypotheses called into question, reputation-based
self-selection could easily explain why liberals are more likely to
go to graduate school, accounting for the finding that possession
of an advanced degree is so important for explaining the liberalism of professors. Looking in more detail at cognitive ability,
Fosse and I also found that while in itself it does little to account
for the political gap between professors and nonprofessors, the
statistical interaction of advanced degree holding with cognitive
ability accounts for just under 60% of the political gap between
professors and others.[32] What this means, on my reading of the
data, is that liberals who are extremely smart are quite likely to
pursue advanced degrees and go on to become professors, while
conservatives who are extremely smart are less likely to do either,
pursuing other options. Self-selection could also explain why religious differences between professors and others matter some for
professorial politics. And it might explain a portion of the politics

gap that our statistical models could not account for, as liberals with graduate degrees could be more inclined than conservatives with such degrees to seek out academic work. Very likely occupational reputation–based self-selection works in tandem with some of the processes discussed in Chapter 2—to do with class, education, values, and personality—to produce the liberalism of the professoriate.

※

But if the factors just considered help explain why it is liberals who often embark on academic careers, what accounts for academe's original liberal reputation? This book is not a work of historical sociology. Nevertheless a preliminary account of the origins of American academic politics is necessary to give the theory of political self-selection some historical grounding.

Ladd and Lipset's *The Divided Academy* began by marshaling various pieces of historical evidence to show that the American professoriate had been liberally inclined since at least the beginning of the twentieth century. There now exists a more systematic data source relevant to this, one that also offers important clues into the timing of the formation of academia's political reputation. Figure 3.1 shows the percentage of all texts in Google Books' American English corpus containing the phrases *liberal professor* or *conservative professor* for the period 1900–2008. Three things are evident from this graph. First, for most of this period there was more discussion of liberal than of conservative professors. Second, there was a significant increase in references to professorial liberalism beginning in the late 1920s. And third, there are two distinct peaks in such discussion, one in the late 1940s and 1950s, the other around 1970. To be sure, published references to the liberalism of

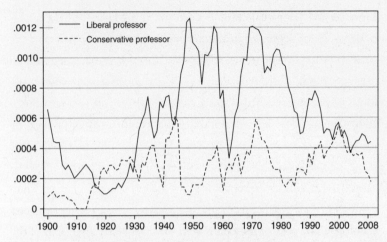

Figure 3.1. Proportion of Google Books texts containing the phrase *liberal professor* or *conservative professor,* 1900–2008 (five-year moving averages). *Source:* Google Ngram American English Corpus.

professors may be driven by a variety of factors, the meanings of *liberal* and *conservative* have shifted over time, and some early twentieth-century usages of the term *liberal professor* were vestigial references to what had been called in the nineteenth century the *liberal professions* and had no political connotations. Still, the patterns revealed by the graph turn out to correspond fairly well with different stages in the American academic profession's engagement with the left.

For the first 150 years of American higher education, the mid-seventeenth century to the end of the eighteenth, the occupation of professor entailed something very different than it does today. There were few higher education institutions—only twenty-five in the whole country in 1800—and they were tiny, educating the sons of colonial elites and preparing them to assume positions of prominence in colonial society.[33] Harvard, Yale, the College of

New Jersey (later Princeton), William and Mary, and the other colleges that dotted the landscape were loosely modeled on Oxford and Cambridge in the sense that they combined "living and learning," and the curriculum and daily regimen to which students were exposed had as their common goal to turn out Christian gentlemen in the manner of whatever Protestant sect controlled the colony and college.[34] Most schools employed few professors, and rarely were they leading intellectual lights. For the most part colonial-era academics were transmitters rather than producers of knowledge, oriented toward classical learning and theology. The lessons they taught were "the proper amalgam of the medieval arts and sciences and of the Renaissance interest in the study of literature and belles-lettres," with most texts in Latin or Greek.[35] It was common for professors to also be ministers.

The number of people employed as professors grew in the decades following the Revolution as new schools were founded, like Thomas Jefferson's University of Virginia, which opened its doors in 1825. But it was not until the second half of the nineteenth century, amid a wave of state university foundings in the Midwest and West, that the professorial role began to change. Influential Americans came to believe that the template for higher education offered by the colonial college had become outmoded and poorly served the needs of an expanding nation. More emphasis, they believed, should be placed on the sciences and on practical fields like agriculture and engineering. Further, they thought that religion should no longer be the centerpiece of a college education. A reform effort ensued, helped along by a variety of powerful social forces, and many institutions, some taking advantage of incentives offered by the Morrill Land Grant Act of 1862, moved in a more modern direction, adding new subjects and revising their course offerings. Private colleges shed ties to the religious denominations that had founded them and ended compulsory chapel attendance for students, while the newly emerging state schools were non-sectarian from the start.[36] These reforms altered what it meant to be a professor. At most institutions professors still were not major scientists or scholars, but increasingly they were expected to be something other than teachers of homilies.

Beginning in the 1870s, reform efforts accelerated. Reformers now argued for an entirely new organizational structure: the research university, inspired by universities in Germany, that would wholeheartedly embrace the challenge of discovering new truths, pulling into a common institutional orbit otherwise informally connected researchers who had been fashioning the apparatus of the American natural sciences over the course of the century, as well a new breed of scholars working on historical and social scientific matters. To maximize scientific exchange, held those like Daniel Coit Gilman, universities should be organized around academic departments, and a key function of such departments should be the training of graduate students who could be given the advanced instruction necessary to pursue scholarship at the highest levels and who could someday go on to become professors themselves. Gilman's Johns Hopkins, founded in 1876 with money from Gilded Age philanthropy, is the premier example of a university built around this reform vision. Slowly, in a patchwork process of imitation, accommodation, and grafting together of old and new elements that varied by region and institutional history, many private and public schools reconfigured themselves along similar lines, while colleges that remained focused exclusively on undergraduate instruction also adjusted in their way to the changing higher education environment.[37]

As they did, the American academic profession as we now know it began to take shape. More professors were expected to have doctoral degrees. Previously diffuse fields of inquiry populated mostly by amateurs crystallized as academic disciplines. The number of academics rose, growing from about 5,500 nationwide in 1870 to nearly 25,000 at century's end.[38] National disciplinary societies were founded to promote and support their members' work. Academic journals were started. And the notion spread of a professor as someone who has specialized knowledge of his field and teaches that knowledge to students while also engaging in a program of research.

For the history of American academic politics, a crucial feature of the emerging professorial role was the stance professors were expected to take toward religion. In Europe, progress toward the development of the university as a research institution had gone hand in hand with secularization. Prior to the late eighteenth century, professors in European schools often faced clerical restrictions on what could be taught and studied. It was in part the close interconnection between religion and European higher education that explained why the scientific revolution of the seventeenth century was also an affair of amateurs with few university ties, and why the great Enlightenment movements of the next century, in Continental Europe and Scotland, stressing the need for freedom of thought, among other things, found academic champions and supporters. As sociologist Randall Collins has argued, the secularization of European academic life was a slow, tension-filled process, more a series of zigzags than a historical straight line.[39] Yet at every turn, intellectual energies were released.

Enlightenment ideals animated the American Revolution, providing thinkers on this side of the Atlantic with some protection against enforced political orthodoxies. But mid-nineteenth-century American higher education reformers felt this was not enough. Throwing off the shackles of monarchy was one thing. In order to be transformed into centers of original research, however, American universities would also have to significantly reduce the amount of influence that religion had over them. Accordingly reformers sought not simply to break off ties with religious denominations but more generally to imbue the university with a secular—though not necessarily irreligious—ethos. Gilman spoke to this concern in his inaugural address as president of the recently founded University of California in 1872 (where he had a short tenure before moving to Baltimore). He distinguished between the spirit of religion and religious doctrine. The former, he said, is that sentiment that pushes mankind toward ever-higher levels of achievement and beneficence; the university would benefit from it. As for doctrine, while in his view there should be professors on campus charged with studying and teaching about the many varieties of religious belief, they must be "scholars, not partisans." In no other way could the demands of religious piety be allowed to interfere with the research and teaching enterprise. While there were "many parents, many religious teachers, many churches" who continued to insist that American higher education maintain itself in the tradition of the "ecclesiastical colleges," setting it up so that "youth at the critical period of college life should be surrounded by positive, outspoken, and persuasive religious influences," Gilman thought this a mistake.[40] The job of the university must be inquiry into truth as revealed by science and disciplined intellectual inquiry alone. In the many public addresses Gilman and other higher education reformers made, in their writings, and in their informal interactions with other social elites, they stressed the need for academic freedom from religious constraints and worked to set up institutional structures in which such freedom would be preserved. As sociologist Christian Smith has shown, freedom from religious pressures was in many ways the watchword of the American higher education reform movement.[41] And as historian Dorothy Ross has noted, writing of this period, the "anticlericalism" of the "educated gentry" who supported university reforms and who were starting to view science "not only as the most authoritative modern knowledge, but as a courageous source of free inquiry, as against an authoritarian, outmoded religion," only "increased as the American churches grew more defensive."[42]

Part of these efforts at effecting what Smith calls a "secular revolution" in American higher education involved attempts to spell out what the appropriate attitude of professors should be toward religion. Most professors would naturally be Christian, Gilman and other reformers assumed. But they should be theologically liberal Christians, open to and tolerant of competing religious views and, more important, willing to keep their religious beliefs more or less in check upon entering their laboratories or seminar rooms. What qualities characterize the professors Cornell should attempt to hire, asked its founding president, Andrew Dickson White, in a report to the university's trustees in 1867? They must "constantly keep in view two great objects," he answered: "first, the discovery of truth; secondly, the diffusion of truth." Filling out what this entailed, White—who would later cause controversy with his 1896 book, *A History of the Warfare of Science with Theology*—insisted that Cornell "must make no man an instructor because he is . . . pious."[43] Only those who put science and learning first merited the title *professor*.

It was theologically liberal Christians committed to secularism and the life of the mind whom American university reformers hoped to pull into the academic profession—and by and large that is who they got, although their success in doing so owed as much to supply- as to demand-side factors and to the sheer fact of ongoing organizational diversification within the university, which pushed against continued recruitment from a narrow pool. Consider what historian George Marsden found when he investigated the changing religious composition of the faculty at Harvard over the course of the nineteenth century:

> Nowhere was the metamorphosis from old-time religious college to modern university more rapid or more dramatic than at Harvard. To paraphrase Henry Adams, Harvard in 1850 was in many ways closer to the Middle Ages than to the Harvard of 1900. At midcentury many of the forms of seventeenth-century Harvard—the tutors, the recitations, the discipline, the strong clerical presence, daily chapel, the classical curriculum—were still in place. The professoriate was largely Unitarian, drawn predominantly from the local eastern Massachusetts aristocracy and their descendants. By the final decade of the century only a fifth of the professoriate were Unitarian. Among others, Catholics and Jews had at least token representation. Perhaps most significant, over a fourth were of no easily identifiable religious persuasion.[44]

What did the hiring into academe of those scholars with liberal theological views and sensibilities—many of whom had had their childhood faiths shaken by the horrors of the Civil War, by exposure to different cultural and religious practices while studying abroad, and by Darwinism—have to do with professors' politics? To some extent, wherever in the world universities became secularized, with reformers and scholars drawing on Enlightenment ideals to justify their claims about the need for distance from religious control, political liberalism of a sort could also be found. Yet in each country, the political effects of secularization on academe came about through a different sequence of historical events, yielding different results.[45] In the United States the hiring of theologically liberal, secular Protestants created a situation in which professors were set up to be among the leaders and key supporters of the Progressive movement.

Caution is in order with this claim. Historians have shown that Progressivism was a complex phenomenon with many competing elements and strands. Some scholars have doubted whether it can be properly described as a movement at all. Where some Progressives sought to tame monopolies and laissez-faire capitalism, others took an accommodationist stance toward big business. Where some were vigorous defenders of autonomy and individual rights, others advocated the preservation of traditional gender roles and restrictive "social hygiene" measures that in retrospect seem sexist, racist, and xenophobic. Some Progressives aimed to rationalize and reform government and harness it for the purpose of social betterment; others directed their efforts toward voluntary organizations they thought more capable of fulfilling the same purpose. Academics could be found involved in all these projects and did not speak in a unified voice.[46]

Still, there can be no doubt that members of the academic profession were major figures marching under each of these banners.

Philosophers William James and John Dewey, sociologists Lester Ward and Franklin Giddings, economists Richard Ely, John R. Commons, and Wesley Clair Mitchell, and historians Frederick Jackson Turner and Charles Beard gave intellectual succor to the movement in its different stages and sometimes practical advice to Progressive policy makers, while one of the movement's most important politicians, Woodrow Wilson, was himself an academic, a political scientist trained at Johns Hopkins who rose to become the president of Princeton before rising higher still.

Scholars like Richard Wightman Fox and James Kloppenberg have argued that, diversity within the movement aside, enthusiasm for Progressivism among educated Americans was underpinned by the same religious sentiment of which Gilman spoke in his address in California—specifically, that sentiment associated with late nineteenth-century liberal Protestantism.[47] Some Progressives, called to act by the "social gospel" theology preached by Walter Rauschenbusch and others, which denounced capitalist greed and saw improving the lives of the poor and disenfranchised as the most direct way to enact Jesus' teachings, clearly had a religious orientation. But others, with more of a secular cast, also thought about their political commitments in terms that liberal Protestantism had bequeathed. Their zeal for reform had an evangelical quality, as Fox explains:

> Liberal Protestantism was a potent social, political, and intellectual force because it was so accommodating. It refused to choose between faith and reason. It helped legitimize a scientific worldview by insisting that no exercise of critical intellect could be at odds with God's purpose. It was fundamen-

tally inclusive. . . . It pushed beyond the limited communal vision of the republican tradition by holding that, in principle, human society could come to approximate a great fellowship. . . . The ability of liberal Protestantism to convey a persuasive aura of spiritual coherence and cultural unity, while laying down a broad welcome mat to an array of secular and religious forces, made it an indispensible ideological bulwark for a diverse and disjointed progressive movement.[48]

Above all, nineteenth-century liberal Protestantism, and Progressivism along with it, stressed the possibility of improving society—bringing to it an element of grace and uplift—through the application not of religious dogma but of scientific principles and findings guided by Christian ethics. This was the same theme on which the American research university and the modern academic profession had also been founded, so it is hardly a surprise that there were many Progressive academics.

Quickly the professoriate became identified with Progressivism and as an occupational group standing on the side of science, rationality, and reform. It would not be long before this distinctive but nonpartisan political reputation took on more of a leftist cast.

Soon after its appearance, the American research university found itself facing a major institutional challenge. Many faculty members were committed to Progressive ideals; the majority would appear fairly conservative when judged by contemporary standards, especially on social matters. Within the faculty, however, were a number of professors—in the social sciences in particular, born of reformist impulses—whose Progressivism was genuinely left-leaning in the sense of favoring significant economic redistribution and market regulation. Their intellectual work was tied to their politics in that it either called directly for overhaul of American institutions or provided general frameworks for the analysis of society consistent with such calls. Yet, as noted earlier with respect to Johns Hopkins, the research university was made possible thanks only to the very Gilded Age capitalism (and its successors) to which, at least in its trust-busting mode, Progressivism sought to respond. Major university philanthropists like John D. Rockefeller and Leland Stanford were fully on board with certain social reform ideas, and the philanthropic organizations and foundations that they and other wealthy industrialists started are a key part of the history of the Progressive era. But when Progressive social scientists pushed their criticisms too far, some industrialists and their representatives recoiled, believing their money should not go toward supporting professors whose ideas and proposals were at odds with their personal commitments and threatened their bottom line. One of the most well-known cases from this time involved the forced resignation of sociologist Edward A. Ross from Stanford University. A critic of the American railroad industry, Ross ran afoul of Leland Stanford's widow, Jane Stanford. The case was widely reported in the press, which correctly described it as an instance in which an outspoken, Progressive professor had been silenced by commercial interests. "In his formal letter of resignation," the *Washington Post* reported in 1901, Ross "intimated that he was being forced out of the university by Mrs. Stanford, who had taken exception to statements made by him in his public addresses on sociological and economic questions."[49]

There is no evidence that the Ross case itself had an appreciable impact on public perceptions of the professoriate, but the growing number of similar cases stimulated leaders of the academic profession, such as Dewey, to make a concerted push for the institutionalization of academic freedom protections that went beyond those envisioned by nineteenth-century reformers.[50] And this push, wrapped up with the founding of the American Association of University Professors and its 1915 declaration of the principles of academic freedom, *does* seem to have been of major importance in shaping public perceptions. Between 1900 and 1915 scores of articles and opinion pieces were printed in newspapers across the country reporting on the academic freedom campaign and debating its merits. Many writers sided with the professors clamoring for protection and with university leaders like Harvard's Charles W. Eliot who believed that the efforts of capitalists to silence professors represented no less of a threat to science and intellectual progress than had earlier clerical strictures. Others thought philanthropists and business leaders entirely within their rights to keep their money out of the hands of academic critics. Whichever side they agreed with, educated Americans exposed to this debate could not fail to come away with the vivid impression that important segments of American academe were on the left. Why else would they have needed protections against moneyed interests?[51]

Intellectual historians like Mary Furner and Thomas Haskell have attributed great significance to these discussions of academic freedom, viewing the tensions underlying them as an important cause of the turn toward scientistic ideals by social scientists at the time, concerned to protect their fledgling disciplines against what often proved the ruinous charge of "advocacy."[52] Yet the debates had another layer: together they composed a social drama that helped imprint the American professoriate with a reputation for political liberalism, a reputation that no amount of gesturing by social scientists in the direction of objectivity would allow them to fully shake. For sociologists, *imprinting* generally refers to the process by which the "technological, economic, political, and cultural resources available" when an organization is first founded continue to "exercise . . . influence over the character of [that] organization" for years to come.[53] Sociologists have mostly been concerned with the consequences of imprinting for the reproduction of organizational structures and practices: a firm that starts out vertically integrated, for example, may have a hard time reconfiguring itself down the line if circumstances call for alternative models of production. Yet occupations can undergo imprinting as well, and their political makeup and political reputations are among the features that may be imprinted. The story of American professorial liberalism over the course of the twentieth century is in large part one of endogenous reproduction based on patterns initially set during the Progressive era, achieved through self-selection around academia's political reputation.[54] Professorial liberalism proved to be self-reinforcing not only in the sense that new cohorts of liberals drawn into academic work confirmed academia's reputation for liberalism, but also in that the reputation intersected with contingent historical developments that drew even more attention to professors' politics.[55]

Space does not permit an extensive discussion of this history, but in broad outline it runs as follows. Seen as a possible home for educated people on the left, academia attracted, in the first decades of the twentieth century, a small number of scholars whose left politics went beyond that of their predecessors. In the context of labor militancy, the emergence of pockets of student radicalism, and the Russian Revolution, these scholars came to the attention of the authorities during the Red Scare of 1919–1920 and in the years immediately following.[56] The censure of radical (and merely antiwar) professors during this time may have reinforced the impression of the academic profession's leftward tilt, as did the fact that prominent academics and intellectuals like Dewey came to the defense of Nicola Sacco and Bartolomeo Vanzetti, however much they insisted they were doing so for procedural reasons and not because they were in political agreement with the Italian anarchists.[57]

After the stock market crash of 1929, academia's reputation for left politics increased still more, and it was in the 1930s that the number of political liberals and leftists in higher education probably began to rise substantially.[58] As was well known then, professors played a major role in Franklin Delano Roosevelt's "brains trust," helping to chart the course of New Deal policy making. This was also a period when liberal, socialist, and communist student groups flourished, with the liberal groups attracting significant professorial support.[59] The former development left little doubt in the public's mind about where academia stood politically—on the side of the New Deal, which was where most Americans stood—while the role of communists on campus would eventually come to light, albeit in a highly distorted fashion, as a result of the investigations of the House Un-American Activities Committee and its state counterparts.

Consistent with the claim that American academia already had a strong reputation for liberalism and leftism during this period, the Google Books graph shows ample references to "liberal professors" in published literature from the late 1930s and 1940s. To select three of these at random: an article in the *American Education Fellowship* from 1938 spoke of the American Legion "bellow[ing] its denunciation of liberal professors at Teachers College," while an essay in the *Christian Leader* from 1942 blamed "the liberal professors, journalists, social workers, teachers, preachers" for many of America's ills.[60] In a different vein, Gunnar Myrdal, a visitor to America, observed in his book *An American Dilemma* in 1944 that the South had many fewer "liberal professors" and editors than could be found in the North, hindering its progress on matters of race.[61] That academia continued to have a reputation for leftism in the 1950s, when Senator Joseph McCarthy went after it full tilt, is not controversial, as noted in Chapter 1.

The late 1960s and early 1970s represented another key period for the reinforcement of the professoriate's political reputation. I will leave most of my discussion of this period until Chapter 7, since the reputation was shaped not simply by political mobilization on the part of students and some faculty members, but also by sharp reaction to it from conservatives, as in Ronald Reagan's pledge as candidate for governor in California in 1966 to "clean up the mess at Berkeley." What can be noted here, and what becomes evident from an analysis of references to "liberal professors" that appear in published sources at the time, are two things. First, although student radicals and others regularly called into question professors' leftist credentials, it continued to be taken for granted by most observers, as it had been earlier, that professors were liberal. "Politically liberal professors . . . dominate the American academic world today," noted Charles Anderson and John Murray matter-of-factly in their 1971 book, *The Professors*.[62]

Second, however, the fact that so much of the protest politics of the era was unfolding on college and university campuses, and that a significant number of professors appeared to be supportive of at least some student demands, created the impression that academia was beginning to veer even further left than before. Protests at Berkeley, Harvard, Columbia, San Francisco State, the University of Wisconsin–Madison, and elsewhere were daily fare in the nation's newspapers and on television newscasts. In most reports professors were depicted as serious scholars doing their best to move ahead with their teaching and research responsibilities in light of campus disruptions. Yet often they were characterized as liberals taking a soft-line stance, rejecting student calls to have a direct role in faculty appointments but willing to hear them out on other issues. And some professors were depicted as being closer to the students than this—as radicals in their own right. For example, an article in the *Wall Street Journal* from 1971 titled "The New Educators" began:

> As college professors go, Fred Snell isn't very typical. His hair flows beneath his collar. When he strolls around the State University of New York's campus here [in Buffalo], he often wears Levi's, leather hiking boots, a pullover sweater and a brown corduroy sports jacket. He prefers lunching at the student union rather than the Faculty Club. Prof. Snell is by no means the local faculty eccentric. At the age of 49, he's a highly respected biophysicist. But Fred Snell also proudly calls himself an activist radical—a type of faculty member found increasingly on the nation's campuses.[63]

The profile was no exaggeration: Snell was a key figure in the antiwar movement at SUNY Buffalo and involved in a variety of other leftist causes. While the rise of the New Left, the antiwar movement, and the civil rights movement—complex phenomena in their own right—were clearly the major factors behind the political mobilization of professors like Snell, news coverage of the trend, and of student unrest generally, may have amplified its effects on occupational recruitment by making it even clearer than before to members of the public and to young people considering different careers that leftism and academe fit together. When the professors brought into the academic fold in this context began pushing their disciplines and institutions in more explicitly political directions in the 1980s and 1990s—and when a new generation of conservative critics called attention to these moves—the political typing of the professoriate was reinforced once again.

Incomplete though this account necessarily is, it suggests that historical contingency has played an important role in explaining why American academia has the reputation for liberalism that it currently does, and therefore why it is as liberal as it is. Had American higher education not been originally religious in nature, requiring a secular revolution, had the modern academic profession not been founded during the Progressive era, had the social movements of the 1960s and 1970s not been so university-based, academia today might well be a less distinctive occupation politically. Here, as elsewhere in society, social outcomes arise out of the intersection of more or less generic social mechanisms, like imprinting and self-selection-based endogenous reproduction, and historical circumstance.[64]

Chapter 4

Political Differences among Professors

The theory of self-selection laid out in Chapter 3 helps make sense of the general tendency of academics to be more liberal than other Americans. In order to really work, however, the theory must also be able to account for political differences among professors. Chapter 1 showed that there is meaningful variation in political attitudes and identities across disciplinary fields and types of higher education institutions. What is more, American professorial politics has trended in a more liberal direction since the late 1960s. What explains these patterns? This chapter offers some answers while also considering the theory that conservative students and professors face bias and discrimination.

Let me begin with differences by field. One of the findings of Chapter 1 was that the social sciences and humanities contain the largest number of radicals; the social sciences, the humanities, and the natural sciences the largest number of progressives; and applied fields like business and engineering more conservatives. Why are some disciplines more liberal than others?

Several approaches have been taken to answer this question. One points to enduring differences in the intellectual content of fields. For example, in *The Academic Mind,* Lazarsfeld and Thielens argued that social scientists are particularly liberal because social science requires a certain mind-set.[1] Aware of social and historical variation in the structuring of institutions—of the great many forms that politics, religion, culture, the economy, and the family can take—social scientists, according to Lazarsfeld and Thielens, tend to be relativists, not assuming that the institutions of their own society are the best possible, as conservatives might. While it would not be hard to come up with similar rationales to explain the liberal tendencies of humanists and natural scientists, a problem with this approach is that the political orientation of most disciplines remains relatively stable over time, changing only gradually within broad historical periods, whereas the intellectual content of fields is often in flux. For example, most social science disciplines today bear only passing resemblance to their mid-twentieth-century counterparts, yet they remain outposts of liberal politics. And this is as true of at least some diffuse intellectual characteristics as of commitments to specific theories and methodologies. Can the majority of contemporary American social scientists, focused on the here and now, be said to be keenly aware of history and national difference as scholars like Lazarsfeld were?[2]

A second approach—Bourdieu's—examines where disciplines stand in relation to the field of power and assumes that this shapes professorial politics through the recruitment of academics from different backgrounds: fields more closely connected to economic and political power draw in academics from higher social class positions, whose family circumstances predispose them to greater conservatism. The difficulty here is that while American academics in different disciplines do vary somewhat in class background, analyses of the PAP data show that this variation does not go far toward explaining why professors in some fields are more liberal than those in others.[3]

A third approach, in line with Bourdieu's emphasis on power but looking less at class background, highlights the connections between fields and external social institutions or whole social sectors. Some disciplines are aligned with conservative-leaning institutions such as big business or the military, in terms of whether academic ideas are drawn on and supported by organizations and individuals in those sectors, while other fields are more autonomous or connected to institutions like those in the nonprofit world that have very different interests and political orientations. The effect of these links, according to this third approach, is to give the work done in different fields a distinctive political hue, drawing in scholars whose personal politics match up.[4]

This approach is promising but vague. How, precisely, does a field's relationship to external institutions shape its intellectual content, and thereby the politics of its members?

Traction on this might be gained by considering a theory I developed with the sociologist Scott Frickel.[5] Our goal was to explain the intellectual change one finds in fields, where new ideas, perspectives, theories, paradigms, and approaches regularly appear. Frickel and I argued that intellectual dynamism could be best understood by conceiving of fields as arenas of collective action. The basic idea was that within disciplines, scholars and scientists are constantly working together to try to get new approaches going, starting what Frickel and I termed "scientific/intellectual movements": laying out their intellectual foundations, recruiting student followers, convincing peers to join with them, building up a base of knowledge, making a splash in journal and book publishing, starting research centers, and so on. The intellectual entrepreneurs who found such movements may hope to win academic glory by doing so; as a social institution science works by using status rewards to incentivize intellectual innovation. But usually they are motivated as well by a genuine sense of dissatisfaction with existing approaches and a desire to set their field on a better course. Because this is so, they can be understood as akin to activists who launch social movements aimed at changing some feature of society that they regard as problematic.

Political sociologists have devoted considerable attention to social movements, and Frickel and I argued that many of their findings and insights could be used to make sense of intellectual change processes in academia as well. For example, political sociologists have shown that whether a movement succeeds or fails depends in part on who launches it. In the West, movements have been more likely to succeed if they are started not by the most marginalized members of society but by activists from the middle class, sometimes looking out for the interests of the disadvantaged, who can put their educational experiences and cultural know-how to use in the service of their activism. In academic life, scientific/intellectual movements are better able to get off the ground when they are started by established scholars holding positions at major research institutions. Academics from throughout higher education may be unhappy with the directions in which their fields are heading and have ideas about what would make for a useful correction. But those in lower status positions usually lack the social connections, reputation, and intellectual capital necessary to get a large number of their colleagues to take up their proposals for change. Political sociologists have likewise shown that social movement success depends on the presence of favorable "political opportunity structures"; a movement may be helped enormously, for instance, if a sympathetic political party happens to be in office.[6] Contingent opportunities play an important role in intellectual change as well, Frickel and I argued, facilitating or impeding scientific/intellectual movement development. The history of any academic discipline, we suggested, is a history of the many and varied scientific/intellectual movements that have occurred within it—a history of movement birth, of significant growth or failure to thrive explicable partly on the basis of social factors, and of success or failure in leaving its mark on the field.

These ideas can be tied to professorial politics through the observation that academic disciplines vary not just in the personal politics of their members but also in whether at any point the research and teaching done within them pushes more in a liberal or a conservative direction, in the sense of calling explicitly for or implying a certain kind of politics. For example, as it has come to be practiced in the United States in the early twentieth-first century, sociology often leans left, having as one of its aims to understand and help reduce social inequality. In the eyes of many sociologists (not all, of course), the ultimate goal of sociological inquiry is to provide organizations, policy makers, and citizens with theories and findings that can inform the creation of a more equal social order. In its current form, economics leads in a more conservative direction. Academics in most fields will tend to be more liberal than other Americans, owing to the general political typing of the academic profession. But above and beyond this, liberal students should tend to opt into more liberally-oriented fields and conservative students into more conservatively-oriented ones, out of an interest in doing intellectual work and being in an organizational environment congruent with their political identity and sensibility. If this is right, then variation by field in the personal politics of professors would be a result of additional self-selection based on perceptions of political and intellectual fit with the content of different disciplines, particularly as this has come to be reflected in disciplinary reputations—in what amount to stereotypes of what sociology or economics or English are like politically as distinct from stereotypes about the academic profession in general. Few students have more than an inkling of such stereotypes before they start college, but many become exposed to them during the course of their undergraduate educations.[7]

But why, in terms of intellectual content, do some fields have a liberal tilt, others a conservative one, and others no readily discernible tilt at all? This cannot be explained merely by gesturing in the direction of the external institutions to which disciplines are linked. These links are important, but they have to be understood specifically in terms of their effects on scientific/intellectual movements. It is inexact to say that whoever is paying the bills determines the kind of work that gets done in a field, politically or otherwise. Even in the most commercialized fields, scholarship has a life of its own. What should be said instead is that the relationship between a field and its various external "audiences"— the users of its ideas, the employers of its graduates, the agencies that fund its research, and so on—affects the likelihood that any particular scientific/intellectual movement, including those with political implications, will succeed, becoming established and institutionalized.[8] Here, generally speaking, the third approach mentioned earlier has it right: disciplines with multiple links to conservative-leaning institutions or sectors are those in which conservative intellectual perspectives are more likely to arise; disciplines linking up more to social welfare, educational, and cultural institutions tend to be places where liberal or even radical scientific/intellectual movements can grow. This is so because intellectual movements often require the resources—funding for research, jobs for graduates, legitimacy—that external audiences can provide, and these tend to be more forthcoming in the context of convergent interests. Whether, on the whole, a field has more of a liberal or a conservative orientation, hence drawing in scholars with different political predilections, is thus a function of the history of the paradigms and approaches that have been pursued under its auspices—a history conditioned by the field's external connections, which also anchor its politics over time amid shifting intellectual fads and fashions (although external connections are not immutable.)

Given space constraints, two examples of this, reflecting disciplines with different political tendencies, will have to suffice. In a chapter for a volume celebrating the hundredth anniversary of the founding of the American Sociological Association, Myra Marx Ferree, Shamus Khan, and Shauna Morimoto trace the emergence of the interest in gender issues that characterizes contemporary American sociology.[9] Feminist sociologists, including the authors, claim that gender relations and gender inequality are not at the forefront of the discipline to the extent that they should be, but all observers agree that there has been a sea change since the 1960s, when gender was often ignored in sociological discussions or treated uncritically. Ferree, Khan, and Morimoto explain the "feminist revolution" in sociology basically as a scientific/intellectual movement started by female sociologists caught up in the wider feminist movement of the 1970s and upset not simply by sociology's neglect of gender but also by the subordinate status of female professors in the field. What explains their relative success in transforming sociology, in making gender and gender inequality commonplace objects of sociological investigation and teaching? Ferree, Khan, and Morimoto highlight several factors, including the growing number of women majoring in the discipline who wanted to see their experiences reflected in textbooks. Also important, however, is that the feminist revolution in sociology coincided with a more general "minority rights revolution" in American society.[10] Spurred into action by the civil rights movement, the feminist movement, and the disability rights movement, among others, the federal government embarked on campaigns in the 1960s and 1970s aimed at protecting the civil rights of women, members of racial and ethnic minority groups, and the disabled, particularly in the workplace and the educational arena. As sociologist Frank Dobbin has shown, organizations large and small scrambled to adjust to the legal and regulatory changes that ensued.[11] All of this created major opportunities for sociologists studying inequalities, including inequalities of gender. While more radical feminist research found only marginal support, by the 1970s mainstream social scientific investigations into the extent and causes of gender inequality were being funded by federal agencies like the National Science Foundation and liberal philanthropies.[12] The minority rights revolution also meant that prominent sociologists working on gender would be accorded respect in the public sphere, their expertise drawn on by liberal policy makers, journalists, and others. And it meant that universities, which had to adjust to the new circumstances as much as any other organization, were under pressure to have sociologists on their staff who were gender experts. Sociology has long-standing links to the American welfare state.[13] In this case, as the state was oriented in a new direction (i.e., toward the redress of gender grievances), sociologists hoping to get a scientific/ intellectual movement going around feminist concerns were able to take advantage of the opportunities afforded by the situation, eventually winning enough supporters for their movement that they were able to institutionalize it. Today the Sex and Gender section is the second largest in the American Sociological Association. The feminist movement in sociology is not the only movement that has given the discipline a strong left orientation—it leaned in that direction long before the 1970s—but it has proven important to the discipline's current intellectual content. Although feminist theories and methodologies have by no means won the day, it would be foolish for anyone with truly antifeminist sensibilities to become a sociologist; such a person would be destined to spend his career bashing his head against the wall, as most undergraduates could gather from taking an introductory sociology course.

On the other side, consider Daniel Stedman Jones's account of the rise of neoliberal economic policy in recent decades—policy stressing deregulation, fiscal austerity, declines in social welfare provision, privatization of government services, and so on—and the role played by academic economists in helping to bring it about.[14] In the United States, economics has undergone remarkable transformation as the institutional economics of the Progressive era gave way to the Keynesianism of the New Deal, and then to the particular version of the neoclassical paradigm championed by the Chicago school that informs neoliberal policy making today. Each of these periods brought economists with different political orientations and perspectives to the fore. How and why did Chicago-style economics gain ground? Stedman Jones argues that in the period after World War II, a number of conservative economists inside and outside academe, along with business leaders, became troubled by what they perceived as the liberalism of economics as it was then being practiced, by what they saw as the scientific inadequacy of its claims and the kinds of policy it was authorizing. Building on ideas developed before the war and on a general critique of totalitarianism, they collaborated to start a "transatlantic" intellectual movement around neoclassical assumptions, pairing these with claims about the intrinsic value of free markets, and worked hard to establish their approach as the only legitimate form of economic knowledge. Funds were donated for positions and centers at leading universities like Chicago, research grants were made available, conference series were funded, and free-market ideas came to be required de facto of economists entering government service or the private sector. Thanks in large part to this coordinated effort, which intensified in the 1970s and 1980s in light of new political-economic realities—and to the credible knowledge the Chicago approach was able to produce—the movement flourished. The point here is that a scientific/intellectual movement that remade a field intellectually and altered its political complexion depended for its success on, and arose partly because of, the connections between the field and other institutional spheres.[15] To an extent, American economics is conservative today relative to other social science disciplines (Democrats still outnumber Republicans in economics, drawing different implications from neoclassical assumptions, but by a less wide margin than in the other social sciences) because its closeness to business and the business side of the state meant that the Chicago school was able to drum up a great deal of support at a crucial moment in its development—at the same time that external connections inhibited the growth of politically countervailing movements in the field.[16]

Variation in the politics of professors across fields therefore depends on the history of scientific/intellectual movements in those fields, although the former feeds back into the latter in the sense that once professors with one political disposition dominate, they may resist new intellectual movements that point in the opposing political direction. At the same time, scientific/intellectual movements can affect the political typing of the professoriate overall, as word of particularly politicized movements, like feminism or academic Marxism, spreads beyond the confines of the academy to influence the reputation of the entire academic enterprise.

But understanding the political leanings of fields to be a consequence of scientific/intellectual movements is helpful in another way as well: it allows us to grasp not only why fields are more or less liberal or conservative, but also why they have particular mixes of political identity. Radicals can be found in relatively large numbers in the humanities and social sciences (outside of economics and criminology) because the distance between these fields and conservative-leaning external audiences has created space for more utopian scientific/intellectual movements to gain a foothold. Despite the efforts of a number of natural scientists in the 1960s and 1970s to remake their fields in radical directions as well—to fuse physics with the peace movement, for example—science's traditional self-understanding as an objective enterprise, along with its ties to industry and to non–social welfare sides of the state, has generally kept radical science movements from winning the day.[17] This has left the natural sciences populated mostly by those progressives and center-lefters who, because of general political typing dynamics, are so likely to pursue academic careers. And several of the engineering disciplines contain unusually large numbers of conservatives because of the close connections that have historically obtained between engineering and nationalist projects of state building.[18]

These claims are meant to be illustrative, not definitive. A full-scale account of why any field has the political leanings it does would have to survey the entire range of intellectual movements to which it has been subject, as well as its multiple external audiences, the individuals and organizations acting as brokers between the field and the outside world, and the field's relationships to other fields.[19]

✦

What about variation by type of institution? Ever since the publication of *The Academic Mind,* and particularly since *The Divided Academy,* social scientists have known that there is an association between academic status and liberalism, with more leftists and liberals located near the top of the academic hierarchy—in elite, PhD-granting institutions—and more conservatives located near the bottom. That is what the latent class analysis in Chapter 1 turned up as well, with the hitch that it found more radicals in liberal arts colleges than in doctoral institutions.

Over the years, three main explanations for these institutional differences have been advanced. The first is Ladd and Lipset's. Professors at elite institutions tend to be the most creative and productive, they argued. This, in their view, reflects dispositional differences between elite academics and others—dispositions that got them top jobs in the first place. Elite professors are typically hired, after all, not primarily for their teaching skills but because of their research record and potential to break new scientific or intellectual ground. Dispositions toward intellectual creativity should make elite professors more liberal, Ladd and Lipset claimed, since intensely creative people would naturally be opposed to the dogmatism of conservative ideology.

Bourdieu, in *Homo Academicus* and his later book, *The State Nobility,* offered an alternative account, seeking to explain patterns of variation by institution different from those in the United States.[20] Just as disciplines vary in their connections to the field of power, so too do academic institutions, Bourdieu suggested. In *The State Nobility,* he analyzed data on the class origins and eventual occupations of students in the French higher education system, and in particular at elite schools that prepared students for high-level positions in the French state bureaucracy. Where some schools, such as the prestigious École normale supérieure—the traditional breeding ground for French intellectuals—served a disproportionate number of students whose parents were in education or the arts and were thus connected to cultural power, others favored students whose parents held executive positions in large companies (connected to economic power). The political attitudes of students, Bourdieu found, differed depending on which corner of the class structure they came from. And the politics of professors varied depending on which class fraction was served by the institution employing them. Scholars at places like the École normale were reliably the most left-wing, expressing the political views of the class grouping composing their core student constituency; scholars at institutions serving students with more economic than cultural capital were more conservative.

The third and final approach focuses on political bias and discrimination. According to researchers such as Stanley Rothman and Daniel Klein, liberal academics essentially took over elite, PhD-granting institutions in the 1960s.[21] Today, they argue, the major research departments in many fields are completely dominated by those on the left, and faculty members in such departments refuse to hire conservatives, who are forced to take less prestigious jobs than their levels of productivity and talent would call for. Bias and discrimination against conservative academics, argue Rothman and Klein, explain not simply the underrepresentation of conservatives at elite schools but also the general dearth of conservatives in the academy: at every stage of the game, from graduate school admissions to the hiring of professors to decisions about tenure and promotion, conservatives are said to be at a disadvantage, particularly in the social sciences and humanities. This is so, they allege, because in many departments processes of "groupthink" prevail in the selection of academic personnel.[22]

The concept of groupthink was initially developed by the social psychologist Irving Janis.[23] Janis's idea was that in some small groups, such as those charged with carrying out military operations or making crucial policy decisions, norms may arise against dissenting from the views of other group members—an undesirable situation since it restricts invaluable debate about the pros and cons of any option the group may be considering. Social scientists analyzing groupthink have typically focused on situations involving high danger, high stress, secretiveness, and rapid decision making, as in sociologist Diane Vaughan's analysis of the organizational circumstances at NASA leading up to the launch of the doomed space shuttle *Challenger* in 1986.[24] But scholars like Klein claim that groupthink can be found in the university too. In academe, he argues, colleagues in a department are generally motivated to get along with one another. Groupthink unfolds as this motivation leads them to favor the hiring of candidates for professorial positions whose work and outlook on life are sufficiently similar to their own and those of their colleagues to not call into question anyone's intellectual choices or broader values. Given that most professors are on the left, particularly in the social sciences and humanities, the normal result of groupthink dynamics in the university, according to Klein, is that liberals will tend to hire other liberals.

Evaluating these three competing claims is more challenging than evaluating other claims about professors and their politics, for reliable data are lacking. Still, it is possible to offer something in the way of assessment.

Ladd and Lipset's argument is intriguing but ultimately too simple. It is certainly correct that professors at elite research institutions tend to publish much more than their colleagues teaching in less prestigious colleges and universities. Is this because elite, PhD-granting schools hire professors who are intrinsically creative and productive, driven by their personality, high cognitive capacity, and work habits to be publishing powerhouses—and destined, because of those same personality characteristics, to chafe at conservatism? To some extent the answer to the first part of this question is obviously yes: it is often evident from students' behavior as early as graduate school which have the motivation, drive, and talent necessary to become star researchers and which do not. At the same time, research by sociologists of science shows that the causality can also run in the other direction, with productivity resulting from institutional position and building on itself.[25] Academics who wind up with jobs in leading research centers teach fewer courses than professors elsewhere and have larger research budgets, better graduate students, and more administrative support; they are also immersed in organizational cultures in which research productivity is prioritized and standards for tenure are higher. Furthermore, once they begin to make a name for themselves, they may find new opportunities for research knocking on their door. How much of the greater productivity of scholars in elite institutions is a function of their creative personality and capacity, and how much is a function of institutional location? It is a mix of both.

Ladd and Lipset's argument also does not accord with the fact that it is professors at heavily teaching-oriented liberal arts colleges who are furthest to the left in terms of their embrace of radical positions. Finally, the point that conservatism and creativity are antithetical is easy to overstate. True, not just professors but also writers, artists, actors, and musicians tend to be on the left. Is this because those who are creative cannot tolerate conservative efforts to restrict autonomy? It might be so. But if, as there is reason to believe, the arts have become politically typed through processes similar to those affecting academia, then it is possible that there are more conservatives with artistic or creative potential than is usually realized but that they have simply channeled it into other arenas. The history of the contemporary American conservative movement shows just how creative conservative politicians, intellectuals, and political strategists have been in developing an ideological perspective, making an emotionally evocative and aesthetically appealing case for it, and innovating new forms of political organization.[26] And are not business entrepreneurs also creative types in their way?

As for Bourdieu's hypothesis, at first glance it seems inapplicable to the American case. The French higher education system differs from its American counterpart in many respects, one being that most leading postsecondary institutions in the United States are not formally tied to the labor market in the way the French Grandes écoles are. In practice, however, there is considerable informal specialization. Private research universities, for example, send a disproportionate number of their graduates into law, medicine, engineering, and high-level corporate positions; liberal arts colleges educate an unusually large number of students who want to go into academe or the arts; lower tier four-year schools send students into less prestigious professions like teaching and nursing and into middle-management jobs; and so on.[27] We also know that, despite claims of meritocracy when it comes to college admissions, students from higher social class positions are more likely to wind up attending elite colleges and universities, such that different types of institutions effectively cater to students originating from different locations in the class structure—which is obviously related to variation in student career choices.[28] Could this explain the institutionally variable politics of professors, with the parents of artsy liberal arts college students, as well as the students themselves, being more willing to tolerate radical academics in the classroom; the parents of high-achieving Ivy Leaguers—many professionals—expecting professors to be Clinton Democrats, as they themselves often are; and the parents of those at less prestigious schools expecting the faculty to look more like America politically?

The explanation is not implausible. We know that people from different social backgrounds view higher education differently. For example, in the public opinion poll Simmons and I conducted, we found that professionals and managers were more likely than other Americans to believe that the main aim of higher education should be to impart critical thinking skills, while those from lower social class positions believe the goal is to provide students the training they need to get good jobs after graduating.[29] To the extent that these expectations are bound up with views about permissible faculty politics, and that parents' and students' expectations influence the kinds of professors selected to teach in different schools, there could well be effects on professors' political beliefs.

But there are also problems with this account. First, while American higher education institutions do vary in the typical class backgrounds and occupational destinations of students, there would appear to be more heterogeneity than in France. Students from highly educated professional families that lean Democratic may be overrepresented in the Ivy League—but there are also plenty of Ivy League students from still more elite backgrounds whose parents are not uncommonly Republicans. Similarly, while well-known liberal arts colleges like Vassar and Oberlin may prepare students for careers in the culture industry, the liberal arts sector of American higher education is in fact far broader than this, encompassing schools as varied as the University of Pikeville in Kentucky, which has a Presbyterian heritage, and Washington and Lee College in Virginia, where four out of five male students belong to fraternities. It seems improbable that we could identify anything about the class composition of the student body within institutional swaths of American higher education as broad as these that would necessarily tilt faculty politics in one direction or the other, since heterogeneity entails competing group interests.

Even more problematic, however, is that Bourdieu's theory is long on claims but short on the specification of causal mechanisms. Thanks to the work of sociologists like Christine Musselin and Michèle Lamont, we have some social scientific understanding of how academics make judgments about other academics.[30] Musselin studied hiring practices in France, Germany, and the United States; Lamont, the peer review practices by which interdisciplinary funding panels make decisions about which research projects to support. The dynamics of these situations differ, but one way in which they are the same is that professors invariably demand autonomy from administrators and other nonacademic groups when it comes to assessing academic quality and potential. One of the hallmarks of a profession, as opposed to an occupation, is that members claim their education and training give them a unique ability to recognize important contributions to their field. Academics assert this with a vengeance, invariably rebuffing outsiders who want to have a say in judgments of academic merit— and nowhere more so than in the hiring process. How, then, would it routinely come to pass that academics whose politics fit with the "class-reproductive" role of their institutions and with the political interests of parents and others end up being selected by recruitment committees?

Finally, is the association between academic status and liberalism, as well as the liberalism of the professoriate more generally, a result of political bias and discrimination? This has been the elephant in the room until now, so common is it for conservative commentators to assert bias whenever the topic of professors and their politics arises.

One piece of evidence consistently cited in support of this assertion is simply the fact that there are more liberals at the top of the academic status structure. For example, in a 2005 article titled "Politics and Professional Advancement among College Faculty," Stanley Rothman, Robert Lichter, and Neil Nevitte set out to test the hypothesis that political "homogeneity makes it more difficult for conservatives to enter and advance in the [academic] profession."[31] To this end, they looked at whether political liberalism among faculty members is associated with teaching at a higher prestige institution once levels of research productivity are controlled for. They found that it is. Summing up the results of their analysis, they insisted that their findings "do not definitively prove that ideology accounts for differences in professional standing." "It is entirely possible," they acknowledged, "that other unmeasured factors may account for those variations." However, they also noted that "the results are consistent with the hypothesis that political conservatism confers a disadvantage in the competition for professional advancement."[32] In other words, there is an association between institutional status and liberalism, and this counts as prima facie evidence of discrimination.

There is also anecdotal evidence to support the bias claim. In January 2011 Jonathan Haidt gave a talk at an academic conference in which he asserted that the political lopsidedness of his field, social psychology, stemmed partly from political bias against conservatives—ironic, since bias is a major subject of research by social psychologists. The talk was reported in the *New York Times,* and in the wake of the ensuing controversy many conservative graduate students and academics emailed Haidt to share their experiences, which he posted in anonymized form on his website, making it a repository of relevant anecdotes. "I can't begin to tell you how difficult it was for me in graduate school, because I am not a liberal Democrat," wrote one person. "As one example, following Bush's defeat of Kerry, one of my professors would email me every time a soldier's death in Iraq made the headlines; he would call me out, publicly blaming me for not supporting Kerry in the election." Another said, "I am a conservative, and like the students you mentioned, I felt very frustrated during my time in grad school. All of the faculty members were liberal, and they constantly made political jokes and comments, assuming that we all shared their ideology. . . . This specific issue affected me so much during my graduate school years that it actually steered me away from research, and I took a teaching position at a local community college after graduation."[33]

Finally, there is some systematic evidence of bias. In a 2005 survey of the professoriate, researcher Gary Tobin asked professors how favorably or unfavorably they felt toward members of different religious groups.[34] Fifty-three percent of academics surveyed stated that they regarded evangelical Protestants unfavorably, while the next highest unfavorable rating, of Mormons at 33%, also went to a conservative group. Interesting as these findings were, they did not speak directly to the selection of academic personnel. Another study, this one by sociologist George Yancey, did.[35] Yancey conducted a mid-sized survey of American sociologists and also surveyed members of other disciplines in smaller numbers. The survey was presented to respondents as a study of what makes someone a good academic colleague, but it was intended as a measure of political and religious bias. After asking his respondents some general questions about colleagueship, Yancey presented the following scenario: "Assume that your facility is hiring a new professor. Below is a list of possible characteristics of this new hire. Many of them are characteristics that you can not directly inquire of prospective candidates. However, if you were able to learn of these characteristics about a candidate, would that make you more or less likely to support their hire?"[36]

The list included things like "The candidate is a Republican" and "The candidate is a Fundamentalist." About three-quarters of sociologists said the party affiliation of job candidates would have no bearing on their evaluations of them. Among those who said politics did matter, however, nearly all said that they would favor a Democratic candidate and disfavor a Republican one, while almost half of sociologists said they would look unfavorably on fundamentalists and evangelicals trying to get a job in their department.[37]

What does all this amount to? Conservative scholars, particularly in the liberal social sciences and humanities, can indeed have a difficult time of it in some situations—just as progressives at some elite law firms might have a difficult time of it. Surrounded by liberals and leftists who may be convinced of the moral and intellectual superiority of their own views and who may hold derogatory stereotypes of conservatives, some conservative graduate students and professors face hostility and inhabit politically uncomfortable educational and occupational worlds. Given what we know about cultural and social psychological dynamics in situations where a large majority of people share a social characteristic, be it a racial or religious identity or a political orientation, this is not all that surprising. In such circumstances in-group membership tends to be celebrated and out-group membership derided.[38] The question is how much the resulting animosity contributes to professorial liberalism and the greater presence of liberals atop the academic food chain. There is good reason to believe that it does not make a huge contribution to either. One study suggesting this is the experiment I carried out with Joseph Ma and Ethan Fosse.

In the sociology and economics literature on prejudice and discrimination in the labor and housing markets, the running assumption is that one has not demonstrated that discrimination contributes to unequal outcomes between groups if one has simply documented unequal outcomes and/or found attitudinal evidence of bias on the part of those making decisions about the distribution of resources. The reason is that there are typically many other factors that could account equally well for the disparity. Concerned to address this problem, social scientists have been turning increasingly toward direct measures of discrimination. The most common methodology they employ is a kind of field experiment called an "audit study." (A field experiment is a social experiment taking place outside the laboratory.[39]) In an audit study the researcher first identifies a large number of decision makers of some sort (e.g., employers or real estate brokers). Then, without informing them that they are being studied, the researcher has testers from the social groups whose unequal outcomes he is trying to explain approach the decision makers to stimulate actual decisions. If the experimental stimuli are manipulated carefully enough, explanations other than discrimination for observed differences can generally be ruled out. Audit studies were first used in the 1970s to measure housing discrimination. Today they are routine.[40]

An excellent example is sociologist Devah Pager's study of race and involvement with the criminal justice system in the entry-level labor market in Milwaukee.[41] Pager hired two black and two white twenty-three-year-old college students, matched in terms of self-presentation, to apply in person to a random sample of job openings. Each week the pair of white testers applied to one set of jobs, the pair of black testers to another. The fabricated résumés of the applicants were matched on job–relevant characteristics, except that for one applicant (but not the other) the application indicated a criminal record. Using voice mailboxes, Pager measured the proportion of applicants in each racial pair called back for an interview or offered a job. She found not only that ex-offenders were discriminated against, but that white testers were called back at a higher rate than black testers: strong evidence that racial discrimination does in fact contribute to unequal labor market outcomes.

Ma, Fosse, and I decided to undertake a similar study measuring political bias and discrimination in academia. It would not be feasible to have fake liberal and conservative scholars apply for academic jobs. In most departments, job applicants—and there can be hundreds for every opening—are evaluated not simply on the basis of their scholarly résumés but also on the writing samples they provide, their academic reputation, and the letters of recommendation composed on their behalf. It would be impossible to create credible, fabricated versions of all this material. But if discrimination in favor of liberal academics or against conservative ones were truly widespread in American higher education, it should be evident in situations beyond hiring, such as the graduate admissions process—worth studying in its own right given the imbalance of liberals and conservatives among graduate students. This gave us an idea.

Every fall, the professors in doctoral programs in the social sciences and humanities who have been asked by their colleagues to serve for a term as director of graduate study (DGS), the professor who has administrative oversight over the graduate program, receive dozens if not hundreds of emails from young people thinking of applying to their departments. In the usual ritual soon-to-be-graduating college seniors or recent graduates introduce themselves and ask a few questions about the program. The unstated goal is to bring themselves to the attention of the DGS in the hope that doing so will give them a leg up in the competitions for admission that happen in the late fall or early winter. These emails *could* be faked, Ma, Fosse, and I realized, and if departmental hostility toward conservatives were so strong and entrenched as to affect the evaluation of academic personnel, the answers received to the emails—or not received—should show it. As explained in the introduction, we proceeded to draft email templates comparable in terms of student qualifications and interest areas, and then sent two emails to each DGS in the top seventy-five American doctoral programs in sociology, economics, political science, history, and literature.[42] One email was a control that mentioned nothing about the fake student's politics, while the other mentioned that the student had worked on either the McCain or Obama campaign in 2008. If we received a response, we had a politically mixed group of three raters code it, blind to what the treatment condition was, on such dimensions as enthusiasm and emotional warmth.[43] On average, the DGSs responded less frequently, more slowly, and less enthusiastically to the conservative applicant. But the magnitude of these differences was tiny; none was statistically significant. For example, on the five-point enthusiasm scale our raters used, responses to the liberal student scored 2.6 on average, while responses to the conservative student scored 2.5. Almost none of the DGSs mentioned anything about the students' politics in their replies. When they did, work on the McCain campaign was praised as much as work for Obama.

By their nature, audit studies involve deception. Since the whole point is to measure discrimination in real-world settings, where people are not being observed by social scientists and do not change their behavior to make themselves look better, any audit study that asked its research subjects for consent before studying them would be self-defeating. But this means that audit studies raise ethical questions.[44] Is it ever permissible for social researchers to deceive their research subjects? Among researchers who employ this methodology, the general understanding—shared by the institutional review boards that must approve their research protocols—is that the deception and lack of informed consent that are part and parcel of audit research are ethically permissible if (1) the subjects of the research are not private citizens plucked from the anonymity of their lives but individuals serving in gate-keeping capacities in public or quasi-public institutions; (2) the discriminatory behavior being studied is illegal or widely seen as illegitimate; (3) a case can be made that social science and/or public policy would be advanced by the findings of the study and that an audit methodology is the best way to study the issues in question; and (4) relatively little is asked of the research subjects and no harm is allowed to come to them as a result of their participation in the research. Predictably, though, when we debriefed our research subjects, some were very angry about having been deceived. Most were not; positive notes in response to the debriefing email outnumbered negative ones six to one. But the negative responses, coming mostly from historians and scholars of literature, were *extremely* negative, with several scholars using choice language to accuse me of ethical impropriety. Two complained to my institutional review board, and one threatened legal action if his case was not removed from our data set. (It was.)

What lies behind this reaction? Some of it is that academics are a principled group and take the idea of scholarly ethics very seriously. Professors who find the idea of any research involving deception abhorrent would naturally react badly to being the subject of such research themselves. Another part of the negative reaction has to do with trust. The interactions that professors have with one another and with current and prospective graduate students would grind to a halt if people in the academic community could not trust that those with whom they are interacting are who they claim to be. Professors have learned not to fully trust undergraduates, having heard one too many stories about grandparents dying the day before research papers are due, but trust does usually extend to students who state their intention of becoming academics. Our study violated that trust, and this understandably made some people upset. Other negative reactions came from DGSs who reminded me how busy they were and said I was wasting their time. At the same time, *some* of the reaction seemed to be defensive, reflecting the sentiment that the inner workings of academia should simply not be subject to outside scrutiny. As I note in Chapter 7, this sentiment is part of what so rankles conservatives about the academy.[45]

When the study was released, proponents of the bias thesis raised a number of methodological objections.[46] It is possible, as some argued, that we would have obtained different results had we somehow managed to study actual admissions decisions rather than email replies. However, research on other forms of discrimination suggests that discriminatory tendencies are most likely to surface in everyday activities—such as the sending of emails in response to student queries—that people do not think will be closely examined by others and that do not require a good deal of careful thought.[47] Another potential problem raised by critics is that DGSs might use boilerplate language to respond to all students or write to all of them enthusiastically so as to encourage more applications, which would decrease their program's acceptance rates and make them look more selective. We did in fact find some use of boiler-plate language when we compared the responses received to the treatment and control emails using plagiarism detection software. But in only about 10% of the cases was the text of both replies substantially similar, and even here the typical pattern was for DGSs to insert some individualized language before or after the boilerplate material. Nor was it true that DGSs responded in a universally supportive manner: there was ample variation on every outcome measure used in our analysis.

In the absence of more compelling objections, the study should count as reasonably strong evidence that most social scientists and humanists in leading departments work hard to keep their political feelings and opinions from interfering with their evaluations of academic personnel. This interpretation is in line with Yancey's finding that three-quarters of sociologists say the political views of job candidates are irrelevant and is consistent with the finding from the PAP survey that 73% of academics agree strongly with the statement "The views of an academic job candidate on national politics should not play a role in whether she or he is hired." It is also consistent with the finding, reported by Rothman, Kelly-Woessner, and Woessner, that only 7% of conservative academics report having been the victim of any kind of political discrimination.[48]

Work to avoid acting in a discriminatory manner is the operative term here. The evidence suggests that some liberal academics may indeed be biased against conservatives in the sense of thinking that conservatives by their nature would not make good professors, and professors are hardly immune from the pressures of homophily, the well-established tendency of people to want to surround themselves with others who are just like them.[49] What seems to be the case, though, is that *most* professors view themselves as professionals and understand that this requires them to keep their politics out of personnel matters. The nature of this understanding varies by field. In the follow-up interviews my research assistants and I conducted with PAP survey respondents, we asked them how they would feel about hiring a colleague with whom they disagreed politically. While the vast majority of interviewees said they would have no problem doing so, biologists, engineers, and economists offered different justifications than did sociologists and professors of literature, corresponding with different conceptions of their work. The biologists, engineers, and economists told us that the politics of job candidates do not matter to them because the subject matter of their discipline is such that political views have almost no bearing on research or teaching (a point to which I return in Chapter 5). Maurice, a fifty-four-year-old professor of engineering at an institution in the South, is a case in point. Maurice describes himself as a left-leaning moderate who is increasingly fed up with the Republican Party. Would he support the hiring of a colleague with differing political views? Yes, he told us.

> We could use somebody here who's a specialist in radio frequency stuff. I dabble in it, but I'm certainly no specialist. But if we wanted to bring in some wireless communications specialist, I don't care if the guy is right wing, left wing, or apolitical. . . . One of the beauties of engineering . . . is there is

no such thing, say, as a Jewish volt, there is no such thing as a Republican ampere. There's no such thing as a conservative kilogram. Or an atheist heater. The atheist looks at the volt meter and it reads 1.26 volts, the ardent Christian conservative reads 1.26 volts, the Muslim reads 1.26 volts. There is some measure of objectivity in this profession.

Most biologists and engineers told us that when they were interviewing candidates for positions, they usually had no idea what the person's politics were. Several stated that they saw no reason to ask.

A different rationale was offered by social scientists and humanists like Linda, a thirty-seven-year-old sociologist who describes herself as a liberal. She too claimed that she would support the hiring of a colleague whose politics are at odds with her own, not because politics do not factor into sociological investigation but because she feels it is her duty, when evaluating other academics, to separate her views about their qualifications and performance from whatever opinions she may have about their political commitments. "I don't think that someone's political views have anything to do with whether they can be an effective and good teacher and faculty member," she told us. "When they're teaching sociology, it's not my business to know how they feel about certain topics." To this she added, "Having a variety of views keeps things interesting in the hallway." The problem with studies like Klein's on groupthink in academe is that they fail to recognize the binding power of professional norms such as those that Maurice and Linda appear to be in the grip of—norms that proscribe direct political evaluation.

Of course, wherever there are norms, there are deviations from them. There are several circumstances in which norms against political evaluation in academe may be weakened. One arises when a specific kind of scientific/intellectual movement takes shape and becomes institutionalized—a movement calling explicitly for the intertwining of academic work and political activism. For example, in an important contribution to the sociology of academic life Fabio Rojas sought to explain the rise of the interdisciplinary field of black studies.[50] Black studies arose out of protests by African American students and scholars in the 1960s who claimed that too little research and teaching was being done about the black experience from a black point of view. This research and teaching, as they saw it, should not be politically neutral but should instead highlight issues of oppression, resistance, and empowerment. Rojas showed how a few select institutions that were targeted for protest, such as San Francisco State, gave in to student demands by starting black studies departments; how this organizational form spread in American higher education in the 1970s; and how, while retaining something of its original political tilt, black studies was transformed in subsequent decades as it was forced to make a case for its continued existence on more strictly academic grounds. Despite these transformations, however, it seems clearly the case that few black studies departments today would countenance the hiring of a scholar with extremely conservative views on issues relevant to African American life; such a scholar would be in tension politically and intellectually with the movement that provided black studies with its raison d'être. Here norms against politicized evaluation might not hold, and the same thing could be true in other academic units, such as women's or labor studies programs, that are also rooted in explicit political commitments and where people may judge the work of potential colleagues and graduate students on the basis of perceived fit with the department's politicized identity and culture.[51] But it is not only in specialized programs that norms against political evaluation may be weakened. Explicitly politicized scientific/intellectual movements arise in larger disciplines as well, and whenever departments and administrators decide that they would like to bring a new professor on board who works from the perspective of such a movement, politics might become a consideration in the hiring process. Because these movements are not uncommon in the social sciences and humanities, populating departments with a minority of scholars who, because of their intellectual and political commitments, may have no problem evaluating candidates politically even when it comes to more standard hires, this expands the potential for political bias and discrimination in hiring, and then tenure and promotion, to have an impact on the distribution of political views in academe.

But to what extent is professorial liberalism in general and the association between academic status and liberalism in particular a function of bias and discrimination? Probably not much. While there may well be cases in which conservative scholars have been passed over for hiring or promotion because of their politics, in terms of professorial liberalism as a whole bias and discrimination could play a major causal role only if liberals and conservatives were applying in anything like equal numbers to academic jobs and if it were usually clear to search committees where job candidates stood politically. But neither of these things is true. We know, again, that liberals significantly outnumber conservatives in the graduate student ranks, and there is no reason to think this is any different among those in the final stages of their doctoral work, searching for academic employment. In liberally oriented fields like those in the social sciences and humanities, the numbers are even more skewed. If there are few conservatives applying for academic jobs, there are few people to discriminate against. Women's studies departments might never hire anyone without feminist credentials, but how many conservatives are there applying for women's studies positions? Conservative critics of academe who acknowledge this point—who recognize that self-selection does contribute to professorial liberalism—contend that conservatives do not pursue PhDs because they realize that they *would* be discriminated against if they eventually sought academic employment. As Peter Wood, president of the National Association of Scholars, puts it, "Conservatives may be self-selecting out of graduate school, but they're doing it on a rational basis."[52] But to return to a finding mentioned in Chapter 3, survey data dating back to the early 1970s show major political differences in the aspiration to become a professor among college freshman who have not yet started school and who have not yet gotten any real taste for what life is like in the ivory tower. At the same time, it is hardly the case that search committees know the politics of everyone who is applying for a job.[53] In the sciences, again, they rarely do, interviews suggest. And yet professors in the sciences are still much more liberal than the American population as a whole.

Nor is the bias and discrimination argument helpful as an explanation of institutional differences. The arguments of Rothman, Lichter, Nevitte, and others have always been somewhat obscure on this point. Even if there is bias against conservative scholars, why should there be more bias at the top? Advocates of the bias theory might respond that the reason is that there are more liberals teaching in top departments, so that here groupthink processes resulting in preferences for liberal job candidates are more likely to operate. But this *is* circular, failing to answer the question of why there are more liberals at the top to begin with. It could be that for resource-related reasons strongly left-politicized departments and programs (which are in some sense curricular luxuries) tend to be found more often in large, well-endowed research institutions, which might account for more politicized evaluation there. But the tendency for there to be more liberals at elite institutions was noted long before any such programs arose. If anything, the greater focus on research excellence in top departments should tend to reinforce norms *against* evaluating candidates on political grounds. This last point is consistent with another of Yancey's findings on bias: he discovered that there is actually somewhat *less* political bias among academics teaching in doctoral-granting programs.[54]

So what is the real explanation for variation in professors' politics across institutions? In a 1949 paper, Friedrich Hayek, one of the intellectual progenitors of the modern conservative movement, observed:

> Nobody . . . who is familiar with large numbers of university faculties . . . can remain oblivious to the fact that the most brilliant and successful teachers are today more likely than not to be socialists, while those who hold more conservative political views are as frequently mediocrities. . . . The socialist will, of course, see in this merely a proof that the more intelligent person is today bound to become a socialist. But this is far from being the necessary or even the most likely explanation. The main reason for this state of affairs is probably that, for the

exceptionally able man who accepts the present order of society, a multitude of other avenues to influence and power are
open, while to the disaffected and dissatisfied an intellectual
career is the most promising path to both influence and the
power to contribute to the achievement of his ideals.[55]

Although Hayek was wrong to claim that those on the left go
into academe because they are disaffected, it does seem to be the
case that liberals who go into academic work tend to have higher
levels of intellectual capital than conservatives who do. If you are
a brilliant student on the left, one of the best and brightest in your
class, you are likely to think of an academic career as a viable outlet
for your energies. If you are a brilliant conservative student, you
are more likely to set your sights on other fields such as business
or law—or politics. Of course there are outstanding conservative
minds who become so interested in academic pursuits that they
persevere in higher education despite the fact that doing so means
going against type. Hayek was one; there are many others. But that
academe is widely understood to be an occupation suitable for liberals should tend to restrict the number of conservatives at the high
end of the intellectual capital distribution who choose academic
careers. To the extent that job candidates are slotted into various
tiers of the academic labor market depending on assessments of
their talents and abilities, this could explain why one finds more
liberals teaching near the top of the academic hierarchy and more
conservatives teaching near the bottom.

There is empirical evidence to support Hayek's contention.
Consider the following. Among professors in the PAP sample, 28%
of liberals received their highest degrees from top-ranked institutions, as compared to 23% of conservatives.[56] Among respondents

to the HERI College Senior Survey from 1994 to 1999, who said they planned to become professors, 46% of those on the left attended highly selective public or private universities or liberal arts colleges, while 30% of conservative aspirants did. Thirty-seven percent of liberal professors in the PAP sample have a father with some kind of graduate degree—a reasonable indicator of inherited intellectual capital—as compared to 32% of conservatives. (Fourteen percent of liberal professors have fathers with doctorates; five percent of conservative professors do.) Furthermore, 78% of liberal professors hold doctoral degrees, as compared to just 46% of conservatives.[57] In a statistical model trying to predict where in the academic hierarchy any given respondent in the PAP study falls (holding disciplinary area constant), the effect of being a liberal—a strong and statistically significant predictor of a more elite location in simpler models—was reduced considerably and rendered statistically nonsignificant when variables measuring father's graduate work, the respondent's holding of a doctoral degree, and attendance at a top school were introduced.[58] *Much of the greater presence of liberals at leading institutions would therefore appear to be a function of differences in intellectual capital between liberals and conservatives who go into academic work.*

But what about the distribution of political clusters across institutions, such as the finding that radicals are overrepresented in liberal arts colleges? Intellectual capital is part of the story here, but a broader social logic is also at play. Analytically helpful is a theoretical framework from the sociology of organizations called "organizational ecology."[59] The idea behind this approach is that it is productive to conceive of organizations in any societal sector as analogous to organisms in a natural environment competing and cooperating to obtain the scarce resources needed for survival. In the case of organizations, resources include things like clients and customers, sales and other sources of revenue, and brand recognition and status. The key to organizational survival, researchers argue, continuing with the ecological metaphor, is for organizations to carve out stable niches for themselves—spaces on the organizational landscape where, thanks to a relative absence of competitors achieved through specialization, they can assure themselves of more or less continuous resource flows.[60] As part of this, organizations seek distinctive identities, things they do and specialize in that give them claims to uniqueness and position them to find their niche. One thing that higher education institutions do as they work to establish a niche is emphasize different aspects of the professorial role. This is not simply a matter of lower-tier schools emphasizing teaching; it is about the total image of the ideal professor that institutions project in defining their identity, an image that becomes prominent in their publicity materials and that forms part of their internal culture. As this has worked itself out in the contemporary American context—and at the risk of major oversimplification—elite research schools tend to stress research excellence and the chances that students will have to come into contact with leading thinkers. Liberal arts colleges promise students a life-transformative experience and, as part of this, professors who will engage them intensively and challenge them to think in new ways. Lower-tier four-year schools often emphasize their regional connections and service and the ability of their faculty to teach material to students from a wide variety of backgrounds and to otherwise promote student success. And community colleges present themselves as way stations to students' futures, stressing the real-world capabilities and insights of their faculty and how these will help students get the education they need to either advance in the labor market or transfer to a four-year institution. These idealized images of the academic role are related to the kind of student constituencies institutions serve, but there is no reason to think, contrary to Bourdieu, that class-related factors are the whole story here; each set of images has a complex and contingent organizational history.

Whether formally or informally, institutionally differentiated images of the ideal professor are in the minds of search committee members when they begin reviewing applications and are widely seen as legitimate standards to which applicants can be held.[61] Harvard wants to hire the next Lawrence Summers, brilliant and a leader in his field but not someone prepared to offer his students a warm and fuzzy learning experience. Williams College seeks the next Mark Hopkins, who was a professor of philosophy and president there for much of the nineteenth century, and about whom James Garfield said, "The ideal college is Mark Hopkins on one end of a log and a student on the other," a phrase that every Williams student comes to know and an expectation that every Williams faculty member is expected to live up to. California State University–Northridge is looking to hire dedicated teacher-scholars who know how to communicate complex material to first-generation college students. Contra Costa College in San Pablo, California, is looking for passionate educators with practical experience who can inspire their students.

Radicals are more commonly found in liberal arts schools, and probably have been for much of the twentieth century, because radicalism fits with the organizational identity of such institutions as providers of intellectually and culturally transformative college experiences.[62] Washington and Lee students aside, could one call oneself a bona fide graduate of a liberal arts college if one had not had one's mind blown by a professor in a course on capitalism and the global South, or feminist theory? Expectations to this effect undoubtedly influence the hiring process, likely via one of the exceptions to norms proscribing political evaluation mentioned earlier. (For example, left intellectual movements may be easier to institutionalize in liberal arts colleges, so that departments there have semipermanent lines to fill in such areas as Marxist literary theory and critical anthropology.) As for the lesser presence of the conservative clusters at elite schools, intellectual capital assessments are probably reinforced by other judgments of academic quality. To the extent that conservatism is seen as incompatible with intellectualism and a rigorous scientific mind-set, schools at the top of the academic status structure concerned to select job candidates who display such qualities may be hesitant to offer positions to those few conservatives who appear on their radar screens.[63]

Finally, what explains change over time in the politics of professors? Two such changes have been mentioned previously: the aggregate increase in professorial liberalism seen since the late 1960s and the tendency among younger academics to not be radicals. Parceling out the causes of long-term attitudinal changes in populations of individuals is always a challenge for social science, not least because, until recently, it was thought impossible to examine simultaneously the effects of age, birth cohort membership, and period (historical developments occurring during a given set of years) in the same statistical model. Although solutions to this problem are now being developed, what has always been clear is that whether one is trying to account for changes in political attitudes, changes in racial attitudes, or shifting views on sexuality, empirically testing competing accounts of attitudinal change using surveys is a data-intensive enterprise, requiring studies with equivalent sampling procedures and measures undertaken at numerous time points.[64] The problem in making sense of changes in professorial politics over the years is that we do not have data that fully meet these requirements.

It is nevertheless possible to make some headway. Consider Table 4.1, taken from higher education researchers Jack Schuster and Martin Finkelstein's book, *The American Faculty*. The table, based on Carnegie survey data, shows changes in faculty political orientation between 1969 and 1997 broken down by broad disciplinary area. Most areas registered an increase in liberal views over this period. What the table also makes clear, however, is that *the bulk of this increase was a result of the growing liberalism of academic women* (and very likely the increasing number of women in higher education). The table shows that the number of male professors in the left/liberal category increased by just 3 percentage points between 1969 and 1997, while the number of women with left/liberal politics jumped by 22 percentage points.[65] In different ratios, as Schuster and Finkelstein note, this same pattern can be found in every disciplinary area except engineering.

What is going on here? Different processes are at play in different fields, but cross-cutting them is a phenomenon of major importance for contemporary American academic life: the feminist movement. Data from the GSS—not just the subsample of respondents who are professors—show that women with advanced degrees are considerably more liberal on average than their male counterparts, and as a group have grown much more liberal since the late 1970s, generally tracking increases in the liberalism of academic women (see Figure 4.1). While causes of the gender gap in politics are much debated, perhaps the most plausible explana-

Table 4.1. Self-reported left/liberal identification among the faculty, 1969–1997

	1969 (%)	1997 (%)	Change, 1969–1997
All faculty	48	57	9
Female	43	65	22
Male	49	52	3
Program area			
Liberal arts and sciences	55	64	9
Female	52	75	23
Male	56	59	3
Fine arts	52	72	20
Female	44	81	37
Male	54	67	13
Humanities	61	75	14
Female	55	79	24
Male	63	71	8
Natural sciences	44	50	6
Female	40	56	16
Male	44	48	4
Social sciences	68	70	2
Female	68	85	17
Male	69	64	−5
Professions	34	46	12
Female	29	53	24
Male	35	39	4
Business	30	31	1
Female	17	45	28
Male	32	24	−8
Education	36	59	23
Female	30	61	31
Male	38	58	20
Engineering	29	33	4
Female	51	46	−5
Male	29	30	1
Health sciences	32	46	14
Female	30	48	18
Male	34	36	2

Source: Jack H. Schuster and Martin J. Finkelstein, *The American Faculty: The Restructuring of Academic Work and Careers* (Baltimore, MD: Johns Hopkins University Press, 2006), 505, 1969 and 1997 Carnegie faculty surveys, sample sizes 60,028 and 5,151, respectively.

Note: Because of rounding, the numbers in the third column differ slightly from those in Schuster and Finkelstein's original table and from those cited in Chapter 1.

tion for women with advanced degrees is that since the 1970s, but really since a phase of institutionalization in the 1980s, academia has been a key home for the feminist movement (as discussed earlier for sociology), a site where many of its leading thinkers have been housed and a venue in which feminists of various kinds have sought to alert young people to the importance of feminist ideals.[66] As both a cause and a consequence of this development, advanced education and academic careers have come to seem particularly suitable goals for young women committed to feminism.[67] The results have been dramatic. Today, according to the PAP data, 63% of female academics describe themselves as feminists. In any period, the mass entry of feminists into academe would have pushed it in a progressive direction, but the growing strength of American conservatism over the past few decades may have led feminist academics to be even more vehement about their politics

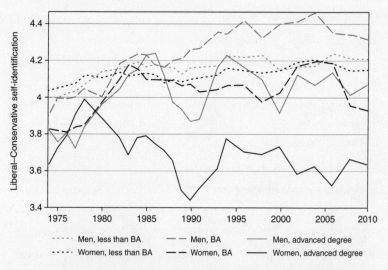

Figure 4.1. Political views by gender and education level, 1974–2010 (five-year moving averages). *Source:* General Social Survey.

than they would otherwise have been given the stance taken by Republican politicians on reproductive rights and other issues. Had there not been a feminist movement, American academia would probably look about the same today politically as it did in the late 1960s: still very liberal and Democratic, given the persistence of political typing and the large number of baby boomers who then entered the academic ranks, or slightly more liberal given dynamics of reinforcement, the growth of other left-leaning intellectual movements in the social sciences and humanities, and the ongoing liberalization of social attitudes among American professionals generally—but not quite so liberal as we see now.[68]

The other change runs in the opposite direction. Relative to their presence in academia overall, radicals are underrepresented in the youngest generation of professors in the PAP study. This development is likely driven by two factors. First, the 1980s and 1990s, the decades when most of these professors were enrolled in college, were not, for a variety of reasons, times of intense left social movement activity in American society or on American campuses, a few non-Marxian movements notwithstanding, such as the South African divestment campaign (and academic feminism). Few academics who came of age then—people whose adolescent "impressionable years" occurred during the Reagan era—were therefore pulled into a far-left orbit.[69] Second, as sociologist Andrew Abbott has emphasized, building on a classic contribution to sociology made by the early twentieth-century sociologist Karl Mannheim, academic generations often engage in efforts to distance themselves from their predecessors.[70] This has significant consequences for ideas, driving no small amount of intellectual dynamism. But it can also matter for politics. The interview data on professors—as well as informal conversations I have had with colleagues—suggest that many youngish academics now find themselves slightly embarrassed by the 1960s-era academic left, by the radicalism and intransigence of its politics and its willingness to subordinate intellectual and scientific concerns to political ones. These scholars, while usually committed to liberal ideals and the Democratic Party, have pegged their hopes on a different, more pragmatic and reformist kind of politics—in a move that some applaud and others view as a capitulation. Whether and how their views will begin to alter the American university when the baby boomers retire remains an open question.

Chapter 5

The Knowledge-Politics Problem

A core argument of the preceding chapters has been that the liberalism of the American professoriate is not an extraneous feature of the occupation but a fundamental and more or less enduring social characteristic, one that has been built into our collective image of what professors are like. Despite the fact that this is so, little research by social scientists asks whether and how professors' politics affect the work they do or its social outcomes.

There are some exceptions. Sociologists of knowledge, for example, concerned to explain why particular ideas, perspectives, theories, and methods develop and become popular at particular junctures, have occasionally factored professorial politics into their explanations. Alvin Gouldner, a pioneer in the area, did this when he sought to account for the ideas of the influential mid-twentieth-century Harvard sociologist Talcott Parsons by highlighting his isolation, in Cambridge, from economic dislocations affecting other Americans—an isolation said to have given Parsons a conservative bent.[1] In line with the work of Daniel Stedman Jones, discussed in Chapter 4, economic sociologists writing about the role of American-trained economists in bringing about neoliberal economic reforms have attended at least in passing to economists' political orientations as well as to their ideas.[2] And a few researchers have explored how faculty politics may have contributed to developments in the higher education sector, such as the rise of the "California idea" for higher education or, later, the growth of multicultural curriculum requirements.[3]

This work is important, but it amounts to a drop in the bucket. Questions remain unanswered. To what extent do professors' political views factor into their teaching—into the content of their syllabi, the ideas and approaches they endorse in class, their pedagogical orientations and goals, their grading practices and relationships with students?[4] In terms of the research process, how exactly do the political commitments of academics affect the topics on which they choose to work, the theories and methods they employ and the kinds of evidence they find persuasive, and the social networks they form and the collaborations they undertake? How does this vary across fields and over time? Turning to other matters, do the typically liberal politics of professors affect the cultural climate on campus, given such countervailing influences as student peer cultures, athletics, and consumerism? And what happens when—as is often the case—professors take their politics into the public sphere, writing op-eds, serving on advisory panels and commissions, working with nonprofits and advocacy groups?[5]

The main aim of this book is not to provide answers to such questions. Doing so would require a massive research effort in its own right. As a step in that direction, however, in this chapter I draw on the follow-up interviews with PAP respondents to examine how professors in five fields—sociology, economics, biology, literature, and engineering—think and talk about the role that politics should or should not play in the research and teaching enterprise.[6] How professors describe the relationship between their personal politics and their academic work is not necessarily indicative of their behavior. That a professor says his political views do not influence his research, for example, does not necessarily mean that they do not; he may simply be unaware of the bleed-over. (A large body of work in the sociology, history, and philosophy of science has been concerned to show that objectivity as traditionally understood is illusory even in the natural sciences and that every field of study is political inasmuch as the assumptions and claims it makes, or fails to make, lend intellectual support to one or another way of distributing power and resources in society.[7]) But understanding academics' beliefs in this regard at least gives us a sense of how they perceive their work roles and tells us something about the kinds of claims and justifications they consider permissible in an academic context. At the end of the chapter, I offer a hypothesis about one of the effects on American society of the ways that professors as a group appear to have melded politics, research, and teaching.

My approach in this chapter is influenced by the work of sociologist of science Karin Knorr Cetina. In an ethnographic study comparing the research practices of molecular biologists and high-energy physicists, Knorr Cetina argued that, sociologically speaking, there is no single, unified scientific method. Instead, using her data for illustration, she claimed that fields of science vary in their "architectures of empirical approaches, specific constructions of the referent, particular ontologies of instruments," and in the nature of the "social machines" they employ to bring knowledge about.[8] In other words, fields vary in their practitioners' shared understandings of what it means to know and in their sense of what is required of those who would advance credible claims to scientific truth. The cultural beliefs and practices that provide the basis for such variation make up what Knorr Cetina called the "epistemic cultures" of different fields.

Most of the research that has been done following Knorr Cetina's lead considers how scientists in different disciplines understand their work and go about crafting knowledge. While commitments to objectivity have been examined under this umbrella, conventional politics represents an aspect of epistemic culture that has not been as carefully explored. In an era when nonacademic scientists, professors, journalists, and others are often accused of ideological bias, no one whose work involves producing ideas can avoid confronting, as a practical issue, the question of whether and how she should allow her personal political commitments to shape her professional practice—what I call "the knowledge-politics problem." Although individuals sometimes innovate novel solutions to this problem, it is more common for them to draw from more or less coherent perspectives on the matter that have congealed within the cultural frameworks they share with others. For producers of academic knowledge, disciplines are the most important groupings in this regard, although subfield and institutional groupings may also be significant. In what follows, I shed light on how the current epistemic cultures of the five fields under study, and to a lesser extent the culture of various institutional spaces within higher education, differ in the typical solutions they offer to the knowledge-politics problem—focusing, again, not on behavior, but on academics' self-understandings.

✦

At the time my research assistants interviewed him, Nathan was a thirty-seven-year-old assistant professor of English at a university in the South. His doctorate is in communications, not literature, but he had been part of an English department for four years. When asked how important objectivity was to him, he replied, "I'm not a big fan of the notion. . . . The idea of [a] separation from interest or situation is . . . suspicious to me." In lieu of claims to objective knowledge, Nathan would "much rather see . . . disclosed interest and disclosed situatedness and . . . being able to . . . work with that . . . in a constructive way." His views on this matter extend beyond his own field to color how he evaluates knowledge in general. "In everything from journalism to the sciences," he insisted, "claims and appeals to objectivity tend to do more to mask interest and situatedness than they do [to] actually assist in knowledge in any way."

At the opposite extreme from Nathan is Jonathan, a twenty-eight-year-old assistant professor of mechanical engineering at a bachelor's degree–granting institution in the Midwest. When we asked what role, if any, politics play in his research, he replied by telling a joke we heard numerous times, always in slightly different form, from other respondents. "It's science," he said. "A chunk of metal doesn't have politics."

The differences between Nathan and Jonathan are not idiosyncratic; they reflect assumptions about objectivity and the knowledge-politics problem that are built into the epistemic cultures of their respective disciplinary fields. Nathan's field, literature, is characterized by deep skepticism about the possibility of objective knowledge; by the sense that at every point in the knowledge-production process, and no matter the nature of the object of investigation, political and other value commitments enter in to inform one's theoretical and methodological approach as well as the substance of one's claims; and by a preference in this context for intellectual practices of "reflexivity," by which one endeavors not to hide one's political interests but to bring them to the fore and frame knowledge claims in terms of them. By contrast, Jonathan's field, engineering, is characterized by a rampant and almost completely taken-for-granted objectivism, by a sense that the nature of the objects studied is such that political or other values can indeed be kept at bay, and moreover that they *must* be kept at bay because the goal of inquiry is to produce knowledge that mirrors the world as it actually is, independent of the standpoint from which one views it. In neither of these two fields is subscription to these epistemological ideals universal, but it is the rare literature professor who thinks of objectivity as unproblematic and the rare engineer who would prefer that engineering knowledge be properly "situated." Objectivism, the interviews suggest, is also widespread among professors of biology and economics. Sociology is best described as an epistemological hybrid, combining elements of objectivism and skepticism.

In one sense it is unsurprising to find professors of literature embracing a culture of skepticism. Literature was one of the most affected of the traditional disciplines by a variety of intellectual movements that appeared in the late 1960s and 1970s, movements such as deconstructionism, postmodernism, neopragmatism,

Lacanian literary theory, and feminist theory.[9] These movements were diverse, but one thing they shared with the history and philosophy of science developments noted earlier was doubt about naïve realism and empiricism as applied to literature or other arenas of knowledge. It is impossible, intellectual leaders of these movements claimed, for those advancing knowledge claims to ever step fully outside the bounds of their own worldviews and assumptions—or, following philosopher Friedrich Nietzsche, to remove themselves in their capacity as agents of knowing from their own practical purposes, designs, and "will to power." Knowledge is never a view from nowhere, and one of the central aims of literary criticism in light of this insight should be the interpretation of texts and cultural objects with a view to the hidden vantage points they express and the power relations they support. Literary studies interviewees were explicit in linking their doubts about objectivity to these theoretical currents. For example, an associate professor of literature at a school in the Northeast recalled, "I was in college in the late '70s, and it was still a period of what's called in literature 'new criticism.' You analyze a text as an autonomous work of art, and you don't contextualize it. And that never felt right to me. Even as an undergraduate, I . . . always vowed that if I ever did go on [in academe] something I would do is work on contextualization." "Art doesn't just arise without being influenced by political events and its cultural context," she insisted, noting that the theoretical "pendulum" in her field swung back toward a recognition of this when she was in graduate school. Her sense of the importance of context led her to specialize in a strain of eighteenth-century literature that "was very clearly at the intersection of political, legal, and economic theories, and the aestheticization of those things." At the same time it undermined her own belief in the possibility of objective knowledge. As far as objectivity goes, she told us, "There isn't any in my field. . . . One of the things we are now teaching is that there is no objectivity. . . . There are fancy words for it, but you bring your personal baggage to a text when you analyze it."

This was not an unusual sentiment among the literary scholars to whom we spoke. Fewer than a third described objectivity in research as unproblematic or desirable. This did not mean that, in their way of thinking about things, faithfulness to textual or historical materials or adherence to high scholarly standards were concepts without meaning. As one scholar put it, "I certainly believe that every text . . . is the product of a person positioned . . . but I also believe that my approach to scholarship does try to be fair and judicious to what others have written and to take that into account." But professors of literature do tend to doubt that their own experiences and worldviews—and as part of this their politics—can ever be bracketed when they undertake research and writing. When we asked one literature professor whether his own politics factor into his research, he replied simply, "They do." His politics, he told us, which he characterized as "very, very liberal," could not help but affect "the way I choose topics. The way I treat topics. The way I write."

Things could not be more different in engineering and biology. Although some of the most trenchant critics of postmodernism have come from the natural sciences—think here of physicist Alan Sokal, perpetrator of the so-called Sokal hoax, in which he managed to get an article of literally meaningless postmodern gibberish about science published in the interdisciplinary humanities journal *Social Text*—almost none of the engineers or biologists we interviewed gave any hint that they were familiar with the kinds of intellectual and philosophical work that have led literary scholars to be so skeptical of objectivity and the possibility of separating knowledge from politics. Only one of the ten biologists we interviewed expressed any real doubts about the possibility of objective knowledge. None of the engineers did. In both fields professors insisted that their politics simply do not enter into their research.

Engineers and biologists ground their claims to this effect in three assumptions. First, they assume that the nature of the objects they study is inherently apolitical. For example, a molecular biologist at a school in the West said, "I'm . . . interested in a topic called abiogenesis, and how a cell can come to function. . . . I don't think that has much of a political take on it." Earlier in the interview, in the context of a question about teaching, he noted that "molecules react the exact same way, whether you're . . . liberal [or conservative]." This view, that the objects of interest to science and the causal processes surrounding them are apolitical, and hence that there is no space for politics to intrude in legitimate scientific research, is what underlies the joke on which we heard so many variations. For Jonathan, the engineer mentioned earlier, the realm of science and the realm of political values are so different that it is literally ridiculous to mention them in the same breath, as in the phrase "A chunk of metal doesn't have politics." A forty-nine-year-old neurobiologist who studies bees expressed the same sentiment, proclaiming, "Honeybees do not have politics." Engineers and biologists obviously do recognize that the enterprise of science unfolds in a political context that may bear on its capacity to yield new findings. In this regard, a software engineer at a PhD-granting school in the West told this story: "I got a grant . . . from NASA . . . a while back. . . . Got the award letter in October. . . . Two weeks to the day before it was supposed to turn on . . . NASA froze all funding that was not active and eventually killed the program." The story was meant to be an example of how politics and scientific research can collide; the nature of that collision is that "politics affects the money that's put into research funding." But this kind of recognition is worlds away from the notion that science itself, in the claims that compose its theories, methods, and findings, could have an inherently political aspect.

A second assumption that grounds the culture of objectivism inhabited by engineers and biologists is more methodological: not only the nature of the objects studied but, as important, the scientific method leave no room for the intrusion of political values or views. When we asked the neuroscientist who studies bees his views of objectivity, he replied, "Being a scientist, we have to be objective. That's the whole thing! . . . I approach everything objectively, and I present the facts. I don't mind if people have a different opinion, but they'd better be able to convince me of that opinion by bringing in scientific facts." For engineers and biologists, the scientific method is not just a matter of following certain procedural conventions, like formalizing and testing hypotheses, but is also about a certain spirit one brings to research. A wildlife ecologist teaching in a biology department told us that for him, objectivity means "designing a study that's well designed, looking at all the possibilities where there could be mistakes, figuring out what assumptions you're making ahead of time, knowing what those assumptions are and clearly stating 'em. And then with your results . . . trying to think of all the possibilities of what [they] really do mean." Someone conscientiously embracing such a spirit and aiming to give an accurate representation of the world could not as a matter of course allow political values to intrude, even if they were somehow relevant. So the ecologist concluded, "In science, I don't think . . . politics really can mesh in there."

Third, a number of engineers and biologists linked their exclusion of political considerations from research to the trust they see as being placed in them by the users of their findings. When we asked the engineer quoted in Chapter 3 what role, if any, politics play in his research, he replied sharply, "None." His work involves "break[ing] things for research and report[ing] on how strong they are." Some of his research has military applications, and while Defense Department "program managers" who make decisions about the use of materials may have biases in favor of this or that "platform," his job as a scientist is to put aside any biases he may have, look the program manager in the eye, and say, "Material A is stronger than material B. I have data to prove it." Only by doing so can he preserve his scientific credibility and fulfill his ethical responsibilities. "In my field," he said solemnly, "objectivity . . . is all we have."

But engineers and biologists were not the only interviewees to inhabit a culture of objectivity. Seven of the eight economists interviewed also characterized objectivity in their research as unproblematic and desirable. Like engineers and biologists, economists view objectivity as grounded in the nature of the object they study, the methods they use, and their responsibilities to decision makers and the wider public. For economists, however, these are not discrete assumptions but are bound together in a coherent paradigm and research program for their discipline: the neoclassical approach that, in one version or another, dominates the field. For economists, it is the fundamental truth of this paradigm, and the requirements it makes of those working under its auspices, that ultimately ensures that economic research, properly carried out, will not be tainted by political values.

Such a claim may sound strange to noneconomists. From the vantage point of other social sciences, such as sociology and anthropology, the assumptions at the heart of contemporary economics are nothing if not political, for at least two reasons. First, these assumptions revolve around an image of human beings as rational utility maximizers that is sufficiently at odds with prevailing views in other disciplines that noneconomists will naturally suspect extrascientific influences. Second, such assumptions seem to carry with them implications about how economies should be run—namely, more or less in line with the principles of free market economics, putting more emphasis on market efficiency than on equitable resource distribution—in which political and economic actors have major investments. But economists do not see things this way. For most, it is simply an axiom of their science that economic actors are utility maximizers and that therefore markets tend to work in certain predictable ways. Because this is so, proper economic research does not admit of political influence.

The clash between these two ways of thinking about economics is nicely captured in an exchange between one of my research assistants, a PhD candidate in sociology, and Brendan, the libertarian economist profiled in Chapter 1.

> *Interviewer:* How if at all do your politics factor into your
> research, such as selection of topics, methodology,
> theory, et cetera?
>
> *Brendan:* Not much at all.
>
> *Interviewer:* Any role in selection of topics, for example?

Brendan: No.

Interviewer: How about theory? I mean, for example, you
  don't take a Marxian economics [approach]?

Brendan: No, I'm a free market capitalist economist, like
  98% of the other economists out there.

Interviewer: So do you think your politics factors into that?

Brendan: No.

Interviewer: Can you explain? If one were to make an
  argument that political bias is everywhere, they'd say,
  well, if you're a leftist, you're going to be a Marxist
  economist regardless of what the facts tell you, and if
  you're on the right, you're going to be a microeco-
  nomic Milton Friedman economist, regardless of what
  the facts tell you.

Brendan: Where politics enter into research agendas in my
  field is . . . in terms of policy analysis and policy
  prescriptions, and that is not an aspect of my professional activity.

Brendan, who saw his politics as influenced by his economics,
but not vice versa, was not alone in believing that economic research is objective and apolitical. In response to a question about
how much politics might influence research, one economist responded, "Not at all. My research tends to be more on the technical
side." Another said, "Virtually none at all." Still another scholar,
a fifty-three-year-old labor economist, told us, "One of my favorite titles in the economics literature is 'Let's Take the Con out of
Econometrics' [the title of a 1983 paper by Edward Leamer].[10]
And that to me is the objectivity part of it. In the process of doing
research you state your assumptions clearly, you build your model

clearly, you share data, and you look for replication of results." In fact the only economist we interviewed who seriously doubted whether economic research is objective was Dave, the radical economist also profiled in Chapter 1.

As several of these quotations suggest, however, economists do recognize that when they move from analysis of the workings of the economy into the formulation of policy prescriptions, they may then be entering the realm of politics and political values. It is here, at the distinction between pure and applied economics, that economists mark the boundary between science and politics. A forty-year-old professor of economics was engaged in this kind of boundary work when she said, "My research is completely away from politics. So far it has looked at marital transactions [in lesser developed countries.] So the only place where it would even remotely come close to politics would be where I formulate policies or I suggest ways to decrease marital transactions." Economists do not appear to believe that policy work is *necessarily* political—if it is strictly informed by economic theory and research, it need not be—but at the very least there is potential for political considerations to enter in.

American sociologists, for their part, are positioned somewhere between literature and economics in terms of the knowledge-politics problem. As many observers have noted, sociology is a fractious, multiparadigm discipline composed of researchers focused on a wide array of problems and employing diverse theoretical approaches and methods. One important dividing line in the field is between sociologists who identify more with the humanities and those who view the discipline as a social science; another is between sociologists committed to an activist agenda and those who have more of a "professional" orientation. Among sociology interviewees, nearly two-thirds said they did think critically about the notion of objectivity, but only one-third told us objectivity is an illusion. The latter tended to be in either the humanistic or activist camp or both and were remarkably similar in their epistemological views to professors of literature—the difference being that their perspectives seem informed more by "standpoint theories," arguing that scholars' views on the social world are inevitably shaped by their race, class, and gender, than by more philosophically sophisticated intellectual approaches. In this regard, when we asked an assistant professor of sociology whether her research is influenced by her politics, she said, "The personal is political. When I teach research methods I tell my students, 'If we were all honest we would admit to the fact that what we all study is based on that which affects us.' I study fringe groups and issues of power. . . . I was born in the projects. We were the only whites and the only Jews in an all-Hispanic, black area. We were regularly beaten. So for me issues of fringe groups and power are important, plus I'm gay. What other ways could I be more powerless? . . . So absolutely, my political, social, personal experiences literally shape my research." For these interviewees, research and politics are intertwined not simply in the sense that Max Weber identified—that one's choice of research topic is bound to be influenced by one's values and interests—but also in the deeper sense that one's personal experiences and values give one a worldview through which research problems are framed and in which different theoretical approaches and empirical claims gain varying degrees of plausibility.

But this was not the dominant position among the sociologists we interviewed. Ben Agger, a sociologist who has criticized the discipline from the perspective of deconstructionist theory, has argued that the epistemic culture of sociology "attempt[s] to imitate the natural sciences in a 'hard' objectivity and indubitability."[11] In a certain sense that may be right, but the majority of sociologists we interviewed said they were aware of the many problems and difficulties associated with the notion of objectivity. Unwilling, however, to descend into what they see as subjectivism, they have forged and now take part in a hybrid epistemological culture in which objectivity as a view from nowhere is seen as impossible to achieve in practice but still held up as a kind of goal, and in which research is understood as being more objective the more researchers acknowledge and come to terms with their own biases and motivations. For most American sociologists, in other words, objectivity remains an ideal toward which they claim to strive, even as they recognize the impossibility of ever fully achieving it. Typical in this regard was an African American sociologist teaching in the South. When we asked how his politics affect his research, he replied, "Well, just in terms of orienting me toward certain topics. Racial identity, racial reparations, health disparities, HIV/AIDS are all problems that . . . affect people in urban centers and African Americans and other groups of color." He was quick to add, nevertheless, "I try to be balanced in my . . . analyses." Does "balance" mean that he considers the results of his research, what he finds after his political and other values have steered him toward a given topic, to be objective? Although this sociologist considers objectivity to be "very important," he also insisted, "It's an ideal type—you know, it's really impossible for humans to be totally objective, but it's a goal. . . . We should strive for objectivity."

The interview data do not tell us anything about whether these nods to the problems of achieving objective knowledge are linked to any meaningful behaviors on the part of sociologists designed to reduce the possibility of bias—or whether, if pressed on the point, biologists, engineers, and economists (and others) might not also concede that objectivity can be difficult to achieve.[12] But they do permit the conclusion, foreshadowed by German sociologist Wolf Lepenies's 1985 book about the history of European sociology, *Between Literature and Science,* that the epistemic culture of sociology is a hybrid, both in the sense that some champions of skepticism and subjectivism can be found in its ranks, and in that among the rest acknowledgment of the difficulty of being objective—coupled with a commitment to grasp for it anyway—is regarded as de rigueur.[13]

✦

In light of these differences in how fields deal with the knowledge-politics problem when it comes to research, a sensible expectation would be to find parallel differences in teaching. One might think professors of literature would readily admit to the role that their political opinions play in their pedagogy and express no great concern about this, that sociologists would recognize the influence of politics but that most would endeavor to minimize it, and that professors in more objectivistic disciplinary cultures would deny that politics affects their teaching at all. This is not what the interview data show. There were differences among interviewees in how they conceived of the politics-teaching relationship, but these differences did not line up neatly with views of research and did not follow automatically from disciplinary location.

As concerns teaching, three groups of professors come into re-
lief from an examination of the interview data. The first and
smallest group consists of those who say they practice some version of "critical pedagogy," in which the explicit goal is to raise
students' political awareness. The second consists of professors
who think that their politics do not factor into their teaching either because the subject matter of their courses does not allow for
it or because they endeavor to conceal their political views from
students even when controversial issues do arise. The teaching
style these professors claim to practice can be described as "political neutrality." The third group consists of professors who recognize the many ways in which their teaching is bound up with
their politics and who think it is fine and good for professors to
share their views with students—as long as they are clear about
defining them as such and not as "truth" and as long as they are
open to dissenting student opinion. The rhetoric around politics
and teaching embraced by professors in this third camp can be
termed "political transparency." The biologists and engineers interviewed were somewhat more likely than the sociologists or
professors of literature to say that the subject matter of their
courses does not touch on the political, but disciplinary location
was not strongly associated with a language of political neutrality
versus transparency; many biologists and engineers teach courses
that go beyond basic principles and research findings to intersect
with questions of public policy, forcing them to stake out positions
on these tricky pedagogical matters.

Only two of the fifty-seven professors we interviewed en-
dorsed critical pedagogy and, in terms of their description of
their teaching, fit the stereotype held by conservative critics of a
radical professor bent on converting students to his political point

of view. Of the two, Dave was the most outspoken. When he was in college, Dave told us, one of his professors asked him, speaking of the conservative views on which he had been reared, "Why do you believe all that stuff?" As Dave sees it, this was the question that started him down the road toward becoming a radical. Dave aims to play the same role for his students. When we asked him whether his politics factor into his teaching, he said, "Well, big time, sure. . . . I tell my students, 'Listen, I could teach you a class of three hundred hours for principles of economics and yet I've only got forty-eight, so I have to choose what I'm gonna teach you.' And inevitably my bias as to what is important and what is not as important is gonna come through." This takes two forms. Dave said he tries to make clear to his students what a Marxian approach to economics entails, and why it is superior not simply analytically but also morally to other approaches—and why a world without private property, without capitalism, would be good. Beyond that, he brings in newspaper articles for his students to read that he hopes will illustrate the contemporary relevance of his point of view. "I bring in articles all the time," he noted, articles that are "pro-environmental, pro-egalitarian, pro–human rights, antiwar." "I do that with no excuses," he continued, because his students "get plenty of the other stuff. Just listen to the radio sometimes on these right-wing talk shows. Whoa! Drives ya nuts." Dave said he does not force his students to agree with his politics on tests and that he tries to engage in respectful debate with conservative students, but he makes no bones about his belief that college is a place where students raised in conservative families should be led to see the error of their ways.

Two of fifty-seven interviewees is not many, however. The vast majority of professors with whom we spoke held more conventional beliefs about the aims of undergraduate instruction, seeing it as concerned with transmitting to students knowledge of a field, giving them familiarity with some of the major issues and debates confronting humankind today, exposing them to classic texts and ideas and works of art, or inculcating skills such as writing and reading well and thinking analytically and critically. They talked about politics and teaching in terms of political neutrality or transparency.

As indicated earlier, the professors we interviewed who could be placed on the political neutrality side of the divide can be divided once again. Some teach classes that they believe are politically neutral in the sense that the subject matter does not seem to bring them into a political orbit. Such professors describe themselves as practicing what might be termed "accidental political neutrality." As they talk about it, it is an accident of fate, a function of their particular specialization and the classes they have been assigned, that politics plays no role in their teaching. This is the case for a forty-eight-year-old professor of mechanical engineering who thought it a sufficient explanation of why politics does not intersect with his teaching to point out, with no further elaboration, that his classes are "in the area of what's called 'mechatronics'—it's a combin[ation] of mechanical engineering and electronics . . . computer science for designing smarter, more reliable, adaptable products." A survey by Bruce Smith and colleagues found that 60% of American professors agree with the statement "Politics seldom comes up in my classroom, because of the nature of the subjects I teach." This suggests that, in the university overall, accidental political neutrality may be the most common pedagogical self-description when it comes to knowledge politics.[14]

The second category consists of professors who claim to practice what could be called "cultivated political neutrality." It is not that such professors say they endeavor to keep politics from being discussed in their classes; some state that they teach on highly politicized topics and encourage political debate. Rather what distinguishes this rhetoric of pedagogy is the idea that no matter the nature of the classroom conversation, instructors' own political views should remain hidden or at least elusive.

Two assumptions seemed to be at work for professors in this category. The first is that college students are impressionable and that professors wield considerable authority in the classroom. To the extent that this is so, if a professor is outspoken about her own views, it may poison classroom discussion or otherwise interfere with the process by which students consider all sides in a debate and rationally form their own beliefs. Second, it is unethical for professors to reveal and argue for their own political views in class because in doing so they are, in effect, using their authority not for the purposes for which it was granted—to instruct—but for political ends. A professor of English with "generally liberal" views was typical of those interviewees who claimed to practice cultivated political neutrality, although the language he used in describing his rationale for doing so was unusually lighthearted. "How if at all do your politics factor into your teaching?" we asked him. "I try to keep it out of my teaching," he replied. "For example, I teach Conrad. And there is a political argument about imperialism that it is possible to make and I try to make it from all sides . . . and be as objective as I can be. But as far as bringing my politics—contemporary politics—into the classroom, I try to leave it out. I've always felt that was obnoxious. . . . I do make an effort to be receptive to all kinds of ideas. . . . But I think it's important that [students] get the education they paid for . . . and not some sort of radicalization camp." More strident was Brendan, the libertarian economist. After asking his views of objectivity in research, we asked whether he felt it was acceptable for professors to argue on behalf of their own political views in class. His response was, "Absolutely not. . . . I have some ethical problems with that [because it] . . . doesn't translate well into imparting critical thinking skills for students. I very strongly believe that eighteen- to twenty-two-year-old college students have a very strong incentive to do whatever they need to do to make the professor happy, and there are certainly perceptions out there that Professor X wants to hear this on an exam or wants you to read this into an essay. . . . Now, I think that most of my students, if they would bother stopping by my office or talking to me . . . they could have a pretty good guess at my political beliefs, but in terms of bringing any of that into the classroom, I try very, very hard to avoid that."

In contrast, many professors we spoke to claim to practice political transparency with their students. If the topic of the class on a given day calls for discussion of political issues, they may, if they deem it pedagogically helpful, reveal to students their own views while also working to ensure that this does not foreclose discussion. A sociologist who teaches at a community college told us that her liberal views do affect the way she teaches. As she sees it, her politics "factor . . . in [to her teaching] by the topics that [she] might address." Viewing sociology as synonymous with the study of unequal distributions of power and resources in society, she elaborated by saying, "I'm a sociologist. I'm going to talk about race and racism. I'm going to talk about sex and sexism. I'm going to talk about social inequality and class in the United States."

When she raises such matters, however, she attempts neither to directly divest students of their conservative views nor to conceal from them her own position. "I really try to be inclusive," she told us. "I don't . . . try to push a particular agenda or a candidate or anything like that. If I find that I have said [something to this effect], I will quickly . . . say, 'You know, this is just my personal opinion and I respect anybody else's opinion and you don't have to agree with me in order to understand the material that I'm try-ing to convey to you.'" By issuing such a disclaimer, she hopes to communicate that her political statements are not to be construed as reflecting the authoritative knowledge she has as a sociologist but are simply the views she has as a fellow citizen. She hopes this goes some way toward removing whatever power asymmetries might otherwise be present in the classroom, and she takes it as evidence that her strategy works that over the years she has had no real conflicts with students over politics. "I remember having discussions with students whose politics were different than my own," she says. These discussions might have become "heated" on occasion, but they ended up being "illuminating" for all concerned because her approach is ultimately "one of allowing and dignifying the other person's perspective." The operative assumption about students for those who claim to be practicing political transpar-ency is that they are not delicate young things prone to indoctri-nation but critical consumers of information and opinion who can understand where professorial authority ends and personal political views begin, and who are capable of taking part as equals with their professors and fellow students in wide-ranging and probing discussion of political matters. Thus it was that an English professor who teaches at a four-year school in the Northeast justi-fied his assertion that it was fine for him to present and argue for his own political views by claiming that students are not going to accept them as gospel: "The students are not stupid, you know? They're . . . human just like the rest of us!" In the same vein, Nathan, the communications/literature scholar quoted earlier, told us he does not have conflicts with students over politics because his goal in classroom discussions is not to "win . . . them over" politically but simply to get them to "argue and think about what their position is."

Examining how the interviewees break down in terms of these profiles reveals, again, that two of the professors in the sample (4%) claimed to be practitioners of critical pedagogy, nine (16%) said they teach in fields or on topics where political issues never arise, eleven (19%) said that professors should not divulge their political views in the classroom, and the rest (61%) indicated that they practiced political transparency to a greater or lesser degree.

Complex statistical analyses are unhelpful on small interview samples, but basic cross-tabulations can reveal interesting patterns. When it comes to attitudes toward politics and teaching, some differences by discipline are apparent, as I have already suggested, and as Table 5.1 shows. Biologists and engineers were more likely than sociologists, literature professors, or economists to claim to teach classes that never touch on political issues, although only a third of interviewees in these two fields could be classified as claiming accidental neutrality. A rhetoric of cultivated neutrality was embraced by a third of engineers and economists, but by only 7% of sociologists, 10% of biologists, and 14% of literature professors. Claims of political transparency were equally common among sociologists and literature professors— about 80% of scholars in both fields made them—but were also relatively common among biologists (60%) and economists (50%).

Table 5.1. Claimed pedagogical practice of faculty by field

Field	Critical pedagogy	Accidental neutrality	Cultivated neutrality	Political transparency
Sociology	7	7	7	79
Biology	0	30	10	60
Literature	0	7	14	79
Engineering	0	36	36	27
Economics	13	0	38	50

Source: Follow-up interviews with sample of respondents to the Politics of the American Professoriate survey, 2006–2007, sample size 57.

Note: Numbers are row percentages and may not add to 100 because of rounding.

As important as these disciplinary differences, however, were institutional ones: half of professors teaching in doctoral-granting universities claimed to practice cultivated neutrality, as compared to 10% of professors teaching in community colleges or four-year schools. This may reflect the greater authority that professors at doctoral institutions understand themselves to have, the lesser intimacy that typically obtains in such institutions between students and instructors, affecting cultures of teaching, or a greater commitment to a certain understanding of academic professionalism. Professors' own political views also appear to be associated with their taking one stance or another. Self-identified moderates in the interview sample were somewhat more likely than conservatives to say they practiced cultivated neutrality (25% versus 20%) but were much more likely to do so than liberals (12%), perhaps because liberals are more likely to view college students as adults and not worry as much about indoctrination.

✵

What is the wider significance of these findings on epistemic culture and the knowledge-politics problem? To bring this chapter to a close, I consider one possible effect of faculty politics on American society.

In *Closed Minds? Politics and Ideology in American Universities,* the 2008 book by Bruce Smith and his colleagues Jeremy Mayer and Lee Fritschler in which the finding mentioned earlier on accidental neutrality was reported, the authors advanced the argument that, if anything, there is too little discussion of politics in the classrooms of America's colleges and universities. Basing their claims not just on surveys measuring professors' views or self-reports of their behavior but also on focus group interviews with students, Smith, Mayer, and Fritschler suggested that most professors are circumspect about revealing their political opinions in class, careful not to treat poorly students whose politics disagree with their own, and concerned to bring to the teaching enterprise the same level of professionalism that characterizes their research activities. While appreciating this professionalism, Smith, Mayer, and Fritschler observed that too often it prevents professors from engaging in the kind of spirited political discussions with their students essential to keeping the fire of democracy burning among the educated. As they put it:

> Americans are normally averse to politics and reveal deep-seated antistatist attitudes. University professors are not immune from those popular sentiments. Americans dislike conflict and controversy and see politics as inevitably involving unpleasant discord and contention. American civic life seemingly has eroded in recent years, and the universities, far from trying to combat the trend, have acquiesced to the erosive forces. . . . The idea that . . . universities are rife with leftist

politics, or any politics for that matter, is at odds with the evidence.[15]

Questions of civic engagement aside, there is reason to doubt whether this description of universities—and the university curriculum in particular—as apolitical is entirely accurate. And this provides a jumping-off point for considering broader consequences. True, if we take professors' descriptions of their behavior to reflect their actual behavior—a questionable assumption— then we would conclude that political issues do not arise in the majority of courses taught in the university. But the fact that most professors say they try not to shove their views down students' throats does not mean that politics is absent from the curriculum.

Consider the case of the Sociology Department at the University of Wisconsin–Madison, my graduate alma mater. The Wisconsin department is known for training students to do careful empirical research, and an undergraduate considering taking classes in the department in the fall 2011 semester would have found several highly demanding methodology courses from which to choose, ranging from a class on computing in sociological research to one on techniques of demographic analysis to several on social statistics proper. But given that the vast majority of American sociologists are on the left, that many think it inevitable and acceptable that their politics will influence the kind of research they do (although not the conclusions that they reach), and that sociology has in fact been receptive over the years to scientific/ intellectual movements with a left tilt, it is not surprising that several of the substantive course offerings the student would have been presented with that semester covered topics of special interest to those on the left, in some cases asking her to learn about research undertaken from a decidedly leftist or liberal point of view. "Marriage and the Family" and "Criminology" could have leaned either way politically (or, depending on one's epistemology and understanding of politics, no way), but that there was a left slant to "Feminism and Sociological Theory," "Intercultural Dialogues," "Environmental Stewardship and Social Justice," and "Class, State, and Ideology: An Introduction to Marxist Sociology" goes without saying. The point can be easily generalized beyond Madison, and beyond sociology: the intellectual content of many social science and humanities disciplines today (with the important exception of economics) has a sufficiently left/liberal orientation that some number of undergraduate courses aiming simply to teach the fields will naturally have a similar bearing, even if the academics doing the teaching are the circumspect professionals highlighted by Smith, Mayer, and Fritschler (and who abound in the Wisconsin Sociology Department). It is hard to find systematic empirical evidence relevant to this claim, but an examination of course offerings and syllabi in many departments of sociology, anthropology, history, literature, communications, education, and geography, in some departments of psychology and political science and in area studies programs, and in nearly all programs in ethnic studies, women's and gender studies, cultural studies, and social work, would turn up validating data. It is certainly not the case that everything that transpires in these fields and that is taught to students is reducible to left/liberal politics. Far from it. But that concerns about inequality, oppression, social justice, diversity, recognition, and tolerance also loom large is not news.

What are the consequences of this—and of the no less significant fact that many courses are effectively taught from the economic right in business schools, departments of economics and engineering, and elsewhere? One hypothesis is that a politically laden curriculum has contributed to increasing divisiveness in the American electorate.

A major debate among political scientists at present concerns the extent of that polarization. On one side are scholars associated with Morris Fiorina, who argue that polarization is more myth than reality.[16] American political elites have grown further apart in recent decades, Fiorina and his colleagues allow, with the Republican Party moving right and the Democratic Party shifting left in the wake of party realignment in the South. But most American voters, they claim, tend to hold middle-of-the-road views on the issues that divide the parties and are not partisans. And they find no evidence that this has changed since the 1960s. On the other side stand Alan Abramowitz and his collaborators, who argue that Fiorina is wrong.[17] Analyzing American National Election Studies data, Abramowitz has found that a growing number of voters are located at either extreme of the political distribution. For example, in the period 1982–1990, 24% of ANES respondents gave consistently liberal or consistently conservative answers to a battery of attitudes questions. By 2002–2004 that number had risen to 33%. Similarly, Abramowitz notes that the correlation between party identification and attitudes has grown much stronger over the years, doubling in strength between 1972 and 2004—an indication of increasing "ideological" thinking in the sense in which political scientists use that word, as referring to a coherent and logically constrained system of political belief. Abramowitz has shown that growing divisiveness within the electorate is not confined to a few states or regions or to primary voters or specific election cycles, and that it has serious consequences, increasing participation in the democratic process (voters tend to get more fired up and involved when there are sharp ideological differences between candidates) while at the same time making it harder for those who get elected to govern (since to compromise is to risk alienating their partisan bases).

Abramowitz goes on to identify several causes of polarization, including internal party dynamics, redistricting, and the slow but steady secularization of American society, which is driving more of a wedge between religious and nonreligious voters. Another key factor, in his view, is the growth of higher education. Political scientists have long known that people with higher levels of education are more apt to take sides politically; they are less likely to have "nonattitudes" on political issues and call themselves moderates.[18] The operative assumption has been that education—higher education in particular—gives you information about politics, which allows you to form a clearer view about where you stand. Also, the educated are *expected* to have strong opinions on political matters. For some people who are truly in the middle, the upshot is that as they gain more education they become more committed to being moderate, but more commonly these factors work to push people toward either extreme of the ideological spectrum. Raise the number of people going to college, Abramowitz says, and the result is going to be a more polarized electorate.

The information mechanism makes good sense, but there may well be another that revolves around the sorting of students into different majors. As mentioned in Chapter 3, studies have shown that politics is an important predictor of college major choice, holding constant demographic characteristics and measures of interest and ability: liberal students are more likely to major in the social sciences and humanities, conservatives in business and other applied fields. To give a sense of the extent of these tendencies, Table 5.2 shows the self-reported political identities of American college seniors for the period 1994–1999 broken down by major area. In the sample overall, there are slightly more liberals (30%) than conservatives (27%). Among social science and humanities majors, liberals outnumber conservatives by a ratio of 2:1,

Table 5.2.   Self-reported political identification of American college seniors, 1994–1999, by major area

| Student major, aggregated | How would you characterize your political views? | | | | |
	Far left	Liberal	Middle of the road	Conservative	Far right
Agriculture	1	16	46	35	2
Biological science	2	31	44	22	1
Business	1	19	46	33	2
Education	1	21	48	29	1
Engineering	2	20	44	33	2
English	7	41	34	17	1
Health professional	1	24	49	25	1
History/political science	4	34	34	26	2
Humanities	6	34	34	25	1
Fine arts	5	32	41	21	1
Mathematics or statistics	2	24	44	29	1
Physical sciences	3	29	41	27	1
Social sciences	3	35	42	19	1
Other technical	2	23	48	26	1
Other nontechnical	2	28	45	23	1
Undecided	3	29	46	22	1

Source: HERI College Senior Survey, 1994–1999, sample size 156,573.
Note: Numbers are row percentages and may not add to 100 because of rounding.

while conservatives are overrepresented among students majoring in agriculture, business, and engineering.

Looking at the numbers for individual majors is even more instructive. Forty-three percent of English majors are liberal; 19% are conservative. Forty-six percent of sociology and 38% of political science majors are liberal; 16% and 29% are conservative, respectively. Among anthropology majors the numbers are 57% liberal to 11% conservative; among geography majors, 44% to 17%. Psychology students are 36% liberal and 20% conservative, while in ethnic studies the numbers are 51% to 20% and in women's studies, 84% to 3%. By contrast, 52% of religion/theology majors are conservative, while just 21% are liberal. Among marketing, management, and other business majors about 30% of students are conservative and 20% liberal. Conservatives outnumber liberals by a ratio of nearly 2:1 among students majoring in aeronautical, civil, chemical, and industrial engineering. And 37% of economics majors are conservative, 22% liberal.

These statistics indicate that, to some extent, undergraduate education in the United States is socially organized around politics. To be sure, in most majors the modal category of student political identity is moderate, no doubt reflecting the large number of students who are tuned out politically. But the point remains that liberal and conservative students can be found concentrated in different fields.[19] In line with my argument from Chapter 4, some of this pattern would seem to be a (time-lagged) function of the political views of professors. Most social scientists and humanists are on the left, and though there is variation in epistemic culture around the knowledge-politics problem, left and liberal social scientists and humanists have clearly stamped their political mark on their disciplines. This means that few conservative under-graduates are going to find the content of these fields interest-ing and worthy of study. At the same time, these fields are linked to occupational pathways that conservatives may not have much interest in starting down. On the other side, while economists and engineers (and business school professors, other data show) may believe firmly in objectivity, the intellectual content of their fields, partly under the influence of their politics, leads in more conservative directions, explicitly extolling the virtues of capital-ism and the market in the case of some economics and many un-dergraduate business courses, and implicitly extolling such vir-tues in engineering to the extent that a major aim of engineering programs is to give students the skills they need to design the products that firms will make and sell, and all the more easily in a pro-business economic environment—and, for other engineer-ing students, the skills necessary to design products with military application. A consequence is that the number of committed liberal undergraduates who will end up majoring in economics, business, or engineering is limited.

This could matter for polarization. The revisionist research discussed in Chapter 2 shows that attending college has less of an effect on political attitudes and identity than previous generations of scholars believed, owing to the failure of earlier studies to ac-count for the factors predicting selection into college in the first place. Yet it is not as though college has *no* effect. In a sophisti-cated recent study economist Javier Arias-Vazquez found that college students "who were liberal and Democratic Party aligned in the senior year of high school are more likely to enroll in the social sciences and humanities, while the opposite occurs for those who major in business, science and engineering."[20] He also found that people who major "in the social sciences and humanities become increasingly Democratic Party oriented over time, while business majors move in the opposite direction."[21] With selection into college controlled for, the magnitude of these changes, he discovered, is not enormous, but neither is it so small as to be completely meaningless.

One way of interpreting Arias-Vazquez's findings is to say that many liberal-leaning students, as a result of their college major choices, end up becoming more firmly committed to liberalism during the course of their college educations, while many conservative-leaning students become more firmly committed conservatives. Two processes are likely at work here. While relatively few students appear to be getting converted from one political camp to the other as a result of their coursework, students may learn, in their majors, stronger intellectual justifications for their prior political intuitions and leanings. For example, someone brought up in a nominally Democratic household who majors in sociology and is exposed to theories of "structural inequality" may, as a result, develop an even deeper, more logically coherent belief about the need for redistributionist economic policies and a firmer attachment to the left.[22] Second, since students not infrequently become friends with other people in their majors—in the HERI College Senior Survey a quarter of students report that "most" or "all" of their friends in college have the same major or academic interest area as they do—students majoring in these fields may become part of politically homogeneous social networks. Research shows that people in homogeneous networks tend to develop more extreme views and to take on those views as highly salient identities.[23] Since about 25% of American undergraduates major in the social sciences or humanities, while another 21% major in business and an additional 5% in engineering, a significant number of students may leave college as stronger, more committed partisans than when they started.[24] If this claim turns out to be right, faculty politics would be implicated in increasing polarization. Ultimately the suggestion is that political balkanization in the university may ramify outward.

In Chapters 6 and 7, I consider another effect of faculty politics on the American political system. Because so many humanists and social scientists are on the left, they have provided conservatives wishing to attack the academy with an easy target. There have been consequences, and not just for academic freedom: had conservatives not had outspoken liberal professors to attack, American conservatism today might be a weaker political enterprise (although it is also true that in other respects the academic left has furthered the cause of liberalism in the United States).

Chapter 6

The Campaign against "Liberal Bias"

In 1955 the effort to root out communists from government service, from America's colleges and universities, and from the arts and other sectors of society, was in full swing. Although Joseph McCarthy had been censured by the Senate the year before and his popularity with the public was waning, dropping from a 50% favorable rating in January 1954 to 35% in November, investigations of disloyalty and communist sympathizing by the House Un-American Activities Committee, the FBI, state and local authorities, and private organizations continued.[1]

Lazarsfeld and Thielens's study of social scientists was one effort by the academic community to come to terms with these events. But it was hardly the only one. Another was *Academic Freedom in Our Time* (1955), a book written by Robert MacIver, then a retired professor of political philosophy and sociology at Columbia. Published by Columbia University Press in conjunction with Richard Hofstadter and Walter Metzger's historical study, *The De-*

velopment of Academic Freedom in the United States (1955), MacIver's book sought to document and decry the many academic freedom violations that had occurred since the breakout of McCarthyism in the late 1940s.[2]

Academic Freedom in Our Time was praised in some quarters, but it was roundly condemned in the book review section of the *New York Times* by the philosopher and ardent anticommunist Sidney Hook. "Although [the book] contains some good things," wrote Hook, "large portions read like the work of an angry partisan." MacIver claimed the current climate on campus, and in the country generally, was not favorable to "intellectual freedom." Hook disagreed; while some professors had lost their jobs, this was because of their political activities outside the classroom. There was little evidence that the intellectual enterprise had been substantially disrupted, he asserted. What is more, MacIver had erred by exaggerating the importance of various anticommunist " 'pseudo-educational' associations" that had recently sprung up calling for a policing of activities in the higher education sector. These groups, which in Hook's view belonged to the "extreme right-wing," were "small, have interlocking directorates, and are so fanatical in their pronouncements as to be self-defeating." The circle of conservative intellectuals that had formed around William F. Buckley Jr. was of a piece with such groups, and would, Hook suggested, share their fate: *God and Man at Yale,* he noted, "had been laughed out of court at Yale and ignored elsewhere." Hook believed that professors who were communists should not be allowed to teach, for, among other reasons, Communist Party membership signaled an abandonment of one's reasoning powers. But since few professors *were* communists, academia as a whole had little to fear from the likes of McCarthy and Buckley, MacIver's "hysterical" claims notwithstanding.[3]

One might think Buckley would have taken offense at Hook's diminution of him. If he did, he kept it to himself. In a piece published in December 1955 in *National Review,* the conservative magazine he and his colleagues started that year, Buckley praised Hook's intellectual rigor and seconded his criticisms of MacIver, describing *Academic Freedom in Our Time* as full of "absurdities." But Buckley did more: he portrayed the book as characteristic of a certain academic mind-set, one that assumed readers would accept statements of fact as true simply by virtue of the intellectual authority of the person making them, even if the evidence was not there to support the claims. Such a mind-set, Buckley felt, showed "contempt for the reasoning process" and was becoming "more and more" evident in "the work of Liberal publicists and scholars." Among the things that irked Buckley about MacIver's book was its hasty rejection of "charges that Lord Keynes' approach to economics is basically collectivist" and its pat "dismissal of widespread complaints by thousands of people about the philosophical biases of modern education on the ground that know-nothings and 'patrioteers' we have always with us—just one more tribulation for an overburdened faculty." There was, as Buckley saw it, an arrogance to these moves, a haughtiness, an unwillingness to dignify conservative complaints about higher education with a careful, fact-based response. And this was all too common in the academic community. "Professor MacIver and the rest of those who refuse to answer their critics except by sneers and clichés, and lofty appeals to the rights of inquiry, are burning their candles at both ends," Buckley concluded. "The community may ask, reasonably, just where the evidence lies that our elite are equipped to discipline themselves even with respect to technical matters involving the canons of sound scholarship."[4]

From the vantage point of the present, there are several notable things about this episode. One is the feeling of déjà-vu it conjures up. It is impossible to read Buckley's piece, written for a regular column in the magazine called "The Ivory Tower," and impossible to read *God and Man at Yale,* for that matter, without thinking how much their critiques of the liberal professoriate foreshadow the work of contemporary critics of higher education. When, in an article published two weeks later, Buckley encouraged readers to send him "evidence of such nature as will clarify the question whether teachers are engaged in indoctrinating their students"— "For example: does your economics teacher refer impartially . . . to the works of Friedrich Hayek, Ludwig von Mises . . . or to those of any other economist of the non-Keynesian school? . . . Does your teacher of sociology urge a particular interpretation of man and his behavior?"—promising that *National Review* would "act as a repository," he was going even further toward creating a playbook from which critics fifty years later such as David Horowitz would draw.[5] Also notable is the uneasy alliance between Hook, a liberal anticommunist and former Trotskyite, and Buckley, a full-throated conservative, presaging similar relationships that would form in the 1960s and 1970s around the so-called neoconservative intellectuals who proved important to the right's efforts during those decades.[6] Of greater significance still, however, is the rhetorical work that Buckley and his *National Review* collaborators did to pair their substantive critiques of academia, of the ideas they thought dominant in college classrooms, with a depiction of academics as elitist snobs looking down their noses at ordinary Americans. Buckley was not the first to invoke these tropes, but he was an energetic, witty, and influential user of them. To understand why criticism of the liberal professoriate remains an important part of the political and educational landscape today requires attention to the role that such criticism continues to play in helping to secure a populist identity for contemporary American conservatism.

✳

On a late September day in 2007, the campus of Columbia University was abuzz with activity. Outside the gates, New York City police officers manned barricades to keep the crowds that had gathered on the sidewalk from spilling out into the street. Satellite trucks from the major networks sat parked along Broadway. Plainclothes federal security agents tried their best to blend in with the usual Morningside Heights crowd. On the campus itself, the scene was anything but usual. Hundreds of protestors—many students, many not—milled about, chanting and carrying signs and banners denouncing the visit of President Mahmoud Ahmadinejad of Iran, who had come at the invitation of the university's president, Lee Bollinger.

In the weeks and months leading up to the visit, the Bush administration had been cranking up its rhetoric against Iran, accusing it of sponsoring terrorism, suppressing human rights domestically, and working to destabilize U.S.-occupied Iraq. Bollinger, a noted First Amendment scholar committed to the ideal of dialogue, had invited Ahmadinejad, himself a former professor, to address an audience of Columbia faculty and students and respond to the charges laid against him. A year earlier, Bollinger had nixed plans for an Ahmadinejad visit arranged by Lisa Anderson, a scholar of the Mideast and dean of the School of International and Public Affairs, but now the timing seemed right. As Bollinger made clear in his opening remarks, delivered in an atmosphere of great seriousness inside Lerner Hall, the invitation to speak was not to be construed as an endorsement. "You exhibit all the signs of a petty and cruel dictator," he told the Iranian president before listing, one by one, the sins of his regime.[7] Beyond repeating accusations of state-sponsored terrorism, he singled out for special attack two of Ahmadinejad's views that protesters outside the hall, many representing Jewish groups, found especially galling: his denial of the Holocaust and his opposition to Israel's right to exist. In his own speech, and in the question-and-answer period that followed, Ahmadinejad addressed these and other charges only indirectly and chided Bollinger for having used harsh words to introduce a guest.

The Ahmadinejad visit occasioned strong and immediate reaction on the editorial pages of the nation's newspapers, from political commentators making the rounds of television talk shows, and in the blogosphere. Many praised Bollinger's tough talk and echoed President Bush's own opinion that the event, whether ill-advised or not, at least served to illustrate the virtues of free speech. More common, however, were critics who argued, as did the editors of the *New York Daily News,* that Bollinger was "damnably wrong to host Ahmadinejad on campus" because in doing so he had given a forum, and some measure of legitimacy, to a man who was a dangerous force in the world. The event was "cheap theater" that "cheapened a great university," the editorial went on to say, suggesting that Bollinger's interest in dialogue with the Iranian leader betrayed the worst kind of academic naïveté.[8]

It was not the first time that Columbia had come under fire for issues to do with Mideast politics. The presence on campus of literary scholar Edward Said, an outspoken champion of Palestinian statehood, had long angered conservatives. More recently, though, a number of individuals and organizations had entered the public arena with a broader complaint: that much of the scholarship carried out by professors in Columbia's Middle East and Asian Languages and Cultures (MEALAC) program involved left-wing, anti-Zionist political advocacy and that undergraduates taking courses from program faculty were receiving a one-sided education.[9] A Philadelphia-based conservative watchdog group, Campus Watch, had been monitoring and critiquing developments in the field of Middle East studies nationally for several years. It escalated its attack against Columbia after several conservative students came forward to claim that their views had been ridiculed by MEALAC professors. A short film documenting these charges, *Columbia Unbecoming,* was circulated, and the issue received extensive coverage in the conservative press, including the *New York Sun,* where Campus Watch founder Daniel Pipes was a columnist. Several prominent members of the Columbia Jewish community, such as longtime Hillel director Rabbi Charles Sheer, expressed skepticism about the MEALAC curriculum, and Abraham Foxman and the Anti-Defamation League became involved when it charged one professor, Joseph Massad, with anti-Semitism. A faculty panel commissioned to investigate found no sustained pattern of misconduct on the part of MEALAC professors, but this did not satisfy critics, who alleged that what was happening with Mideast studies at Columbia was symptomatic of a larger national problem: the fact that on many issues American academe consistently displayed a "liberal bias."

Indeed, as remarkable as these events around Columbia were, even more remarkable is that in the first decade of the twenty-first century—when many scholars were busy declaring America to be a knowledge society in which professors and other members of the creative class would be universally lauded for their role in stimulating economic growth—similar events involving searing criticism of American academics and their liberal politics could be found unfolding on campuses across the country.

At Harvard, Lawrence Summers's comments about women in math and science set off a firestorm. In response to them, and to other comments and behavior, the university's Faculty of Arts and Sciences voted to rebuke Summers, passing a "lack of confidence" motion in his leadership that eventually forced his resignation. Conservative commentators had a field day. Cathy Young, writing in the *Boston Globe,* described the "anti-Summers backlash" as "a scary display of know-nothingism, an embarrassing spectacle of academics rushing to denounce the mere statement of an unortho-dox hypothesis," while Nat Hentoff in the *Chicago Sun-Times* chalked the incident up to "political correctness" run rampant in the ivory tower.[10] Some impolitic liberals even got in on the drub-bing. Cultural critic Camille Paglia explained to *New York Times* readers that the lack of confidence vote came about as "feminist pressure groups" at Harvard "rose en masse from their lavishly feathered nests and set up a furious cackle." Summers's only mis-take, according to Paglia, was in daring to challenge "the liberal orthodoxy" that prevails on campuses like Harvard's, where "ide-ological groupthink" is the order of the day.[11]

Far from the Cambridge limelight, in Boulder, Colorado, a faculty committee was set up that same year to investigate the research activities of Ward Churchill, then a tenured professor of ethnic studies. A prolific author and frequent public speaker, Churchill is a scholar and activist whose writings focus on the historical mistreatment of Native Americans. He became a cause célèbre for conservatives after publishing an essay about the terrorist attacks of September 11, 2001, titled "Some People Push Back." The essay characterized the attacks as an understandable response to years of U.S. foreign policy in the Mideast and suggested that many of those who died that day in the Twin Towers— whom he referred to as "little Eichmanns"—were not innocent victims but willing participants in a global capitalist empire in the service of which that foreign policy had been forged. Conservative commentators seized upon the essay, treating it as an example of how dangerous, unpatriotic radicals had managed to insinuate themselves into America's higher education system. Churchill was denounced night after night on Bill O'Reilly's Fox News TV show, *The O'Reilly Factor,* as well as on conservative talk radio and in newspapers nationwide. During this time, allegations surfaced that Churchill had engaged in practices of shoddy scholarship, misrepresenting the historical record. It was these charges the investigative committee took up, ultimately finding some of them to have merit, though when University of Colorado president Hank Brown—a former Republican senator—used the findings as the basis for firing Churchill, many on the left suggested the investigation had been little more than a pretext for ridding the university of a tenured radical, and someone who had become a public relations nightmare.[12]

Meanwhile, at DePaul University in Chicago, Norman Finkelstein, a political scientist, was engaged in a pitched battle for tenure. Finkelstein's parents had been Holocaust survivors, and as a liberal, anti-Zionist Jew, he saw as part of his life's work to show how claims about the Holocaust had been manipulated to support an Israeli nationalist agenda and deflect criticism away from Israel's treatment of the Palestinians. This was one of Finkelstein's major concerns in a series of books that began to appear in the mid-1990s, garnering him attention in and out of academic circles.[13] He soon found his work attacked on scholarly and political grounds, not least by Harvard law professor Alan Dershowitz, author of the 2003 book, *The Case for Israel,* who ended up lobbying the DePaul administration to deny Finkelstein's tenure bid. Critics charged that Finkelstein was more a political advocate—and an immoderate one at that—than a political scientist, and undeserving of a scholarly post. Like Churchill, Finkelstein lost his job.

As the controversy surrounding these cases flared, David Horowitz was in the midst of a major campaign to reform American higher education. His goal was to alert people to what he saw as the indisputable fact that in many humanities and social science fields, leftist or liberal advocacy too often passes for scholarship, and indoctrination for teaching. While acknowledging that the majority of professors are "professionals," Horowitz contended that in fields like literature, sociology, women's studies, African American studies, and Mideast studies, a significant number could be found whose research is inseparable from their leftist politics, whose teaching tends to be politically one-sided, and whose radical views in some instances pose a threat to national security. On his popular website FrontPageMag.com, in bestselling books like *The Professors: The 101 Most Dangerous Academics in America* (2006) and *Indoctrination U.* (2007), and in appearances on television and on campuses around the country, Horowitz named names, identifying those academics whom he saw as behaving irresponsibly.[14] To shield students, he drafted an "Academic Bill of Rights" asserting that true academic freedom entails "the protection of

students—as well as faculty—from the imposition of any orthodoxy of a political, religious or ideological nature."[15] Through his
advocacy organization, the David Horowitz Freedom Center
(previously called the Center for the Study of Popular Culture),
he also started a student group, Students for Academic Freedom,
that, a few years after its founding, claimed to have members at
more than 150 colleges and universities. Horowitz and his allies
persuaded legislators in twenty-two states to consider making the
Academic Bill of Rights law. Several states—most prominently,
Pennsylvania—held hearings to assess whether Horowitz's charges
had merit. In the end, no legislation was enacted, although im-
passe on Horowitz's proposals did not occur before the issue of
liberal bias in academe received additional media coverage at the
state and local levels.[16] And while Horowitz was pressing his case
against the liberal professoriate, other organizations, from the National Association of Scholars (founded in the late 1980s to protest
"illiberal ideologies" on campus) to the Intercollegiate Studies
Institute (started in 1953 to promote conservative values among
college students) to the American Council of Trustees and Alumni
were doing the same. These groups, working in conjunction with
conservative journalists and commentators, produced a deluge of
material charging that the present and future of American higher
education were imperiled by the imbalance of liberals to conservatives on the faculty, by discrimination against conservative
professors, viewpoints, and students, and by the takeover of many
academic fields by radical political agendas, which had displaced
the traditional liberal arts curriculum and watered down academic standards. Often these criticisms were paired with the arguments that professors do not work hard enough, that they are
overpaid, that they should be spending more time on teaching,

and that the institution of tenure, said to protect the incompetent, should be abolished.

The issue of liberal bias surfaced again in the 2008 presidential campaign. Conservatives sought to portray Barack Obama, a former instructor at the University of Chicago Law School, as an intellectual out of touch with the real world and the values of Middle America. One way they did this was by emphasizing his ties to academe, which were many. In August 2008 the Center for Responsive Politics reported that in June and July alone educators gave $2.3 million to the Obama campaign, making them the second leading occupational group to back Obama financially, behind lawyers. The Center also reported that employees at nine major universities had collectively given more to the campaign than employees at nearly any other workplace.[17] Conservative commentators suggested the high level of academic support for Obama was evidence of something amiss with his values and policies. "It's no secret that academia is in the tank for Mr. Obama," wrote Jason Mattera, spokesman for the Young America's Foundation, in an op-ed piece.[18] Noting a number of vitriolic comments made by academics about Sarah Palin after she was announced as John McCain's running mate, Mattera went on to assert that while "liberal professors have a right to say whatever they want," it was reasonable to ask whether "we want people who exhibit . . . narrow-minded [partisan] perspectives teaching our young minds." Like so many other conservatives, Mattera also raised the question of Obama's connection to William Ayers, a professor whose political views and past behavior conservatives held to be beyond the pale.[19]

Dozens of other incidents and controversies, some taking us right up to the present day, belong to this same wave of conservative critique: lecture invitations issued to leftist professors that were quietly rescinded; Ivy League job offers to scholars critical of American foreign policy that were pulled, apparently after conservative uproar; Freedom of Information Act requests made by conservative think tanks seeking access to liberal professors' email accounts; demands made for curricular reforms, including changes to the list of books that some colleges and universities ask incoming students to read prior to freshman orientation; denunciations of pernicious liberal trends in the nation's elite law schools by prominent jurists, including Supreme Court Justice Clarence Thomas; the attacks made by Glenn Beck on the leftist sociologist Frances Fox Piven and her collaborator (and deceased husband) Richard Cloward, whose ideas were discussed at least fifty times on *The Glenn Beck Show* (which stopped airing on Fox News in June 2011) and on Beck's popular website, The Blaze, which were followed by anonymous death threats against her; and considerable talk during the Republican primary contest in 2011–2012 from candidates Newt Gingrich and Rick Santorum of colleges and universities as "indoctrination mills" for the left.[20]

It is a sign of how intense this criticism has been that members of the academic community, far from feeling safe behind campus gates, felt compelled to respond. In the run-up to the financial crisis that began in 2008, when attention shifted to other matters, academics could sometimes be found taking to the op-ed pages to castigate Horowitz and his compatriots.[21] Going beyond editorializing, other professors mounted collective responses. High-profile conferences were put on with titles like "Academic Freedom after September 11th" and "Free Inquiry at Risk: Universities in Dangerous Times."[22] At such events major public intellectuals declared their opposition to conservative "interference" in academic affairs. New advocacy groups were also formed, such as the Ad Hoc Commission to Defend the University, whose founders—Joan Scott of the Institute for Advanced Study in Princeton, Jeremy Adelman of Princeton, Steven Caton of Harvard, Jonathan Cole of Columbia, and Edmund Burke of the University of California–Santa Cruz—issued a petition in 2007 calling upon academics everywhere to resist "outside groups seeking to influence what is taught and who can teach." More than 650 scholars, many at similarly distinguished institutions, signed on.[23]

Established academic organizations also jumped into the fray. Throughout the first decade of the century disciplinary societies like the American Historical Association, the Modern Language Association, and the Mideast Studies Association would come out of their annual meetings with rhetorical guns blazing, denouncing conservative attacks in no uncertain terms. Equally outspoken were unions with significant academic representation, such as the American Federation of Teachers, which issued a series of reports calling conservative claims untruths and exposing what it saw as the dangers of the Academic Bill of Rights and other proposed reforms.[24]

Taking the lead in all of this, however, was the American Association of University Professors, despite having experienced a major drop in its membership numbers beginning in the 1980s.[25] Roger Bowen, a historian by training and former president of the State University of New York at New Paltz, who served as secretary general of the organization from 2004 to 2007, became a tireless opponent of Horowitz and other conservative critics. In a typical interview he gave on the Academic Bill of Rights and related efforts, Bowen described Horowitz as a "wolf in sheep's clothing . . . [who] has shamelessly plagiarized from the AAUP's statements on academic freedom, but added a totalitarian codicil that would make government, or university administrators, regulators of speech in the classroom."[26] Others associated with the AAUP, such as its elected president, English professor Cary Nelson, were every bit as vocal, condemning Horowitz whenever the occasion presented itself and drawing parallels to previous moments in our nation's history when academic freedom was under attack from the right.[27]

As further indications of the energy of conservative critiques in recent years, consider four more systematic sources of evidence. The first is simple: Google *liberal bias* and *higher education* and you will get a list of more than sixty thousand links. As a second piece of evidence, Figure 6.1 shows the number of articles in major U.S.

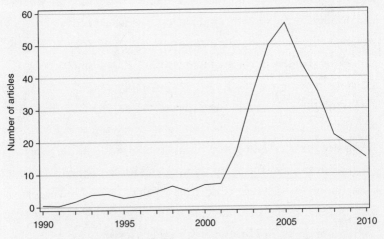

Figure 6.1. Co-occurrences of the phrases *liberal bias* and *higher education* in major magazines and newspapers, 1990–2010 (three-year moving average). *Source:* LexisNexis.

magazines and newspapers for the period 1990–2010 containing those same phrases. The spike around 2004–2005 is clear, although earlier waves of criticism—for example, around political correctness in the late 1980s and early 1990s—are not captured with such a measure.[28]

Third, in our 2006 survey of the professoriate, Simmons and I borrowed a question from Lazarsfeld, asking respondents, "In the past few years, how much have you felt that your own academic freedom has been threatened in any way?" Twenty-eight percent of respondents said they felt either a "lot" of threat to their academic freedom or "some" threat—a higher percentage than gave the same answers on Lazarsfeld's survey at the height of McCarthyism.[29] The follow-up interviews suggest that for many respondents, conservative critics were the main source of threat they had in mind, as in the case of Margene, the moderate biologist profiled in Chapter 1 who told us the only time her academic freedom had been threatened was when her college administration, wanting to avoid conflict with students and outside forces, asked members of the biology department to teach evolution in a watered-down way. Margene had acceded to the request, but some of her colleagues did not, resigning in protest.

Finally, consider what the opinion poll that Simmons and I conducted, and follow-up interviews to it, reveal about the extent to which conservative criticism of the academy had penetrated public consciousness. At the time of the poll confidence in American colleges and universities remained high: 42% of respondents said they had "a lot of confidence" in higher education institutions—a higher level of confidence than was expressed in any institution except the military. Notable about the confidence numbers, however, was that they showed a clear partisan divide:

48% of Democrats, as compared to 31% of Republicans, had a lot of confidence in colleges and universities. In terms of ideology, self-described conservatives were almost three times more likely than liberals to say they had hardly any confidence.

Confidence aside, what proportion of Americans bought into the conservative argument that academia is politically biased? Chapter 3 mentioned the finding that about two thirds of Americans believe colleges and universities favor liberal professors—evidence suggesting academic work is politically typed. Even more relevant here is a finding mentioned in the notes to the introduction: 37% of respondents to the poll said political bias in the classroom was a "very serious" problem facing higher education, while another 38% said it was a "somewhat serious problem." In the eyes of the public, political bias was by no means the *most* serious problem facing American colleges and universities. Just 8% of respondents described bias in the classroom in those terms; 43%—the plurality—said the biggest problem was the high cost of college tuition. Nevertheless that more than a third of Americans saw the issue of political bias as very serious is not a finding to be taken lightly. Here again partisan and ideological differences were evident: 49% of Republicans and 39% of Independents told us they saw political bias in the classroom as a very serious problem, as compared to 27% of Democrats. The numbers for conservatives and liberals were 47% and 37%.

Follow-up interviews to the poll, conducted in Colorado and Wisconsin, make clear that at least in states that saw a large amount of media coverage of the liberal bias issue, members of the public really were following it.[30] In the interview sample, which had more moderates and fewer liberals than the national polling sam-

ple, 25% of respondents described political bias in higher education as a very serious problem, while 45% said it was somewhat
serious. What stands out, however, is that a remarkable 80% of the
Colorado interviewees and 60% of those in Wisconsin told us they
had heard something in the media about controversy surrounding
the politics of professors. Often what they reported having heard
was fairly specific, as in the case of a sixty-two-year-old Colorado
resident formerly in plumbing sales who told us, "We have Churchill
here at CU. There is a big to-do about him. He was influencing
things . . . and they tried to fire him." Other interviewees mentioned the media sources from which they had heard about the
controversy, including Fox News and local talk radio. All told,
thirty-two of the sixty-nine interviewees were able to recall something about one or more high-profile cases involving professors
and their politics. Why and how did conservative charges of political bias in higher education come to have so much energy behind
them and command public attention? Scholarly discussion of this
question has generally revolved around three hypotheses: one to
do with anti-intellectualism and status politics, another with political tolerance, and a third with elite influence.

✦

The first hypothesis would locate conservative attacks in a long-
standing American tradition of anti-intellectualism and see them as
having been stirred up by recent changes in American society. It
would inevitably be informed by Richard Hofstadter's seminal 1963
book, *Anti-Intellectualism in American Life*.[31] Although published as the
1950s were fading into the distance, *Anti-Intellectualism*, like *Academic
Freedom in Our Time*, was very much a response to McCarthyism.[32]

To understand recent events in American history, including McCarthyism, Hofstadter claimed, one had to begin with the recognition that disparagement of intellect is woven deep into the American cultural fabric. By intellect Hofstadter meant roughly what Ladd and Lipset meant by intellectualism: the "critical, creative, and contemplative side of mind." Anti-intellectualism entailed "suspicion of the life of the mind" thus understood: skepticism toward "those who are considered to represent it; and a disposition constantly to minimize the value of that life."[33] Such a tendency, Hofstadter held, could show up in a variety of claims, gestures, attitudes, beliefs, and behaviors. Lending some coherence, however, was the fact that American anti-intellectualism tended to be organized around three distinctive cultural frames: one linked with fundamentalist Protestantism, distrustful of the cool rationality of intellectuals and their secularism; another arising out of the nineteenth-century fascination with commerce and industry, valuing practical intelligence and know-how but finding little to admire in more abstract forms of inquiry; and a third, rooted in agrarian populist movements, also of nineteenth-century origin, that called out intellectuals for being elites having insufficient respect for the common man.[34]

To some extent, argued Hofstadter, all three elements could be found in McCarthyite witch hunts and related phenomena, such as the growth of the John Birch Society, the rabidly anticommunist and nativist organization founded in 1958 by businessman Robert Welch. Yet the way these elements had fused suggested something about the unique circumstances behind the present moment. Anti-intellectualism may be a latent tendency in American culture, but Hofstadter believed it is activated only under specific historical conditions. In *Anti-Intellectualism,* but also in the essay collection he published in 1964 under the title *The Paranoid Style in American Politics,* Hofstadter invoked what was then a popular social scientific theory to explain the current activation: the theory that movements for the preservation of the status quo or for restoration of the status quo ante arise when significant swaths of the population experience anxiety about their declining social status relative to other groups.[35] Embraced as well by Lipset, not least in his 1970 book, *The Politics of Unreason,* a sociological account of more than two hundred years of right-wing activity in the United States, the theory of status anxiety was often deployed alongside the psychoanalytic claims advanced by Theodor Adorno and his colleagues in *The Authoritarian Personality* (1950) to make sense of how social and personal insecurities might get translated psychologically into racist beliefs, far-fetched conspiracy theories, obedience to charismatic authority figures, and a predisposition toward violence and the suppression of dissent.[36]

As Hofstadter saw it, McCarthyism had become a force in American life because the postwar nation was changing in ways that threatened to erode the social status of the groups composing the movement's base: members of the working class, those with low levels of education, people living in rural areas, Irish Catholics, and some Anglo-Saxon Protestants. Although some of these groups would benefit from efforts made in the 1960s to enhance social mobility—including, ironically, the expansion of higher education—the half-conscious perception among their members at the time, according to analysts like Hofstadter, was that they were shaping up as losers in the emerging American order. In the "mass society" said to be coming into formation, white-collar jobs were gaining ground, small businessmen were being displaced by large firms, local markets were giving way to national and international ones, rural areas saw further declines in their population, and people with advanced education and expertise, including many Jews, were being showered with prestige in the age of the atomic bomb and other technological innovations. Insecure, the groups that felt they were being left behind rallied around McCarthy and his allies. Their members bought into the scapegoating of intellectuals, into the portrayal of them as heavy-handed social planners or, worse, as a dangerous fifth column. Intellectuals, with their cosmopolitan ways, seemed to embody the very forces and changes that those insecure about their own status found so worrisome. It was this that accounted for the nature of 1950s-era anti-intellectualism. As Hofstadter put it in an essay in 1954 on what he called the "pseudo-conservative revolt":

Is it not status aspiration that in good part spurs the pseudo-conservative on toward his demand for conformity in a wide variety of spheres of life? Conformity is a way of guaranteeing and manifesting respectability among those who are not sure that they are respectable enough. The nonconformity of others appears to such persons as a frivolous challenge to the whole order of things they are trying so hard to become part of. Naturally it is resented, and the demand for conformity in public becomes at once an expression of such resentment and a means of displaying one's own soundness. This habit has a tendency to spread from politics into intellectual and social spheres, where it can be made to challenge almost anyone whose pattern of life is different and who is imagined to enjoy a superior social position—notably, as one agitator put it, those in the "parlors of the sophisticated, the intellectuals, the so-called academic minds."[37]

Needless to say, Hofstadter believed McCarthyism and the "radical right" had to be resisted, not simply because of the dangers they posed to intellectual life but for two other reasons as well. First, their actions threatened to stop the forward momentum of New Deal liberalism and the expansion of social, political, and civil rights that it entailed—a project to which Hofstadter had given his support. Second, the "paranoid style" of politics practiced by the right, revolving around "feeling[s] of persecution" in which a "hostile and conspiratorial world" is seen as "directed against" one's "nation . . . culture . . . way of life," and further characterized by overheated rhetoric, ideological thinking, and a disregard for facts, was in Hofstadter's view at odds with the requirements of a pluralist democracy.[38]

Might anti–intellectualism, when paired with an updated version of the status anxiety argument, provide an explanation for the most recent round of conservative critique? Although the notion of status anxiety is not nearly as popular with social scientists today as it once was, many have noted significant social and political changes that occurred or intensified in the first decade of the twenty-first century (before the onset of the recession)—changes that could well have made some groups insecure. Perhaps some of that insecurity was displaced onto academics. Among other things, the period saw the emergence of a mature knowledge economy in which science and engineering jobs grew much more quickly than those in other sectors.[39] The proportion of Americans with a bachelor's degree continued to climb, as did the wage premium associated with a college education.[40] And it was becoming clear that cities and regions heavily populated by knowledge workers were now the nation's key zones of economic growth.[41] Perhaps attacks on the liberal professoriate were able to gain traction because people in certain segments of American society—those without much education, those living outside knowledge-work hubs, fundamentalists and evangelicals—saw these changes taking place, realized they would only further erode their already precarious social positions, and became quick to jump aboard the "Blame the professors" bandwagon, viewing academics as symbols of the new and threatening world coming into being.

In a similar vein, the past two decades have witnessed major shifts in the standing of various sociodemographic groups in the United States. Although still paid less than men, women have made remarkable strides in a wide variety of occupational domains, are permanent fixtures in the full-time labor force, and have rates of educational attainment that now exceed those of men. A sizable black professional class has made its presence known, and America's Hispanic population continues to grow. Gays and lesbians have won rights and gained social acceptance to an extent unimaginable thirty years ago. Scholars like Robert Horwitz, as well as a number of popular commentators, have argued that the status anxiety generated by these changes, particularly among straight white men, was a crucial factor propelling the rise of the Tea Party after Obama's election in 2008, and with it the distinctive style of politics—which some have described, not without reason, as paranoid and anti-intellectual—that Tea Party supporters have practiced.[42] Could not subscription to conservative critiques of academia arise from similar sentiments, with professors deserving blame, in the eyes of white men in particular, for having played a role in bringing about these changes through their support for affirmative action, their championing of diversity and tolerance, and their commitment to feminism?[43]

While these arguments make some theoretical sense, the evidence is not overwhelming that Americans who agree with conservative critics like Horowitz are insecure about their status. Consider what the opinion poll tells us on this front. To get more traction on the polling data, Simmons conducted a latent class analysis using a number of attitude measures.[44] The analysis distinguished three groups of respondents: those "concerned" about liberal bias (34%), those "unconcerned" (51%), and those with "no clear views" on the matter (14%). Table 6.1 shows how respondents in these three clusters are distributed across social groups by education. There is an educational gradient here. For example, there are more white men and white women without a bachelor's degree in the concerned than the unconcerned cluster. But there is no single low-education group whose members make up an obvious core of supporters for anti–liberal professor rhetoric. All told, 77% of respondents in the concerned cluster have less than a bachelor's degree, but so do 66% of those in the unconcerned cluster. Paralleling these real but not massive educational differences, among respondents who were employed at the time of the poll those in the concerned cluster were only slightly less likely than the unconcerned to hold professional or other white-collar jobs. For example, 20% of the concerned were professional workers, as compared to 23% of the unconcerned. The concerned could be found more commonly in rural areas than in cities, but by a difference of only 2 percentage points.

Perhaps more in line with the notion that the concerned may be hostile toward or fearful of the knowledge economy, 66% of them, as compared to 42% of the unconcerned, stated that too much of the research conducted by professors is irrelevant to the needs of society, while 70% of the concerned, as compared to

Table 6.1. Clusters of American adults on "liberal bias" in higher education by education, race, and gender

Education level	Unconcerned about liberal bias (51%)	Concerned about liberal bias (34%)	No clear views (14%)
Less than high school			
White men	1	7	3
White women	3	4	12
Nonwhite men	2	4	4
Nonwhite women	2	3	3
High school			
White men	10	14	16
White women	11	12	24
Nonwhite men	4	2	4
Nonwhite women	4	4	3
Some college			
White men	12	7	5
White women	10	14	10
Nonwhite men	3	3	1
Nonwhite women	4	3	2
Bachelor's or more			
White men	14	11	3
White women	13	9	8
Nonwhite men	2	2	0
Nonwhite women	3	1	1

Source: Attitudes toward the American Professoriate survey, 2006, sample size 1,000.
Note: Numbers are column percentages and may not add to 100 because of rounding. Percentages in parentheses are cluster sizes.

53% of the unconcerned, were of the view that faculty should spend more time on teaching and less on research. But this could just as easily reflect subscription to the full package of conservative criticism and the view that much academic research is irrelevant *because* it is politically biased as hostility toward knowledge per se. And indeed the poll showed few differences between the groups in the propensity of their members' children to go to college, suggesting that the concerned are not boycotting the knowledge economy or being left behind by it.

Turning to other factors, the poll revealed some differences by race and gender. Across educational levels the concerned cluster contains disproportionately more whites than nonwhites, more men than women. But as Table 6.1 also indicates, these differences are not large. Two more significant differences are that the concerned tended to be older than the unconcerned (mean age forty-eight versus forty-three years, respectively) and were more likely to identify themselves as evangelical Protestants. With regard to the latter, perhaps evangelicals are leery of professors because they fear they are out to secularize students and the country? Evangelicals in the poll were more likely than nonevangelicals to disagree with the statement "American colleges and universities welcome students of faith" (29% versus 16%) and more likely to believe that the typical college or university professor is not religious at all (35% versus 27%). But since more than two thirds of evangelicals think that colleges *do* welcome the faithful, there would appear to be no widespread perception among them that higher education per se represents a threat to Christian values or their way of life, an interpretation that corresponds with the fact that growing numbers have been going to college in recent years.[45] More generally, it is probably an indication that fears about shifting levels of power among social groups are not the main thing driving support for conservative critique that the concerned and the unconcerned in our poll were indistinguishable in their levels of satisfaction with the direction in which the country is heading overall.[46]

As a further test of the status anxiety hypothesis, I had one of my research assistants comb through transcripts of the follow-up interviews to the poll, to see whether any interviewees expressed—even in a veiled fashion—frustration with their life situation or a sense that contemporary society was leaving them in the dust. None did. (We would surely have found more frustration had the interviews been conducted during the economic downturn.) Frustration was not something we asked about directly, but if status anxiety were a major factor underlying popular support for critique of the professoriate, one might imagine that at least some of this anxiety would have come out in an interview about professors.

Lack of strong empirical support for the status anxiety hypothesis was exactly what political scientist Michael Rogin found when he scrutinized a range of polling data to shed light on the McCarthy phenomenon for his 1967 book, *The Intellectuals and McCarthy*. Finding a lack of clarity among theorists in which groups specifically were said to be insecure and throwing their support behind McCarthy, as well as inconsistent empirical evidence that these groups really constituted McCarthy's base, Rogin argued that McCarthyism was not properly understood as a mass phenomenon at all. "From 1950 through 1954," he wrote, "Joseph McCarthy disrupted the normal routine of American politics. But McCarthyism can best be understood as a product of that normal routine. McCarthy capitalized on popular concern over foreign policy, communism, and the Korean War, but the animus of McCarthyism had little to do with any less political or more developed *popular* anxieties. Instead it reflected the specific traumas of conservative Republican activists—internal Communist subversion, the New Deal, centralized government, left-wing intellectuals, and the corrupting influences of a cosmopolitan society. The resentments of these Republicans and the Senator's own talents were the driving forces behind the McCarthy movement."[47] The account I develop in Chapter 7 of the movement against the liberal professoriate likewise puts more emphasis on the activities of political movers and shakers than on social psychological stirrings in the population, however much it, like Rogin's, also tries to explain why those activities resonate for some Americans.

✦

A second hypothesis—one that dovetails with the first—revolves around the concept of political tolerance. Political scientists and sociologists define tolerance as "a willingness to extend the rights of citizenship to all members of the polity—that is, to allow political freedoms to those who are politically different."[48] There is debate among scholars of tolerance as to whether the American public has grown more tolerant over time.[49] Some claim that it has, citing declines since the mid-twentieth century in the proportion of Americans who favor restricting the civil liberties of socialists and communists. Other scholars claim that while tolerance of socialists and communists may have increased, intolerance of other groups has grown. Even if scholars in the first camp are right, however, there can be no question that even today a substantial number of Americans think the rights of political dissidents ought to be curtailed. As it happens, one of the questions commonly used in social science surveys to measure tolerance asks whether respondents believe that dissidents of one stripe or another should be allowed to teach college. A question to this effect, focusing on communists, has been asked since 1972 as part of the GSS. At that time, 64% of Americans said that a college teacher found to be a communist should be fired. The number has since declined, but in 2006 it still stood at 37%. In the public opinion poll Simmons and I conducted, we found that 45% of Americans strongly agree that public universities should be able to dismiss professors who join radical political organizations like the Communist Party. Combine such a level of intolerance with the fact that many academics *are* much further to the left than most Americans—if almost never today communists—and you get a recipe for recurrent political conflict over higher education.

But why does such conflict wax and wane, and why was it on the upswing in the first decade of the century? Another important finding from research on tolerance, one with roots in the ideas of Georg Simmel, a German sociologist at the turn of the twentieth century, is that levels of intolerance increase during wartime. As Simmel put it, "Groups in any sort of war situation are not tolerant. They cannot afford individual deviations from the unity of the coordinating principle beyond a definitely limited degree."[50] During wars, or periods when national security is otherwise felt to be threatened, citizens of a country rally together to fight a common enemy and look at dissidents as traitors. In a test of this idea, political scientists Marc Hutchison and Douglas Gibler, using cross-national survey data, found that people living in countries that have recently gone to war, been seriously threatened by war, or been embroiled in territorial disputes are far less tolerant of political dissenters than people living in countries that have been relatively free of conflict.[51] How might this apply to the controversy over liberal professors?

Figure 6.1, discussed earlier, indicates that concern about liberal bias in academe was most intense in the aftermath of September 11 and in the early years of the Iraq War. Perhaps it is no coincidence that some of the professors targeted, like Ward Churchill, were called traitors precisely for their views of the terrorist attacks and the invasion. A hypothesis derived from research on dissent and tolerance would hold not simply that we should expect tension around professors' politics but that such tension would have been heightened as a result of external threat to the nation and mobilization for war. Certainly the idea that McCarthy was able to win support in the 1950s by playing off cold war fears is a standard claim of American historiography.

This hypothesis is insightful but has its limits. For one thing, according to a number of different measures, including those used in the Hutchison and Gibler study, levels of political tolerance are higher in the United States than in most other countries of the world.[52] Within the United States, tolerance varies by geography: Americans living in the South and in rural areas tend toward greater intolerance, probably a function of religion, regional culture, and lower levels of education.[53] Political conservatives and the elderly also tend to exhibit less tolerance. But compared to citizens of many other nations that do not have democratic traditions as long-standing as those in the United States, Americans overall are more willing to extend basic rights and freedoms to dissidents. That no other advanced industrial democracies, including those with lower levels of attitudinal tolerance, like Germany, have had the same kind of campaign against professors calls into question whether intolerance alone could explain the phenomenon (although the greater political distance between American professors and the American public than between professors in more social democratic nations and citizens there might account for a good deal of this discrepancy).

A related problem is that levels of tolerance for political dissidents in the United States, as measured by surveys like the GSS, showed no signs of precipitous decline after September 11. In

2000, 38% of GSS respondents said that a communist college teacher should be fired. That figure was virtually unchanged in 2002, and in 2004 dipped to 34%. Regarding dissent over the war specifically, in March 2003, after the invasion of Iraq was under way, a majority of Americans, according to the Gallup organization, supported the free speech and assembly rights of antiwar protesters.[54] Religious and ethnic tolerance did not fare as well: anti-Muslim and anti-Arab sentiment spiked in the wake of the attacks on the World Trade Center and the Pentagon—although it was reasonably high to begin with.[55] But few of the professors targeted by conservative critics have been Muslim, and while academics like Churchill and Kevin Barrett at Wisconsin were depicted as sympathetic to radical Islam and to terrorism, the bulk of the criticism of liberal professors has revolved around other issues.

The tolerance hypothesis also does not square entirely with data from the opinion poll. There is *some* confirmatory evidence. When Simmons and I ran a statistical model on the polling data, we found, in line with the numbers discussed earlier, that lower levels of education, age, and political conservatism were statistically significant predictors of membership in the concerned versus the unconcerned cluster. In other words, criticism of the liberal professoriate tends to be more pronounced within groups known to be less tolerant politically. Yet when we looked to see whether people in the concerned cluster were more likely to support action clearly designed to stamp out political dissent on campus, evidencing intolerance directly, we found they were only somewhat more likely to do so. Sixty-five percent of the concerned think public universities should be able to dismiss professors who join radical political organizations, but so do 56% of those in the unconcerned cluster. Fifty-seven percent of the concerned agree there is no room in the university for professors who defend the actions of Islamic militants, but so do 49% of the unconcerned. By these measures, Americans worried about liberal bias in higher education do seem to have lower levels of political tolerance, but there is far from a perfect correlation between intolerance and such worry.

Finally, even if the campaign against the liberal professoriate is tied to tolerance in the sense that conservative critics have struck a chord with elements of the public that are less tolerant of dissent, the intolerance hypothesis reveals little about why threat-induced reaction against dissenters resulted in targeting professors specifically. While not focusing on intolerance directly, a third hypothesis, to which I turn in Chapter 7, seeks to illuminate the mechanics of this targeting.

Chapter 7

Why Conservatives Care

In 1994 historian Alan Brinkley could note, in an observation that applied as much to other disciplines as to his own, "The American right has [not] received anything like the amount of attention . . . that its role in twentieth-century politics and culture suggests it should."[1] Times have changed. Today an enormous scholarly literature exists, spanning the fields of history, political science, and, to a lesser extent, sociology on the contemporary American conservative movement.[2]

In this body of work, no concern has been more central than to explain the right's ascendance in the second half of the twentieth century. To be sure, conservative political figures feature prominently throughout our nation's history. But conservatism as we know it today—as a movement and political ideology inextricably tied to the Republican Party and entailing belief not simply in the virtues of business, wealth, and tradition, but also in an enervated state, which is different from the "neomercantilist" conservatism of the nineteenth and early twentieth centuries—is a relatively recent phenomenon.[3] At the height of New Deal–era liberalism and in the years immediately following the end of World War II, a common perception was that a vigorous and intellectually credible right was nowhere to be found on the American political stage.[4] Conservatism as a political identity did not have the cachet with voters that it currently does and, as a corollary, conservative politicians were not routine contenders for political power at the national level in the same way they are today. The Democrats, though admittedly a different breed than they are now, controlled the White House from 1933 until 1969, except for an eight-year interlude when moderate Republican Dwight D. Eisenhower was in office; the Democrats held majorities in both houses of Congress throughout the 1930s and 1940s; and the Republican Party was for all intents and purposes controlled by moderates from the Northeast.[5] In fact McCarthyism and the appearance of conservative intellectuals like Buckley garnered so much attention from social scientists in the 1950s because the brand of conservatism associated with both seemed like a novel development, notwithstanding the fact that thinkers like Hofstadter sought to connect it to earlier waves of discontent.

Scholars of conservatism have offered a range of explanations for the right's rise. While many depict the nomination of Barry Goldwater for the presidency in 1964 as a turning point, signaling the GOP's capture by strong conservative elements, a common argument is that conservatism was able to gain real ground only in the 1970s, and this because of economic changes occurring during that decade.[6] As corporate profits dwindled in the face of growing international competition, the OPEC-induced oil crisis, and inflation, the argument goes, business elites began withdrawing from the New Deal bargain with labor and government that had held sway for more than thirty years.[7] Increasingly they threw their support behind politicians championing free market policies. In the wake of Watergate and as successive presidents failed to tamp down inflationary pressures, kick-start growth, or solve the nation's mounting social problems, the confidence of ordinary voters in the power of government to rise above corruption and get things done also faltered, lending credibility to conservative calls for greater reliance on market-based solutions.[8] The declining strength of labor unions in the 1970s, part of a longer term trend tied to shifts in the economy and a reorganization of manufacturing, is also important, as it made it harder for unions to reliably channel the working-class vote toward the Democrats. These developments are said to have paved the way for Reagan's election in 1980.

For a second group of scholars, by contrast, it is not primarily the economy but racial cleavages and other social and cultural divides that explain the rise of conservatism. In their eyes, Goldwater was able to win the nomination for one reason alone: his opposition as senator to the Civil Rights Act of 1964. In the aftermath of the civil rights movement, southern whites and so-called ethnic whites in the Northeast and elsewhere began fleeing the Democratic Party—which had backed the movement—and came to regard liberalism as the enemy, either because of direct racial antipathy or because they perceived a mismatch between the values they held dear and those they saw embodied in liberal legislation and social policies designed to improve the social and economic standing of African Americans.[9] This is thought to have presented major opportunities for conservatives within the GOP and to have set the stage for the party's "southern strategy" of wooing disaffected southern white voters with veiled appeals to racial solidarity—a strategy that would give the Republicans a leg up in national elections for years to come.[10]

Other scholars highlight different cultural factors, such as the vast distance that opened up in the 1960s between evangelicals and the counterculture, leading many evangelicals to become politically mobilized against what they perceived as pernicious social trends.[11] The anti–Vietnam War movement, the Black Power movement, the feminist movement, and, somewhat later, the gay rights movement are also portrayed in this literature as having spurred conservatives to action. Finally, one scholar, historian John Andrew, argues that conservatism was able to harness the same 1960s-era youthful radicalism and optimism that powered the growth of New Left groups like Students for a Democratic Society. This occurred, Andrew claims, as conservative college students flocked to organizations like Young Americans for Freedom—started by Buckley and others in 1960—outraged not just by the disruptions taking place on their campuses but also by the overall direction in which they saw the country heading.[12]

For a third set of scholars, however, economic and cultural factors alone could not have given rise to a movement as powerful as contemporary American conservatism. Also required was the construction of a vast ideological and institutional infrastructure to support the movement—and it is in relation to this institution-building effort that several analysts locate conservative critiques of higher education. In order to amass power, political movements need backers and followers and allies, and this requires, among other things, compelling ideas to which people can cleave. Although conservatism might never have made inroads were it not for economic and cultural circumstances, another condition for its success, some argue, was that conservative elites invested in building up the movement's idea base, founding a large number of think tanks, media outlets, and advocacy organizations that worked to elaborate and disseminate conservative ideology and push American thinking to the right.[13]

On at least some accounts, systematic criticism of the liberal professoriate—of the sort seen over the past decade, and before that in debates over political correctness and multiculturalism—emerged amid these institutional developments. The argument goes like this: Leading conservatives in the 1970s and 1980s recognized that if they wanted their movement to make even larger gains, they would have to take on academia, since it was a main center of American leftist and liberal thought. So, in cooperation with the big conservative philanthropies that began making their presence felt during this time—especially the "four sister" philanthropies: the Smith Richardson Foundation, the (several) Scaife foundations, the John M. Olin Foundation, and the Lynde and Harry Bradley Foundation—they worked to put in place structures through which the academic left would be attacked and discredited. This entailed starting specialized pressure groups that could devote themselves to bashing liberal professors, working closely with conservative students and faculty, nurturing the development of conservative-leaning higher education institutions and programs, and encouraging conservative think tanks and writers and reporters to take on liberal professors whenever possible. Ellen Schrecker, in her latest book about academic freedom, highlights in this regard an influential memo written in 1971 by Lewis Powell, who would soon be nominated by Richard Nixon to the Supreme Court but was at the time an attorney employed by the tobacco industry. The memo was sent to a friend of Powell's in the U.S. Chamber of Commerce and argued that if the goal was to give conservative ideas greater currency,

> the business community would have to "be far more aggressive than in the past" and engage "in careful long-range planning and implementation . . . over an indefinite period of years, in the scale of financing available only through joint effort, and in the political power available only through united action and national organizations." It would have to mount a sophisticated public relations campaign to insert conservative ideas into the nation's public discourse. It would also have to monitor textbooks, campus lectures, and television newscasts, as well as establish its own network of speakers and scholars. "Perhaps the most fundamental problem," Powell explained, "is the imbalance of many faculties. Correcting this is indeed a long-range and difficult project. Yet it should be undertaken as a part of an overall program. This would mean the urging of the need for faculty balance upon university administrators and boards of trustees." Conservative business leaders, thus, had a double mission: they would have to create their own intellectual infrastructure while at the same time they would also have to destroy the credibility of the already existing academic one.[14]

Although it took some time for the second element of this double mission to be implemented, Schrecker argues that by the late 1980s and early 1990s it was: the National Association of Scholars had been founded, David Horowitz was on the scene, conservative writers like Roger Kimball and Dinesh D'Souza were receiving support for their stabs at the shibboleths of the academic left, Lynne Cheney was attacking political correctness in higher education from her position as head of the National Endowment for the Humanities, and the idea began to spread that academia was too liberal for the nation's good. As Schrecker sees it, the current hubbub about liberal bias is a function of the conservative movement's investment in the project of trying to silence or at least marginalize academic radicals, liberals, and other "squeaky wheels." Versions of this argument have been advanced by others as well.[15]

One of the things this hypothesis has going for it, as against the two discussed in Chapter 6, is that it attends closely to the conservative organizations and activists involved in mounting critiques of liberal professors and to the flows of money going toward them. To my knowledge no one has put together a list of all the organizations that have pressed for political reform of higher education. But Free Exchange on Campus, a coalition of left-leaning groups, including the American Association of University Professors, the American Civil Liberties Union, the American Federation of Teachers, and the Modern Language Association, compiled data on some for a report they issued titled "Manufactured Controversy."[16] Alleging that "since the terrorist attacks on Sept. 11, 2001 . . . attacks on the academy have escalated well beyond a vigorous back-and-forth about the curriculum and the 'canon' into a full-scale assault on the credibility of U.S. colleges and universities," the report went on to list key organizational "players" and detailed the extent to which these organizations had been supported by major conservative funders.[17] Figure 7.1 displays graphically the numbers from the report, which come from tax filings. They are fairly staggering, although not all of the organizations listed are concerned exclusively with higher education, so that some of the millions of dollars that Olin, Bradley,

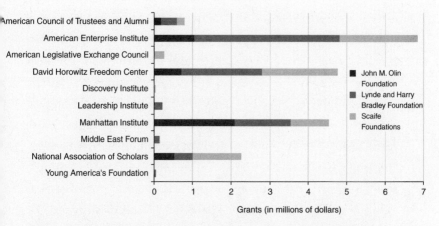

Figure 7.1. Money given to higher education reform groups by major conservative philanthropies, 2001–2006. (The John M. Olin Foundation closed its doors in 2005; donations illustrated here are for 2001–2005. Scaife Foundations include Scaife Family, Sarah Scaife, Carthage, and Allegheny.) *Source:* "Manufactured Controversy: An Examination of the 'Academic Bill of Rights' Movement," 8, http://cdn.publicinterestnetwork .org/assets/1VWEvg8YSPXfmG3nZL28TA/Manufactured-Controversy .pdf (accessed 5/18/12).

and Scaife poured into these entities were in fact directed toward other efforts.

Chapter 6 briefly discussed several of the organizations that appear in the graph: the David Horowitz Freedom Center, the American Council of Trustees and Alumni (ACTA), the National Association of Scholars (NAS), and Middle East Forum, home of Campus Watch. Another notable entry is the Center for the American University, based at the Manhattan Institute, which runs a website compiling information relevant to conservative critique of higher education and provides fellowships to conservative journalists and others who write on the issue. For its part, the Young America's Foundation, which emerged out of Young Americans for Freedom, "currently focuses on training young conservative activists, fostering conservative activism on college campuses and providing networking opportunities for these activists. [It] also provides a conservative speakers bureau for on-campus speakers and has featured David Horowitz at some of its events."[18] Not included in the figure is the John William Pope Center for Higher Education Policy in Raleigh, which has supported higher education reform efforts in North Carolina and elsewhere; and the Intercollegiate Studies Institute (ISI), which, among other things, issues a report aimed at conservative students and parents called "Choosing the *Right* College: The Whole Truth about America's Top Schools" (emphasis added), in which schools are assessed by the political suitability of their faculty and student body.[19] The ISI too—whose first president, when it had a different name, was William F. Buckley—is heavily supported by conservative funders. There has been no detailed analysis of the affiliations and social network connections of all the conservative intellectuals, writers, and journalists who have taken part in the campaign against the liberal professoriate, but many seem to have links with one or more of these organizations. Is all this evidence of a coordinated and manufactured attack against American higher education—of what amounts to a vast right-wing conspiracy to attack left-leaning professors?

The numbers in Figure 7.1 leave no doubt that the campaign against the liberal professoriate has been reasonably well-financed. But there are problems with characterizing it, as Schrecker and others do, as little more than a top-down affair orchestrated by political and business elites. First, while my data on the subject are indirect, there appears to be less than unanimous agreement among such elites that going after liberal academics is a worthwhile enterprise. For example, when I interviewed David Horowitz in the

spring of 2008 in his southern California home, he spoke repeatedly of his frustration with the fact that so few Republican politicians had gotten on board with the Academic Bill of Rights.
Describing what had transpired in Pennsylvania, he said he was
able to get hearings held into the question of whether professors
there were indoctrinating students only because he had the ear of
Gib Armstrong, an investment advisor then serving in the Pennsylvania State Senate. Republican lawmakers proved unable to
move the issue forward, however, and Horowitz called them
"lame, stupid, weak." In his memoir of the campaign, *Reforming
Our Universities: The Campaign for an Academic Bill of Rights* (2010),
he elaborated on what he meant by this. In his version of events,
Democrats were in effective control of the committee that ran
the hearings, and in the end they drafted a report concluding that
no evidence had been found of political indoctrination by professors in Pennsylvania and that existing policies were sufficient
to protect students. Horowitz wrote:

> For me, the most dispiriting aspect of the episode was the
> fact that the Republicans did not protest this travesty, but
> actually validated it. Once the Democrats had the upper hand,
> the Republicans on the committee capitulated to the major-
> ity and voted to ratify the . . . report. It is true that they were
> demoralized by their defeat in the elections two weeks ear-
> lier, which was driven by a backlash against pay raises legisla-
> tors had voted themselves that year. The Republicans lost
> fourteen seats, including those belonging to Gib Armstrong
> and Tom Stevenson [an Armstrong ally]. Armstrong explained
> to me afterwards that the Republican members were too
> embarrassed to vote against the report of a committee on

which they were a paper majority. . . . But I also was of the opinion that, with the exception of Gib Armstrong, the Republicans on the committee—unlike their Democratic counterparts—never took the battle seriously, and were always just trying to get through the hearings with as little damage to their resumes as possible.[20]

Later in his interview with me, Horowitz reaffirmed his view that "the Republican Party is out to lunch on the issue" of indoctrination on campus. To explain this, he told a story: "About fifteen years ago, I called up—maybe it was the head of the conservative party in New York, maybe it was the head of the Republican Party. I can't remember. Probably Republican. It was about vouchers. I said, 'You know, these kids, they're dying in these public school systems. There's got to be competition.' He says, 'education isn't a Republican issue.' Those were his exact words." While there obviously has been strong Republican support for vouchers, Horowitz's point was that the core concerns of American conservatism have been taxes, business regulation, the military, and social issues like abortion.[21] More generally, he claimed, "conservative [politicians] are gun-shy when they're moving into left-wing territory," like that surrounding higher education. "They don't know how to fight. They think they're going to get nothing but grief. You know . . . they're business school majors—not all of them are businessmen—or they're scientists. They don't move easily in the[se] kind[s] of [academic] discussions." In a later conversation, he detailed the various ways in which, as he saw it, the Academic Bill of Rights had been undermined by his fellow conservatives: in his estimation, half of the board members of the NAS had been opposed to the Academic Bill of Rights;

though his campaign for it was covered extensively in the mainstream press, neither the *Weekly Standard* nor *Commentary*—major organs of conservatism—had devoted a word to it; his work was attacked in a piece in *Reason;* and the *Wall Street Journal* had come out with an editorial warning of the dangers of the Academic Bill of Rights.[22] Horowitz said that he certainly had allies, including people at foundations like Bradley and in organizations like the Young America's Foundation, and among conservative media figures like Sean Hannity. But it did not seem to him as though the conservative movement, which he described as a "very diverse coalition [that] ranges from anarchist libertarians to religious authoritarians," had rallied behind his campaign in a serious way at all.[23]

Other people who interact regularly with major players in the conservative movement told me they think Horowitz is right about this. For example, one observer of the Washington scene who did not want to be identified wrote to me, "My sense is that a subset of conservatives care a lot about these issues, but that it's really not widespread (or the top issue). I always look at where these folks send their kids, and they are all lining up to send their kids to Harvard (Anne Neal's daughter [Anne Neal, the president of ACTA]), Yale (Bush's daughter, continuing family tradition) or publics like U of Texas at Austin (other Bush daughter). If the conservatives really believed that liberal terrorists were running the leading universities, damaging everyone they can, would they send their kids there?" *New York Times* columnist John Tierney made the point that while some influential conservatives are incensed about the state of American academic life, "a lot of conservatives in Washington don't worry much about intellectual diversity on campus because it seems like a hopeless cause and also fairly irrelevant politically." And Peter Wood of the NAS told me that in his experience "only a minority among people who could be considered 'conservative elites' take these matters seriously. . . . A major line of division is whether higher education should be thought of as primarily preparation for the workforce, or whether its role in shaping culture should also be taken seriously."

One sign of this less than unanimous support is that the main advocacy organizations involved in criticizing the liberal professoriate are forced to be selective in which conservative donors they turn to for help. Horowitz has been receiving funding from Bradley and Scaife for many years (and from Olin before they closed in 2005) and sent me copies of the short proposals—sometimes only four pages—he has used to get money from them in the range of several hundred thousand dollars. But his organization is large and expensive to run, and typically, he told me, no more than about 10% of his funding comes from big foundations.[24] The rest comes from a variety of other sources, including wealthy individuals, direct-mail campaigns, and Internet donations. Soliciting donations has required hard work. Horowitz said that in the early days he put a great deal of time into fundraising. Now two members of his staff are tasked with the responsibility. He said that raising money is not terribly difficult for him, but this, he told me, is because over the years he has built up a loyal following of supporters. His success at fundraising comes from knowing who in the conservative community to ask for help and who not to bother asking—and he reiterated that there are many well-to-do conservatives who "shrink from . . . conflicts" over the university. By contrast, the people who run the NAS said that raising enough money to operate has always been a challenge for them.

What they share with Horowitz is the experience of operating on a complex and heterogeneous conservative funding landscape; the leaders of the organization, Wood and NAS founder Stephen Balch (about whom more shortly), stated that over the years many conservative foundations, including that run by billionaire Charles Koch, had "repeatedly" turned down their funding requests.

Even at the well-heeled Manhattan Institute, a citadel of conservative thought, the lack of unanimous support among conservative elites for the campaign against liberal professors is apparent. Journalist John Leo began writing about political correctness as a columnist for *U.S. News and World Report*. He now runs a website called mindingthecampus.org—"dedicated to the revival of intellectual pluralism and the best traditions of liberal education"—from his position at the Center for the American University. When I interviewed him back in 2008, the website was just getting off the ground. Leo noted that it was a shoe-string operation at that point—just him and a former intern he had brought over from *U.S. News*—and that their budget was not much to speak of. While he said that the leadership of the Manhattan Institute had been eager for him to join the think tank because it sensed a gap in its issue coverage, he also said he did not believe very many influential people in the conservative community were aware of the work he had been doing on the website. When I asked him how mindingthecampus.org was viewed by other conservatives, he replied, "Well, those who have noticed us, I think, are impressed, but [the number] of people that haven't noticed us is frankly very large. [With] the uproar of media, it's so hard to keep up with things." That Leo felt he was having a hard time getting attention, despite his connections, suggests again that not all power players in the conservative community are riveted to higher education matters or keen to rock the higher education boat.[25]

But there is a second problem: timing. If the elite influence account offered by Schrecker and others told the whole story, we would expect modern-day attacks on the liberal professoriate to have begun in earnest in the 1980s and 1990s, after the contemporary conservative movement had picked up steam and its funding structures were in place. Yet criticism of academia, typically moving beyond the McCarthyite themes so well documented in Schrecker's earlier work, and beyond the occasional criticisms lobbed at left professors during the Progressive era, became commonplace in the late 1950s, when the conservative movement was still in its infancy. It continued throughout the 1960s and into the 1970s—as Schrecker's own analysis of academic politics shows.

Consider some additional examples drawn from *National Review*. In a column in July 1957, Buckley railed against the American educational establishment, charging that it was dominated by collectivists, with "Columbia Teachers College . . . still the center of the educationalists' patronage network," just as it had been in the days when education professor Harold Rugg, "a socialist . . . , a pragmatist, a relativist, a social architect," worked there, helping to establish the nation's social studies curriculum.[26] An anonymous report from that October noted that a conservative student group at Harvard had been formed to offer an alternative to the "one-dimensional view of contemporary politics which the Harvard faculty as a whole gives to its students."[27] Conservative writer and former academic historian Russell Kirk, author of the 1953 book *The Conservative Mind,* declared that the most recent generation of students might be referred to as "the defrauded generation," since many of them "feel that they have been defrauded of their intellectual and moral birthright: defrauded by social indoctrination in the guise of scholarship, by shabby standards, by coddling of the stupid and lazy in our colleges and universities."[28] In July of 1958 Willmoore Kendall, a former political scientist at Yale who had been one of Buckley's teachers and had helped him start *National Review,* poked fun at the work of political scientist Herbert McClosky, who had just published an article in the *American Political Science Review* arguing that conservatives suffer from personality problems. "Its findings," wrote Kendall, "will, over the next years, admirably serve the purposes of any Liberal who either a) wants to take his Conservative friends and acquaintances down a notch or two, or b) wants to reinforce his smugness about his own supposed moral and intellectual superiority."[29] A column by Allan Ryskind, a graduate of Pomona College, in November 1959 explained how that institution had been taken over by collectivist professors.[30] And Buckley wrote a piece later that month with the self-explanatory headline, "As the Left Goes, So Goes Harvard," following this up the next year with an essay asking whether the declines seen in student religiosity at places like Harvard stemmed from the fact that "students submit, as we have seen they do in political matters, to the indoctrinational verve of their teachers."[31]

Skipping ahead a few years, Kirk wrote a column in July 1964 titled "Little Academic Tyrants." A student, Kirk insisted, has "a right to a certain professorial toleration of the student's private opinions; and a right to receive genuine instruction in a discipline, not to be the victim of secular indoctrination. . . . But certain academic gentlemen behave as squalid oligarchs, gauleiters of the classroom, whenever they discover a student who dares dissent, even silently, from their own secular dogmas."[32] In an unusually long contribution, heavy with sarcasm even by *National Review* standards, a scholar named Susan Buck complained about having been fired from her job at Hunter College for her conservative views. "Hunter College is clearly a dictatorship of the Liberal elite," she began.[33] Similarly, as New Left activities began heating up, former communist turned conservative Will Herberg wrote an article charging that a new development was evident in American academic life: "The fact of the matter is that a sizable group of our professors do not like to think of themselves simply as scholars and teachers in their various fields. They yearn to be recognized as *philosophes* in the eighteenth-century sense, that is, as self-appointed journalistic publicity makers, free-wheeling policymakers responsible to no one and to nothing, except their own good opinion of themselves."[34] It was these professors—part of a dangerous "New Estate"—who were abandoning their academic responsibilities to take part in teach-ins around the country.

But it was not only in the pages of *National Review,* or in the other, less influential conservative magazines that popped up around the same time, that one could find conservatives attacking liberal professors; throughout the 1960s critique of the professoriate was a mainstay of conservative political discourse. Two examples will have to suffice. In his book *America's Political Class Under Fire* (2003), historian David A. Horowitz (no relation) notes that even after the "loyalty" issues of the McCarthy era passed, conservatives expended great energy chastising the "knowledge elite": "an assortment of government planners, public administrators, social service providers, policymakers, academic specialists, and knowledge professionals comprising an influential segment of the civic intelligentsia."[35] As Horowitz observes (with many others), the idea that in mid-twentieth-century America a New Class of knowledge workers was coming into being was embraced as fervently by thinkers on the right, such as Hayek and neoconservative Irving Kristol, as by social scientists on the left. But it was not only intellectuals who found the New Class concept, and the ideas surrounding it, meaningful. In a chapter on the politics of race, Horowitz shows how transformative political figures like Goldwater, Phyllis Schlafly, and George Wallace depicted the civil rights movement, ensuing government efforts at desegregation, and President Lyndon Johnson's "Great Society" program as attempts by a predatory and corrupt group of northeastern intellectual and policy elites to push the country in directions that ran contrary to its nature and that would lead ultimately to socialism and an infringement of individual liberty. These policy developments, in other words, were not simply bad on their own terms—threatening, in the view of conservatives, to destabilize the social order and undermine American traditions—but were also to be resisted for their antidemocratic origins. "By offering to rally ordinary people behind an antielitist banner that borrowed from Franklin Roosevelt as well as the lesser known John Bricker," Horowitz argues, "Goldwater [and other politicians] restored populist conservatism to a central role in the Republican Party."[36]

Professors were not the only ones implicated in these attacks, but they took center stage in Reagan's 1966 gubernatorial campaign in California, my second example.[37] Unrest at Berkeley began with the free speech movement in 1964, when police arrested some eight hundred protestors. As noted in Chapter 3, Reagan made the restoration of campus order a key component of his campaign. As he saw it, the insistence by student protesters that they were exercising their rights to free speech and to untrammeled academic inquiry did nothing to change the fact that they were behaving lawlessly, in ways that disrupted university life and violated the moral standards and expectations of California taxpayers, who were footing the bill for the UC system. "What in heaven's name," Reagan asked, "does 'academic freedom' have to do with rioting, with anarchy, with attempts to destroy the primary purpose of the university which is to educate our young people?"[38]

Reagan did not stop at blaming students. As historian Gerard DeGroot has argued, on the basis of archival research with internal campaign documents, Reagan

> recognized that he had little to gain from merely lambasting militant students. If, however, those students could be shown to be supported, or "indoctrinated," by radical, or "Communist" professors, the problem could be magnified, and his call for tough action would seem more appropriate. And if the radical professors were defended—in the name of academic freedom—by liberal colleagues, then the list of enemies would grow conveniently longer. The UC administration could, in turn, be blamed for failing to uphold "the high and noble purpose of the University" and [Democratic Governor Pat] Brown for his "policy of appeasement . . . dictated by political expediency in this election year." From such small acorns of innuendo did the big oak of a political campaign grow.[39]

After he was elected, Reagan tried to make heads roll on campus, forcing the ouster of UC president Clark Kerr before he came up against the limits of gubernatorial power in matters of university governance.

What is the significance of the fact that conservative critics of the liberal professoriate could be found throughout the late 1950s and 1960s, when the contemporary American conservative movement was still gathering strength? The possibility I will consider momentarily that such criticism played an important role for the movement, helping its ideologues carve out a coherent collective identity for conservatism. But the implication with more immediate relevance is that while conservative advocacy groups in the 1980s and since have certainly been busy pushing the anti–liberal professor line, it is not as though these groups invented it, and not as though social and political circumstances of recent years uniquely brought it about.

Third and finally, Schrecker and others who emphasize elite influence err by depicting the conservative intellectuals and activists involved in critique of the professoriate as puppets of more powerful forces in the conservative community. The best way to think about people like Horowitz or Daniel Pipes or Balch is as "moral entrepreneurs," and this requires that we take seriously their role in developing the organizations around them and calling attention to the issues that grieve them. The term *moral entrepreneur* was coined by sociologist Howard Becker. It refers to "crusading reformers" who are "profoundly disturb[ed]" by "some evil" in the world and devote their lives to eradicating it.[40] Horowitz, Pipes, and Balch fit this image well; Balch can stand as an example.

Balch was trained as a political scientist, receiving his PhD from Berkeley in 1972. He began his career teaching at John Jay College in New York. A moderate liberal when he started, he soon came to believe that the faculty at John Jay was more left-leaning than at other schools and that many of his colleagues were bent on laying the groundwork for radical social change by trying to form their students into a class-conscious proletariat. This worried him greatly, he told me. He was beginning to see the "manipulative" aspects of radical politics and increasingly viewed the left as utopian, not clear about its own interests, not willing to be held accountable. Besides, even in the post-1960s era, the classical aim of education—the transmission of the heritage of civilization from generation to generation—remained important, and he believed politics in the classroom undermined it.

Around this time, Balch had an epiphany while reading sociologist Paul Hollander's 1981 book *Political Pilgrims*.[41] The book tells the story of intellectuals—academics, writers, and others—who traveled to communist societies like the USSR and Cuba only to come back entranced and oblivious to the atrocities committed there. Hollander's goal in writing was to lessen the appeal of this sort of "magical thinking" on the part of the intelligentsia (Hollander's phrase, although it was no more unique to him than to Joan Didion). With Hollander and French sociologist Raymond Aron, whose similarly themed *The Opium of the Intellectuals* had been translated into English in the late 1950s, Balch was coming to see the intelligentsia as having betrayed the cause of freedom.[42] The book was a turning point in Balch's life (at least in his retrospective account of his political development). He was "tremendously moved by it," he told me, and "felt like [he] had to do something" about the problem Hollander had identified and that seemed so clearly evident around him at John Jay. He set to work.

By this time Balch had become a subscriber to a neoconservative newsletter called *Contentions,* which was published by Midge Decter, the conservative writer and wife of Norman Podhoretz. Balch got the idea to approach Decter to find out whether there were other academics in the New York area on her mailing list. He thought he might call them up, see whether their views about contemporary academic life were similar to his own, and ask whether they would join with him in doing whatever could be done to stand up to the academic left and urge a restoration of traditional academic ideals. Decter gladly shared her list, and Balch had a series of lunches with the professors on it, people like conservative humanist (and one time New York gubernatorial candidate) Herbert London, literary scholar Carol Iannone, and humanist Peter Shaw. Balch found common ground with these scholars, and they soon started a newsletter of their own.

In Balch's recollection, it took about two years before the group received its first outside funding, with which they held a conference. Two years later they held another conference. Finally, about five years in, they got their first truly significant grant, from the Smith Richardson Foundation.[43] The grant was big enough that it enabled Balch to take a leave of absence from John Jay, open a small office, and hire a secretary. Things picked up from there: the group, originally called the Campus Coalition for Democracy, changed its name to the National Association of Scholars to signal that it was interested only in academic matters; a journal was founded; sympathetic academics from around the country, including some liberals and neoconservatives upset by the academic consequences of the 1960s, were encouraged to become members and take part in the conversation; and, in a period when conservative philanthropies were flush with cash and some were willing to give, more grants were secured. Balch left his academic post and devoted himself full time to advocacy.

In the course of his work, Balch has interacted with many conservative elites: foundation representatives, wealthy businesspeople, politicians, pundits, people like Lynne Cheney. But while it is true that NAS would never have gotten off the ground without elite backing, and while it is not a grassroots organization, any more than Students for Academic Freedom is, it is also true that it would not have existed without the entrepreneurialism, commitment, and energy of Balch. In no version of the NAS's history that I have been able to reconstruct could conservative elites be said to have willed it into being.[44] Nor has the sense of moral outrage that motivated Balch and his early collaborators diminished as the organization has changed hands. When I asked Peter Wood, Balch's successor, to explain how he became involved with the issue of higher education reform, he told this story:

> I had a rather traumatic experience in my first weeks of college. And that was some form of strike called by the black student association at Haverford. Haverford is a Quaker College and the black student association chose a tactic of saying that they were going to take a vow of silence and would not speak to any white person until their grievance was addressed. And they also wouldn't say what their grievances were. Their original statement said we'd have to look to ourselves to answer that question. . . . In the days that followed, I had my first encounter with . . . mass hysteria. I saw many students my age or slightly older—many white students—publicly accusing themselves of . . . what we would call hate crimes. . . . They paraded around campus with bed sheets with blood—red blood on them denouncing themselves as racist.
>
> This went on for several days and then we were assembled in the meeting hall for the campus, Roberts Hall. And I guess that was a horribly hot October day. The Quaker tradition

kicked in that we were not going to leave the hall until consensus had been reached; consensus meaning no dissenting
voices here, whatsoever. And what was sought was a kind of
general agreement that all the whites were racist and that the
institution was institutionally racist. At which point, if we all
agreed to that, we would be permitted to disaggregate and go
our ways. So I guess in the fall of 1971—though I didn't have
these words for it—I had a face-to-face encounter which I
later learned to call "political correctness." I went in relatively
short order from being kind of passive leftist to someone who
had real doubts about the spirit of freedom of thought and
freedom of conscience that might exist within a community
that defines itself on the basis of these supposedly liberating
principles.

This sense of having experienced the academic or student left as
a personal affront is common among conservative activists; it too
fits poorly with a portrayal of them as ideological mercenaries in
the employ of the power elite.[45] An alternative explanation for
mobilization against the liberal professoriate—one that can account for the passions of the campaign's moral entrepreneurs,
alongside the inconsistency of elite support and the history of conservative complaints—is in order.

✴

If you want to understand the origins of the twenty-first-century
campaign against the liberal professoriate, you have to understand
why conservatives like Buckley were engaged in a similar campaign in their day. Some of the anger that *National Review* authors
directed at left-leaning academics reflected the same impulses and

strategic calculations that sustained McCarthyism: the sense that the nation was under threat during the cold war; the view that the ranks of the American left were filled with communists or former communists who were either outright traitors or simply not to be trusted, especially with the impressionable minds of youth; and the awareness that even if there was a meaningful difference between communists and liberals, the distinction could be blurred to good political effect. Buckley, after all, was one of McCarthy's most vigorous defenders, coauthoring in 1954 (with Brent Bozell, his brother-in-law) *McCarthy and His Enemies,* which a reviewer for the *New York Times* appropriately described as "the most extraordinary book yet to come forth in the harsh bibliography . . . of 'McCarthyism,'" given its point-by-point defense of some of McCarthy's most outlandish claims.[46] However, *most* of the criticisms of academia that appeared in *National Review* did not allege subversion per se by professors, and this was particularly the case from the 1960s onward. What lay behind the alternative lines of critique that Buckley and his collaborators pursued?

First, as someone intensely committed to invigorating the conservative movement, Buckley took seriously the notion that he had to engage the American left in a war of ideas. Intellectuals, he believed, play vital roles in politics by articulating conceptions of the good and theories of the world that may filter down to average people and shape their political predilections, through their direct educative functions, and as advisors who sometimes have the ears of policy makers and politicians. As Kirk put it in 1962 in a regular column he wrote called "From the Academy," "Today's lectures in the classroom become tomorrow's slogans in the street."[47] The American professoriate, Buckley and his colleagues felt, had in recent decades strongly backed the cause of liberalism not simply in terms of professors' personal political commitments but also in their behavior in the public sphere. Given these beliefs, going after liberal academics was an entirely natural thing for them to do.

Indeed Buckley's assumptions about the importance of the intelligentsia to the American left were not without some basis in fact. On the one hand, the 1950s and 1960s were decades of major expansion in the American college and university sector. Expansion of the nonacademic intellectual class was almost as large, fueled by the growth of government bureaucracies and the cultural consumption needs of an increasing number of educated, white-collar workers, which created new markets for journalists, writers, and others.[48] As creators and disseminators of ideas, intellectuals were playing a more significant role in American life than ever before.

On the other hand, many intellectuals at the time really were on the left and lent their services to liberal causes. To give one example, academics and intellectuals had been key supporters of Henry Wallace's Progressive Party campaign for the presidency in 1948. Academic Wallacites included Rexford Tugwell, the "brains trust" economist who had taken a position at the University of Chicago after a term serving as the appointed governor of Puerto Rico; Harvard astronomer Harlow Shapley; and Harvard literature professor F. O. Matthiessen. Support for Wallace, it is true, was a minority position within academe, despite an article he wrote in the *Annals of the American Academy of Political and Social Science* making a case for his campaign. Lazarsfeld and Thielens's survey data make this clear.[49] More anecdotally, many influential professors came out against Wallace, including Harvard economist John Kenneth Galbraith and Harvard historian Arthur Schlesinger Jr., charging that his calls for peace with the Soviets meant that he was doing their bidding. But these critiques, issued in conjunction with the work that scholars like Galbraith and Schlesinger were doing for the recently formed liberal organization Americans for Democratic Action, were as much about the need for unity among liberals as anything else: academic critics of Wallace were every bit as enthusiastic as he was about continuing the program of New Deal liberalism and ensuring civil rights for blacks.[50]

When civil rights issues gained even more prominence a few years later, academics and intellectuals once again stepped forward to act on behalf of liberal ideals. Gunnar Myrdal's *An American Dilemma,* written with the support of the Carnegie Foundation, had come out in 1944, helping to convince academics (as well as many others) who might have been on the fence that civil rights was an essential national goal. Later, academics like Horace Mann Bond, Kenneth Clark, John A. Davis, John Hope Franklin, Mabel Smythe, and C. Vann Woodward were tapped by the NAACP to support its efforts in *Brown v. Board of Education* by writing briefs and providing expert testimony, including testimony about the psychological effects of segregation on black children. In the early 1960s the Southern Nonviolent Coordinating Committee, a more radical organization, saw the value in recruiting both college students and scholars for their efforts. Historian Staughton Lynd, the son of sociologists Helen and Robert Lynd, became coordinator of SNCC's "freedom schools," working closely with Howard Zinn. And in 1965 professors such as Richard Hofstadter, Walter Johnson, and C. Vann Woodward were among those who marched with Martin Luther King (whose activism was greatly influenced by his academic experiences as a graduate student at Boston University) to Montgomery.[51] While these efforts placed academic activists on the right side of history, to conservatives who opposed the civil rights movement they represented an abomination. The fact is, as David A. Horowitz (the historian) concludes, there *were* a great many intellectuals in the postwar period throwing their weight behind progressive efforts at social change, a group whose collective ideological work was helping to sustain and deepen American liberalism and keep conservatism from gaining ground. There is nothing all that surprising about Buckley's going after them: nefarious elite conspiracies or not, when academics seek to make their mark in the political arena, either directly or indirectly, they can expect to be attacked by some of their opponents. Such is politics, although it is also inevitable that Buckley's depictions of them would be overblown—partisan writers are not given to balance, nuance, and restraint.

But what explains the tenor of the attacks, specifically the fact that they were couched in a language of anti-elitism? A second factor is the rhetorical function that opposition to liberal professors, cast as representatives of the knowledge elite, played for the emerging conservative movement.

Historians of conservatism have noted that a key condition for the movement's getting off the ground was the formation of a collective identity capable of binding its various strands. In the post–World War II era, when the ideological foundations were being laid for later advances, different groups of conservatives could often be found at one another's throats, with the biggest debates breaking out between traditionalists and libertarians. Histories commonly observe that *National Review,* through the efforts of

Buckley and editor Frank Meyer, was instrumental in articulating a conception of conservatism capable of bridging some of these divides and enabling coalition building.[52] The "fusionist" philosophy developed by the magazine focused on what all American conservatives ostensibly had in common, including patriotism, opposition to collectivism, and a strong belief in the principles of federalism and local self-determination, as well as recognition of the value of Western, Christian civilization and an objective moral order. All this is right: had *National Review* with its fusionism not come along, the conservative movement would have been slower to coalesce.

But missing in these historical discussions is recognition of another point. The sociologist Jeffrey Alexander has argued that while much of politics revolves around material concerns, American politicians and other political actors are constrained at every turn by culture, by a deep code at the heart of American political discourse that identifies certain themes, values, and narratives as sacred and to be cherished, and others as profane and immoral.[53] Drawing on contemporary and historical materials, Alexander argues that this code centers around democracy. Whether they are on the left or the right, American political figures must find a way to wrap their beliefs, claims, and proposals around democratic ideals of freedom, self-governance, and equality if they are to gain traction with voters. In fact, argues Alexander, in a book about the 2008 presidential race, a significant part of any political campaign involves the effort by politicians to paint themselves in democratic hues and depict their opponents as somehow undemocratic.

Cultural constraints of this sort posed a major challenge for the emerging conservative movement, particularly in a historical context where many Americans habitually associated democratic values with liberalism or at least with the center-left. How could a movement that explicitly sought to defend the rich and to preserve long-standing social hierarchies against the ideals of egalitarianism avoid the charge that it was undemocratic? Buckley and other conservative intellectuals did so by painting restrictions on capitalist activity and attempts at mandating progressive social change in other areas as violations of liberty: the liberty of property holders—a category with which many Americans could identify in the prosperous 1950s—to do as they wanted with their property, including profit from it, and the liberty of local communities to continue with their cherished traditions, not least their religious traditions. This way of framing things gained considerable rhetorical force when it was paired with populist themes. In a recent article, sociologist Robert Jansen attempted to define populism in a manner that is useful to scholars of both the left and the right and who study populism in the United States and abroad. According to Jansen's definition, a style of political engagement can be considered populist if seeks to "mobilize . . . ordinarily marginalized social sectors into publicly visible and contentious political action, while articulating an anti-elite, nationalist rhetoric that valorizes ordinary people."[54] It is unclear whether postwar American conservatism meets Jansen's first criterion, although the mobilization of evangelicals in the 1960s and beyond would seem to be an example of bringing a previously marginalized group into the political fold. But Buckley and his colleagues did speak frequently in a language that sung the praises of ordinary Americans. It was precisely ordinary Americans who, in their depiction, found their liberty most threatened by collectivism and who would rally under the banner of conservatism to restore their rights and re-create a just social order. Hand in hand with this idea was the identification of an enemy of the people said to be lording power over them, an enemy the people would work to vanquish. Left populism found its enemy in economic elites. As cold war hysteria cooled, conservatives increasingly found theirs in liberal intellectuals and their allies in government, the press, and the judiciary said now not to be communists but to be leading the charge toward collectivism in other ways. Intellectual and cultural elites and their bankrupt ideas, claimed *National Review* authors, posed major threats to freedom.

Part of what is so remarkable about this is that elsewhere in *National Review* could be found articles that *championed* elitism, that sung the praises not just of the rich but of the conservative cultural elite. Buckley, like his wealthy oilman father, had been influenced by the writings of Albert Jay Nock, who described all those educated conservatives who defended individualism through the lonely night of New Deal statism as constituting a "remnant"; eventually they would be the ones to lead the country out of darkness. *National Review* was written for just this group, in a sophisticated and urbane style. In the end, though, that the magazine spoke out of both sides of its mouth on the populism question is perhaps not mysterious. The idea of a remnant might be useful for rallying a small and privileged cadre, but in its unadulterated form it could hardly provide the basis for a mass political movement.[55] Populist elitist bashing could, and *National Review* gave voice to both rhetorics.[56]

Savvy and strategic though Buckley and others in his circle were, it is doubtful that they consciously decided to target intellectuals in order to score populist points.[57] After all, Buckley had started doing so during his days writing for the *Yale Daily News,* before he sensed the wind of national political change. More likely is that the tactic, which built on established anti-intellectual tropes and on conservative populist themes that were bubbling up elsewhere, emerged from what amounted to experimental efforts by those in the *National Review* network at finding a collective identity for conservatism that would gain traction.[58] In other writing, Jansen has argued that populist mobilization should be viewed in terms of practices that political actors develop as they work through the practical problems and challenges that political life throws at them under particular social and historical conditions; these are practices that may not be carefully planned in advance by the social actors who enact them but that tend to be hammered out over time through experimentation and that may then become routinized if they prove successful.[59] This is an apt way of thinking about the language used by Buckley and those around him. Going on about the depravity of the liberal elite worked in the sense that it seemed to resonate for many readers of the magazine and segments of the broader public and helped to position conservatism—despite its origins in the remnant—as a democratic alternative to the liberal status quo.[60]

One aspect of this resonance demands particular attention. Chapter 3 mentioned the finding from Amy Binder and Kate Wood's research that opposition to the liberal professoriate is a common thread that helps unite many conservative collegians. It is not clear that this is any more the case now than it was in the late 1950s and early 1960s. *National Review*'s attacks on the professoriate may have rung especially true for college-educated conservatives at that time because they provided a language and a coherent narrative for understanding experiences they themselves could have had as students. During this buttoned-down period, scholars in the social sciences and the humanities were hardly preaching radicalism. But they may have been doing something that conservatives found every bit as insidious. Historian Andrew Jewett has argued that midcentury liberal social scientists and humanists, writing when overt partisanship in scholarship was very much frowned upon by the academic community, sometimes endeavored to "naturalize" their politics, smuggling their political commitments into their academic writing by arguing in one way or another that a left-leaning, pluralistic society and a left-leaning, pluralistic worldview were objectively good and healthy—as in the claims of Hofstadter, Adorno, and others—and that deviations from these ideals represented forms of degeneracy or abnormality.[61] This was not lost on smart conservative students who took social sciences and humanities courses only to find that on some occasions the material they were asked to read simply took for granted that their views were wrong, while implicitly characterizing them—and their families and friends—as immoral or psychologically flawed. *God and Man at Yale* was Buckley's first sustained attempt at expressing the grievances of young conservatives who felt mistreated during their college days. *National Review* critiques extended this effort, and the same themes and concerns were important in the early days of Young Americans for Freedom (YAF).[62]

Buckley's critiques of higher education, and those of his *National Review* colleagues, soon became staples of American conservative discourse. One way to think about this is with a concept developed by the historical sociologist Charles Tilly: "repertoires of contention." In his book *Popular Contention in Great Britain* (1995), Tilly argued that between 1758 and 1834, the manner in which British citizens went about making claims on those who held power—claims for more rights, for higher wages—underwent a fundamental shift. In the eighteenth century, Tilly discovered, "vengeance against moral and political offenders occupied a prominent place in the contention of ordinary people," while "local people and local issues, rather than nationally organized programs and parties, entered repeatedly into . . . collective confrontations."[63] By the early nineteenth century things were different. There was no less political agitation, but it now took a different form. More of it centered around pubs and coffeehouses, public meetings, rallies, and marches. Political associations that could register citizen complaints and petition Parliament grew in size and influence. More claims were national in scope. More or less spontaneous and isolated attacks on employers thought guilty of worker mistreatment gave way to coordinated turnouts and strikes. Violence was not uncommon, but it did not accompany contentious politics as often as before.

According to Tilly, these were not disconnected historical facts but signaled important changes in citizens' underlying "repertoires" for making claims: the routines, practices, and habits they typically employed as they articulated their grievances and went about pursuing redress. What brought about the shift? Tilly's basic answer is the rise of capitalism and the growing administrative capacity of the British state. As industry and Parliament loomed larger as centers of social power, citizens found that only through coordinated action could they make their demands heard. But repertoire change did not occur automatically in response to these pressures. As Tilly portrays it, in line with Jansen's account of the emergence of populist practices, it was an instance of collective learning born of struggle and trial and error.[64]

Buckley and those around him were important in shaping modern American conservatism's repertoire of contention, including its collective identity, the way it saw itself as a movement. Through the influence of *National Review,* YAF, and allied organizations, opposition to liberal academic elites became part of what it meant for a substantial number of conservatives to *be* conservative.[65] Built into the conservative repertoire at a foundational moment, this theme would echo in conservative thought and politics for generations to come, though with continual adaptations.

In the late 1960s its salience only increased amid campus unrest. We should not underestimate how troubling conservatives found such unrest to be. Reagan liked to claim he would never have made the disturbances at Berkeley a campaign issue had he not frequently been asked his thoughts about them while on the campaign trail. This may or may not be true, but there is no question that most conservatives regarded the student protests with abhorrence, particularly as their intensity increased near the end of the decade. For example, in his history of YAF, Gregory Schneider notes that "growing radicalism on campus, such as the siege of Columbia University and the University of Wisconsin's 'Dow Days' riots during the spring of 1968, pointed to a need to resist student activism. A breakdown in authority and the fear of revolution gripped the air as classes resumed in the fall of 1968; the campus was more politicized than ever before, and a hard-core active Left was making inroads among formerly apathetic students disenchanted about the war, the draft, and the growing oppressiveness of American society and government. For the next several years, YAF would turn to combat the Left on campus."[66] YAF antiradicalism was particularly strong in California, Schneider reports, given that it had Reagan's backing and the fact that the New Left had been so active on campuses there. Standing up for law and order, conservative students in California wore buttons in support of S. I. Hayakawa, the "embattled" president of San Francisco State, and at least temporarily overcame their factional differences to denounce leftist students, their faculty supporters, and liberal campus administrators who, in their view, had not been as courageous as Hayakawa in trying to stem the tide of dissent.

But it was not only conservative students who felt scandalized. So did a great many conservative professors, according to Ladd and Lipset's data, who objected to both the goals of student protest and the protestors' tactics of educational disruption. Some political and economic elites on the right were equally incensed, clearly. The Powell memo discussed earlier provides one indication of this; other evidence is not hard to come by. An article about the Olin Foundation by historian Jennifer de Forest, for instance, notes that the organization's commitment to higher education reform grew out of the experiences of the 1960s. Founder John Olin, who had inherited his father's munitions fortune,

> matured into an activist philanthropist in 1969 in response to events at Cornell University, his alma mater, to which both he and his father gave generous donations. That year a group of black student protesters occupied the student union building. Pictures of the student leader holding a shotgun and wearing a bandolier filled with ammunition appeared on the front pages of newspapers nationwide. American conservatives were infuriated when Cornell's president not only negotiated with the students but also absolved them of individual responsibility for damaged property. In reaction to these events, the 78-year-old Olin decided to focus his giving on promoting conservatism in American higher education. In

this way he hoped to leverage his funds, as he put it, to check "the creeping stranglehold that socialism" had gained over America.[67]

The 1960s were also a spur to the philanthropy of the Bradley Foundation. Michael Joyce, its entrepreneurial president during its most active years of giving—the mid-1980s to the early 1990s, after Rockwell International purchased the Allen-Bradley Company in Milwaukee, infusing the organization with cash—had been converted to the right after thinking about what he saw as the failure of 1960s-era social policies.[68] That conservative students, academics, some elites, and rank-and-file voters often blamed the left-leaning faculty for encouraging student radicalism—not a logically necessary move, given that, as Ladd and Lipset's data also showed, a reasonably high percentage of liberal academics too disagreed with student protest tactics—testifies to the influence of National Review's framing of the situation.

How does all this relate to the most recent period of conservative critique? In one sense, there is nothing more surprising about Horowitz or Pipes or any other conservative commentator going after liberal academics than there is about Buckley going after them. Academia is a strongly left-leaning occupational group, and its members are active politically. What is more, as Chapter 5 observed, some number of social scientists and humanists today, freed from the constraints of their midcentury predecessors by scientific/intellectual movements that sprang up in the 1960s, 1970s, and 1980s, explicitly bring their politics into their academic work and claim strong intellectual justification for doing so. At the same time, some faculty research, while not political in nature, draws factual conclusions with which conservatives disagree. In this context, it would be surprising sociologically if conservative commentators did *not* go after academics (which is not to condone conservatives' behavior).

Still, the intensity of recent attacks is noteworthy, as is their social organizational basis. How should we explain the drumbeat of criticism coming from the NAS, ACTA, the David Horowitz Freedom Center, the Center for the American University, and so on?

Schrecker is not wrong to highlight the relevance of a greatly expanded infrastructure for conservatism in the 1980s and beyond. But there is a better way of explaining its role. Chapter 4 offered a thumbnail sketch of the sociological approach to the study of organizations known as organizational ecology. Just as that approach can be used to make sense of higher education, so too has it been used to leverage an understanding of politics. For example, sociologists who study movements for social change have noted the common tendency for successful movements to transform themselves over time into nonprofit advocacy organizations, or what are sometimes called "social movement organizations" (SMOs). Scholars have used the organizational ecology framework to identify the social conditions that make it possible for SMOs to arise and acquire the resources needed to survive, and have considered such issues as how the appearance of multiple SMOs, sometimes competing with one another for supporters, financial resources, and influence, can constrain the activity of any one of them, with implications for success and organizational longevity.[69] The framework also provides a fruitful way of thinking about American conservatism.

The best way to understand the conservative movement as it took shape in the last third of the twentieth century—and as it continues to exist today—is to see it as comprising a complex ecological field of political organizational activity consisting of the Republican Party at the state and national levels, politicians and political operatives, conservative donors and philanthropies, political action committees, lobbyists, conservative media organizations, religious organizations and educational institutions, and a wide variety of think tanks, advocacy groups, and voluntary associations. Different elements of the movement sometimes act in a co-ordinated fashion, but this is a contingent outcome that must be achieved, as there are a great many centers of activity, with different interests, commitments, ideologies, and beliefs lying behind each.

There was indeed a growth of conservative war of ideas–type institutions during this period. But this was not simply because, in response to the Powell memo and to the social upheavals of the 1960s and 1970s, conservative elites worked to create new institutions of ideology production to better serve their cause. After all, while conservative think tanks and advocacy groups multiplied then, so too did liberal and nonideological ones (although not at the same rate as their conservative counterparts).[70] Another important factor in their expansion, as political scientists Theda Skocpol and Paul Pierson have argued, was the dramatic growth of the American state, whose increasing size and power after World War II—a function of exigencies of governance as much as ideology—made it a more important stake than ever in political struggles, leading to a proliferation of all manner of organizations concerned to steer it in one way or another. This was a key structural change providing a historical backdrop to Powell's call and to the rise of conservatism generally.[71]

Specialized conservative advocacy organizations that took on the liberal professoriate arose as the conservative field became reconfigured in this context not because, at least in the cases I have examined, their founding was directed from above, but because the midlevel moral entrepreneurs behind them—each of whom connected in a deep personal way to the line of critique Buckley pioneered—sensed that they could carve out niches for themselves on the conservative landscape by becoming specialists in the rhetoric of professorial attack that had already become a well-established part of the conservative repertoire. They were able to get the funding and support and airtime that they needed to operate because a distinct subset of conservative philanthropic leaders, donors, and media figures were as wedded to the identity Buckley had helped forge for the movement, and as keen to take on liberal professors, as they were. Strategy and interests no doubt mattered here, but so too, we may theorize, did beliefs, personal experiences (such as being a loyal Cornell alumnus), social relationships, and moral commitments.[72] An additional reason support may have been forthcoming from some, though not all, quarters is that the organizations these entrepreneurs started performed important latent functions for the conservative movement (i.e., functions that are sociologically identifiable but not generally obvious to the social actors involved). In conjunction with other conservative groups attacking the "liberal" judiciary and the press, they continued to shore up the movement's populist credentials by identifying an elite to which conservatives could stand opposed—a task that grew in importance as populist elements within the Republican Party gained even more prominence. They continued to provide a vocabulary for conservative college students (and their parents) to express frustration with their higher education experiences. And they helped to call into question the credibility of academic knowledge, which made the growing number of conservative intellectuals in think tanks working on topics like taxes or energy policy or financial deregulation seem more reliable and trustworthy by comparison. Inasmuch as the conservative movement has been able to accommodate and support rhetorical efforts that have these latent effects, it can be considered not merely a field of action but also an emergent complex system—capable, on occasion, of functioning in a more or less spontaneous fashion to ensure its own survival and prosperity. In sum, as the conservative field came into being, moral entrepreneurs like Horowitz and Balch saw the opportunity to advance what they saw as important political goals—and at the same time to make new and exciting careers for themselves—by becoming full-time critics of the professoriate, in effect professionalizing an activity that had previously been carried out by other conservatives on a somewhat more ad hoc basis.[73] The organizations they founded, each of which came at the problem from a different angle, took on lives of their own and acted as hubs connecting a range of figures with complaints against liberal professors.[74]

That there may be important latent functions served by the work of people like Horowitz helps to explain, among other things, the general pattern of support for anti–liberal–professor rhetoric one sees in the public. What distinguishes those Americans who have bought into criticism of the professoriate is not first and foremost a set of sociodemographic characteristics (although, again, critics are more likely to be white, male, less well-educated, evangelicals) but instead identification with conservative populism generally, which takes different forms depending on levels of education and other factors.[75] Consider, from the interviews in Wisconsin and Colorado, two representative cases of conservatives who believe liberal bias in academe represents a serious problem. The first is Elsie, a sixty-two-year-old retiree living in central Wisconsin who went to college for two years but never received her associate's degree. She is a former office manager who describes herself as somewhat conservative and a political Independent. She is a mainline Protestant but does not attend church regularly. When we asked whether she thought that public universities should be able to dismiss professors who espouse radical views, she said she did. "This is America," she told us. "We are Americans and we are Christians and these are our views . . . and if you are going to be a communist go to a communist country and teach. . . . If you are going to teach radical Muslim beliefs then you should be in that country teaching them." Professors who hold such views, Elsie said, "are a danger."

Yet in the course of the interview with Elsie, it became clear that she did not think most professors are either communists or defenders of radical Islam. When we asked her whether the term *radical* describes the typical college or university professor, she said it did, but her reason for saying so was that in her view professors were trying to cram their liberal—not communist or Islamicist—politics down students' throats. "I don't think [professors] are teaching tolerance," Elsie said. "They are not teaching to express both viewpoints. . . . It seems like when I see Berkeley on TV and I see the University of [Wisconsin] . . . there is no room for diversity. It is my way or the highway." What really seemed to make Elsie

294 Why Conservatives Care

mad about liberal professors is not their politics—as long as they are not extremists, she said later, "I don't think that anybody should be fired solely on their beliefs"—but that they are using their positions of influence in society to advance their political interests, and in the course of doing so are trying to get ordinary people to believe things that simply are not true. Many professors, Elsie stated, "are . . . politicizing things instead of just teaching things. They are expressing opinions instead of just expressing what is history." Elsie's prime example of this is Ward Churchill, who, she said, "was paid $5,000 to come to the University of Wisconsin and speak, plus all of his expenses, when he didn't speak anything that was truthful." There were also some professors at Madison who she had heard were teaching things that were "absolutely off the wall . . . teaching that there wasn't a Holocaust. It is ridiculous." (There are in fact no Holocaust-denying faculty members at UW-Madison; the university is a rich center for research on Judaism.) Equally problematic, in her view, was that many liberal professors require their students to agree with their politics in class. It is fine to have a classroom debate about the war in Iraq, Elsie said, but she had heard stories in the conservative media of professors marking their students down unless they agreed with their antiwar stances, which she saw as a major abuse of power. Elsie's anger at elites is not restricted to her views of the professoriate; for example, she also told us she does not "have a lot of faith in our politicians today" since "they will tell you anything you want to hear as long as they get elected." But it appears to be the frame through which she interprets the controversy over liberal bias in higher education. It is not unreasonable to suppose that the liberal bias issue has stitched her more tightly to the right.

A slightly different set of concerns was flagged by Mark, a sixty-one-year-old Colorado resident who works in sales and holds a bachelor's degree in computer science. Mark, a Republican, describes himself as somewhat conservative. He launched into a complaint about liberal bias early on in the interview, when we asked him to explain why he does not have much confidence in higher education institutions—despite the fact that he, his wife, and both of his children have college degrees. Colleges and universities, he said, "tend to be cloistered environments" in which "there is a lot of pressure brought on . . . faculty and students to conform in their thinking." In many institutions, he continued, there is a "general intolerance for conservatives. There are a few schools that are oriented that way, but most aren't." When we asked him to give us some examples, he mentioned how when "David Horowitz was invited to speak at [Boston College] he was shouted down."[76] As Mark seemed to see it, echoing themes that college-educated conservatives have articulated for decades, intolerance among academics for conservative students is not just unfair but is fundamentally undemocratic, since it involves a privileged group using its position for political gain. This, Mark thought, has had disastrous effects: "I think that history, economics, political science, et cetera are very important fields of study and political bias in these fields completely distorts the subject matter of what is being taught." "History is always open to interpretation as well as economics," he said. But too often, in the hands of liberal academics, knowledge "is not being presented in a balanced way," and in these fields common sense is forced to take a backseat to political fantasy. Mark was genuinely angry about this, and it does not take a strategic genius to recognize that having a lot of Marks out there is generally a good thing for the right.

Nor are Elsie's and Mark's cases unique. In eight of the other Wisconsin and Colorado interviews research subjects spontaneously described professors as elitist, arrogant, haughty, or over-privileged, sounding conservative populist tropes.[77] Turning to studies with larger sample sizes, although the opinion poll Simmons and I conducted contained no direct measure of conservative populism, it did contain measures, as noted in Chapter 6, of levels of confidence in several American institutions. Relative to those unconcerned about liberal bias in the academy, respondents who were concerned tended to have more confidence in the military, in organized religion, and in the White House under President Bush and less confidence in the press—as well as, of course, less confidence in higher education.[78] This is just what one would expect to find among people with strong nationalist and religious commitments who have doubts about the knowledge elite. Along similar lines, a 2012 survey by the Pew Research Center for the People and the Press found that among Republicans and Republican-leaning Independents, the view that colleges are having a negative effect on "the way things are going in the country" was substantially higher among Tea Party supporters—a group committed to conservative populist rhetoric if there ever was one—than among those who disagreed with the Tea Party or had no opinion about it (47% versus 28%).[79] To be sure, not everyone in the public who is critical of liberal bias in the academy is a conservative populist voter; some people just think it is a problem, on less ideologically charged grounds, that there is an imbalance of liberals and conservatives on the faculty, while a number of well-educated conservatives who shun populism are equally critical, seeing in the intellectual trends spawned by post-1960s academic leftism a perversion of the cultural heritage of the West. But subscription to the critique seems most common among those with conservative populist sensibilities.

Why does conservative populism resonate for a substantial minority of Americans, especially working-class and lower-middle-class white men and evangelicals? Status politics may be part of the answer, but another part has to do with meaning. With the help of the conservative movement, religious institutions, and the culture industry, many whites from the lower echelons of the class structure (men in particular and retirees) have come to subscribe to a collective identity that depicts them as virtuous carriers of traditional American values—including the value of hard work and of pulling yourself up by your bootstraps—in an increasingly corrupt world. Freeloaders of all kinds figure as threats here, but first and foremost as symbolic threats to a worldview born as much of a felt need to maintain a sense of distinctiveness, dignity, solidarity, and connection with the past as anything else.[80] Conservative populism, with its disparagement of liberal elites, portrayed as apologists for moral laxity and as architects of a new and unsavory moral order, has become the natural form of political expression for people with such views.

True though it may be that anger at the professoriate has been useful for conservatism, there is something quite ironic about all the effort the right has put into attacking academia for being politically lopsided and biased. Although one of the aims of this criticism has been to open up space in the university for conservative thinkers and ideas, it is likely that decades of antiprofessorial rhetoric have made academia seem an even less desirable home for young conservatives than it would otherwise be. Elsie and

Mark would not have encouraged their children to become professors. There is, then, an interesting relationship between the social processes discussed in Chapter 3, having to do with the reproduction of academic liberalism, and those considered in this chapter. Academic liberalism has multiple roots, but to some extent conservatives' criticism of higher education for being politically one-sided has become a self-fulfilling prophecy, reinforcing the occupation's preexisting reputation for liberalism and steering conservatives into other fields, despite rearguard actions by organizations like ISI to nurture conservative students' interests in academic careers.[81]

Finally, what accounts for the fact that while conservatives have been attacking the professoriate for a long while, the intensity of such criticism ebbs and flows, varying not just between Buckley's day and our own but within the most recent period as well, reaching peaks like that seen around 2005? In a classic essay, political scientist Anthony Downs wrote in 1972 of an "issue-attention cycle" in American politics involving "heightening public interest and then increasing boredom with major issues."[82] Downs's focus was on social problems; he saw the primary factor accounting for the inevitable drop in attention to a problem to be public recognition of the difficulty of tackling it. Yet his general point applies to cultural-political controversies as well: no issue will remain on Americans' radar screens in the same fashion indefinitely. Over time, social and political changes render some controversies irrelevant. Others simply lose energy as all the arguments, pro and con, and the related stories and claims are rehearsed ad nauseam.[83] Conservatives running organizations that attack liberal professors or working alongside such organizations have had to navigate issue-cycle dynamics. They have found it harder to get coverage for their efforts when other, rhetorically non-complementary controversies have captivated the nation's attention. And they have run up against significant constraints after a given wave of attacks begins to lose energy, as the political correctness controversy did by the mid-1990s and as the debate over liberal bias per se did by 2008 or so.

Higher education journalists I interviewed were keenly aware of such cycles and contributed to their operation by giving diminishing coverage to conservative efforts after they perceived a given cycle had run its course. For example, Scott Jaschik, the editor of *Inside Higher Ed.*, told me in 2008 that he had closely covered the liberal bias controversy because there had been so much "public debate over . . . [the] bias issue." "At the same time," he continued, "because of that, there's so much out there that there becomes a selectivity factor. And so for instance, when groups like David Horowitz's group started going around and checking voter registration at different college's faculties, it's interesting the first time. Then you hit a point where it's like—okay, so we've learned that the philosophy departments at all the Ivy League universities lean Democratic. Is it a shock that NYU's does too? And so then, you have sort of the flipside of all the interest—it's starting to say the same thing." Jaschik told me he was then getting several op-ed submissions a week weighing in on liberal bias or on the culture wars and higher education more generally, and that he was constantly being bombarded with press releases detailing relevant new studies or reports. Most of these he ignored, since, a few years into the controversy, they no longer seemed "fresh." Because conservative activists working on higher education have faced these constraints, they have had to reinvent their criticisms over time, focusing on newly emerging cultural themes or historical developments and taking advantage of whatever soft targets within academe may present themselves. Examples are the wave of postmodern theory that hit in the 1980s and 1990s, the excesses of which certainly made some academics look foolish, and the controversy surrounding Ward Churchill. In other instances, conservatives have worked to soften up targets, as happened with Beck's no-holds-barred treatment of Piven, which was denounced by the American Sociological Association as "demagoguery."[84]

Conclusion

In Chapter 3 I mentioned research from the 1960s showing that high school aspirations toward college completion are an important predictor of educational success and that working-class kids are less likely to aim for bachelor's degrees. To say that this research, spearheaded by University of Wisconsin sociologist William Sewell, has been influential among sociologists who study higher education would be a major understatement. Although many have found fault with the specifics of Sewell's approach, the broader insight developed in his work—that in a credential-based society higher education institutions may play inadvertent roles in perpetuating social inequality—has become the cornerstone of the entire subfield. Today the majority of sociologists of higher education grapple with questions such as: Why do college completion rates vary not just by class background but by race and ethnicity as well? What factors in childhood and adolescence (socialization by parents? neighborhood differences in school quality? peer group effects?) account for these differences? What are the consequences for people's long-term life chances of attending an elite college or university, and why, when institutions are formally committed to meritocracy in admissions, are students from higher social class backgrounds more likely to be admitted to elite schools? In short, as Mitchell Stevens, Elizabeth Armstrong, and Richard Arum observed in a recent review essay, the sociology of higher education has in many respects become the study of educational inequality.[1]

Without denying the importance of this research agenda, Stevens, Armstrong, and Arum argue that it is ultimately limiting. Colleges and universities are indeed linked with what sociologist Douglas Massey calls "the American stratification system," under some circumstances working to reproduce inequality while at other times serving as ladders to mobility.[2] But in sociological terms they are so much more: they are places where training for some of the most important technical occupations in American society takes place; settings in which millions of Americans each year undergo formative experiences (although not often, as I have argued, experiences in the classroom that fundamentally alter their political orientations); sites for the production of knowledge and culture and for the carrying forward of learned traditions; complex organizational entities; and more. "Sieve, incubator, temple, hub," say Stevens, Armstrong, and Arum. Higher education is all these things.

One way of reading this book is to see it as following Stevens, Armstrong, and Arum's call for a more expansive and ambitious sociology of higher education, one that would attend to the full range of higher education's social effects and functions. Specifically, the book has explored some of the connections between higher education and politics. This is not untrodden scholarly ground.[3] But one of my goals has been to show that the connections run deeper than previously recognized. This is so in that the occupation of professor—an occupation at the core of what higher education is about—is socially defined in relation to politics, while American political life would arguably be different if left/liberal views were not so highly concentrated in the professoriate, making it easier for conservatives to mount targeted attacks on the intellectual elite.

Beyond this general point, however, what are some of the specific implications of the claims advanced in this book, both for social science and for higher education? I address the question of implications in this conclusion. But before doing so, I review the book's main findings and arguments and discuss future avenues of research.

✴

Conservatives often portray the academy as a bastion of liberalism. In Chapter 1 I showed that they are essentially correct—with a few important caveats. Between 50% and 60% of American professors can be classified as some version of liberal in terms of self-perceptions and attitudes. When it comes to party preferences and voting, the academy is overwhelmingly Democratic. But to the observation that the professoriate is the most left-leaning of the major American occupations must be added that there are many fewer radicals in the academic ranks than some conservatives charge; that that there is an underappreciated center-left and moderate bloc in the professoriate; and that there are several equally if not more influential occupations that are bastions of conservatism. Also, there is real variation in political views across disciplines and disciplinary areas, while, contrary to some impressions, the academic profession has become only somewhat more liberal since the late 1960s. To formulate these claims, I drew on survey data and interviews with professors, tying them together with an alternative way of conceptualizing political orientation, one that highlighted political identities.

Chapter 2 considered some of the most common explanations offered by social scientists for the tendency of academics (and other intellectuals) to be on the left. Pierre Bourdieu argued this was a function of the ratio of cultural to economic capital held by intellectuals, whose firm command of high-status knowledge and taste and relatively empty pockets make it in their interests to denigrate and want to restrict the power of the business classes and to increase state spending. I argued, mostly on empirical grounds, that this explanation does not work well in the case of American professors, whose political views are typically formed before they start down an academic career track. Are professors made liberal by their exposure as students to so many years of schooling? While this may be the experience for some, the liberalizing effects of higher education ought not to be exaggerated. Perhaps the liberalism of professors is a result of value differences between liberals and conservatives? This explanation is also limited. Finally, while cognitive and personality differences might have some role to play, evidence I presented suggests that such differences do not explain the bulk of the phenomenon.

Chapter 3 laid out the alternative theory that Ethan Fosse and I developed: over the years academia has acquired such a strong reputation as a liberal occupation that many more liberal than conservative students form the aspiration to pursue an academic career, seeing it as a better fit with who they are politically. The chapter also offered a preliminary historical account of how the American academic profession developed its reputation for liberalism, becoming "politically typed" in the first place.

Chapter 4 sought to make sense of patterns in the distribution of political views among professors. Professors in the social sciences and humanities tend to be the most left-leaning, I argued, not because there is something intrinsic about these fields that makes them so but because over the years the distance between them and conservatively inclined sectors such as the military and the business world has enabled radically or liberally oriented scientific and intellectual movements to gain ground, rendering the moving content of these fields especially appealing to scholars on the left. Conservatives are less likely to be found at elite schools not because of bias or discrimination against them but because those conservatives who go against type to become academics often have lower levels of intellectual capital than their liberal peers. As for the uptick in academic liberalism seen since the 1960s, this is largely a function of the entry into academe of women influenced by the feminist movement, while recent declines in radicalism among younger professors stem from the paucity of other kinds of social movement activity on American college campuses during the 1980s and 1990s.

In Chapter 5, I used interview data to explore how professors in five fields—sociology, economics, literature, engineering, and biology—think about the role that politics should play in research and teaching. Sociologists and professors of literature tend to believe it is inevitable that politics will influence their research, although the majority of sociologists say it only influences their selection of research topic, not their findings. Very few professors in these two fields, or in the other three more objectivistic ones, express an interest in indoctrinating students politically. Still, a case can be made that politics does affect undergraduate instruction. Partly in consequence, liberal students are more apt to major in liberal fields, and conservatives in conservative ones, in a process that may be contributing at the margins to the polarization of the American electorate.

Chapter 6 turned to the major public controversy at present over liberal bias in the academy. I used data from a public opinion poll to call into question the claim that the controversy stems primarily from backlash against changes in American society or has its origins in post-9/11 decreases in public tolerance for dissent. Chapter 7 found problems too with the theory that the controversy is nothing more than a top-down, manufactured affair created by conservative elites. To be sure, some elites have been instrumental in backing the many organizations contesting liberal dominance in higher education. But those organizations are best explained as resulting from concerted efforts undertaken by midlevel moral entrepreneurs deeply attached to an antiprofessorial identity that became an established part of the conservative repertoire in the 1950s. That identity continues to thrive today and find resonance with conservative voters because it serves a number of latent functions for the conservative movement, including that of bolstering its populist credentials.

✦

Empirical research supports each of these arguments. But in the social sciences, even more than in the natural sciences, no single study on any topic can be definitive, and my book is based on a series of single studies, each focused on a different aspect of the professorial politics problem. What additional research could put the claims made here on even more solid empirical footing? The next steps for research involve more social description, further investigation of patterns of association among variables, and direct observation of social processes.

Regarding description, we could do with more data on what professors' politics are like. The Politics of the American Professoriate study may have been strong methodologically, but it is now seven years old. American (and world) politics have changed since the study was carried out, with issues of income inequality and fiscal austerity looming larger and the Republican Party more fractured than at any point in its recent history. Given the relative constancy of American professorial liberalism over the past half-century, as well as the tendency of partisan attachments to remain stable over the course of people's lives, one would not expect these changes to have dramatically altered the complexion of academic politics. But an updated survey would still be helpful, not least for what it might reveal about the proportion of center-lefters and moderates who, in the context of the economic downturn, may have been drawn into the progressive camp. Interviews with a wider array of professors could also be useful, shedding light on more fine-grained ideological differences and identity groupings than the six identified in Chapter 1.

The other major topic on which there is a need for additional descriptive research is the intersection of politics, research, and teaching. The interviews carried out for this book tell us something about this matter. But, as mentioned in Chapter 5, while these interviews give us a sense of how professors think and talk, we know little about their behavior. In what ways exactly do individual literary scholars bring their political commitments to bear on the research process? To what extent do economists do the same despite their protestations to the contrary? When academics say they make sure not to pressure students into accepting their own politics as gospel, what does that mean in practice? Do professors' views of their pedagogy on the "knowledge-politics problem" square with student perceptions? Close observational research would be needed to answer these and related questions.

Other descriptive data could help us understand better how politics colors professors' engagement in the public sphere, as well as the positions they stake out around university governance.

More work is necessary as well to confirm that the patterns of statistical association reported in this book—for instance, those found in my study with Fosse using General Social Survey data—hold up using other data sources, other ways of measuring key variables, and alternative statistical techniques. Especially important, in light of all the energy around political psychology at present, would be studies of the aspiration to become a professor and of graduate school attendance that are able to measure personality traits and cognitive characteristics in a more nuanced way than my data sources allowed. Studies with better measures of attitudes toward science and scientific reasoning are also in order. And, given how controversial it is likely to be, it would be good if future surveys of the professoriate could confirm the finding that conservative professors have lower levels of intellectual capital on average than liberal ones, including lower rates of doctoral degree holding, and that this goes a fair way toward accounting for their lesser presence in elite institutions.

Future research might also seek out more direct evidence of the many social processes that I have argued are at the core of professorial liberalism and conflict over it. Concerning the former, the theory of political typing puts heavy emphasis on perceptions by undergraduates of political fit with different occupations, as well as on processes of occupational imprinting and reinforcement. However, while there is circumstantial evidence that perceptions of fit matter, no one has done the kind of longitudinal study (with an interview-based or ethnographic component) that would be necessary to observe such perceptions operating in real time as they work to shape aspirations and life trajectories. More detailed historical work on how the academy acquired its reputation for liberalism would also be of value, as would further investigations of academic hiring practices, building on the audit study that Fosse, Joseph Ma, and I carried out and on the work of Christine Musselin.

On conflict over the professoriate, I offered an interpretation focused on the emergence of a distinctive repertoire for modern American conservatism and the eventual founding of advocacy organizations around elements of it. Although research on the right has flourished in recent years, little of this work has examined repertoires and their consequences for political ecology. Here too more inquiry, delving more deeply than I have been able to do into the history of conservatism and contention around academic freedom, would be worthwhile.

Finally, and cross-cutting this three-part classification of future lines of work, it would be good if research could place the claims advanced in this book into comparative perspective. I have said little about professorial politics in other countries—about the views of professors outside the United States, the processes that led to the formation of those views, and the extent of political conflict over the academy on other shores. To some sociologists, this may seem a serious omission, not least because there is a small but influential body of scholarship from the 1980s and 1990s exploring intellectuals' politics on a comparative basis.[4] The omission has been a conscious one, however, guided by a belief that the data requirements for mapping and explaining professorial politics are such that anything more than very preliminary comparative analyses are impossible at this juncture. A coordinated effort at surveying the political views of professors and other intellectuals in a number of different countries would help us overcome this problem and might, among other things, elucidate some of the broader social and historical conditions in the United States that serve as a backdrop to the dynamics I have outlined.

✴

Suppose, though, that once all this research is completed, the upshot is that the explanations developed in this book turn out to be largely correct. What would be the implications?

Let me begin by discussing three of special interest to sociologists. The first concerns the phenomenon of class politics. In all the work they have done to assess the degree to which people's positions in the social structure influence political preferences and voting, in the United States and elsewhere, scholars of class politics have never devoted much attention to the possibility that for members of some occupational groups job and politics may be linked not because of the "interests" associated with particular lines of work or because of workers' class backgrounds but because of processes of political typing and political self-selection of the sort described here for professors.[5] Most jobs are not politically typed. But if there were others beyond the professoriate that are this could have significant bearing on studies of politics and class. Preliminary analyses that my research assistants and I have carried out using HERI College Senior Survey data suggest that there are several career aspirations associated with student politics—associations that do not appear to be a result of differing levels of academic ability or job values. Beyond professor, these are, on the left, social worker, writer/journalist, and actor; on the right, clergy member, accountant, and military officer (and homemaker).[6] It would not be surprising if more sophisticated studies based on general population data turn up other politically typed fields. The proportion of voters in such occupations is likely not overwhelming, but neither is it likely negligible. Would estimates of the amount of class voting change if the distinctive nature of these occupations were brought to the fore? Would theories of class politics—of the processes at its heart—have to change as well, paying more attention to the contingent cultural and historical dynamics by which occupations become politically typed and their political reputations reinforced or remade over time? These are important questions for political sociologists to address.[7]

The second implication has to do with the sociology of knowledge. Chapter 5 noted that over the years some sociologists of knowledge have examined the significance for knowledge production of professors' political commitments but that much more work needs to be done on this topic. This could go well beyond my earlier call for studies of how individual academics bring their politics into their research and extend into analyses of how major trends in disciplines and subfields might be linked with professorial politics. To give just one example, throughout the 1980s and 1990s many sociologists resisted the argument that culture had a role to play in the intergenerational transmission of poverty, thinking that to acknowledge this would be to blame the victim, as in anthropologist Oscar Lewis's well-known "culture of poverty" thesis.[8] Today resistance appears to be softening, and one of the explanations sometimes offered is that the new generation of sociologists is not as partisan as its predecessor. Is that claim right? What could we likewise learn about intellectual change and ideational paths taken or not taken in anthropology, political science, or history, say, if we put the politics of academics front and center in our analyses? Intellectual historians sometimes do this, of course, as do academics writing about their own lives.[9] But sociologists of knowledge have yet to do so in a systematic way, except when they depict academics as ideologues expressing the veiled "political" interests of their class, race, gender, or sexual orientation.[10] Were they to focus more on conventional politics, sociologists of knowledge might give us insight into a powerful set of social mechanisms guiding and constraining the evolution of academic thought, though surely more so in some fields than in others.[11]

Third and finally, if the arguments I have made are correct, they help to highlight one of the ways Americans are deeply divided over politics—that is, with respect to their occupational choices. Yet people's social identity as liberal or conservative, and variants of these, may influence more than just what jobs they take and who they punch a ballot for in the voting booth. Evidence from political science and other fields suggests that politics may also affect where people consider living, who they become friends with, their cultural consumption habits, and more.[12] To date, sociology has not been much concerned with liberalism or conservatism as identities with significant consequences for people's lives and life choices, aside from studies of those on the far left or far right. What do these ways of thinking of oneself politically and of positioning oneself symbolically in relation to others mean to Americans? How do these meanings vary by region, class, race, gender, and other factors? Where and how do people acquire mainstream political identities, for what proportion of the population are they salient, what are the everyday practices associated with them, and how exactly do they thread through social interaction? These are vital issues for sociology to take up in a divisive political era, building on but moving beyond work by political scientists on political socialization, and I hope that my book may nudge the discipline in the direction of doing so.

Beyond implications for sociology, though, do the arguments of the book have any practical bearing?

Over the course of many years studying professors and politics, I have often been asked whether I agree at all with conservative critics who claim that the left tilt of the academy is a problem. I have usually refused to answer, not wanting to weigh in on the very polemics I was analyzing.

Still, it seems possible to note at least one practical implication of my findings without crossing the line too much between social science and advocacy. My research suggests that conflict over the liberalism of professors is not going to go away anytime soon. David Horowitz's Academic Bill of Rights may be dead in the water, but it will not be long before enterprising conservatives, capitalizing on the fact that liberals continue to stream into academe, find another group of professorial enemies to take on. Will it be progressive or radical scholars who say nice things about Occupy Wall Street? Climate scientists who wear their politics too much on their sleeves and can be cast as biased? Hiring committee members or academic administrators who let slip their doubts about conservative job candidates? Only time will tell, but in the current economic climate the conservative movement needs its populism as never before, and we can expect that moral entrepreneurs like Horowitz (and his successors) will continue to find support for their work.

Whatever one thinks of the substance of their attacks, the academic community must stand ready to meet them if it wants to assure itself of continued public goodwill and flows of money for research. With the American Association of University Professors in decline, and with the major scholarly societies as well as many individual colleges and universities lacking the expertise necessary to respond meaningfully to conservative criticisms, it is not clear that the academy will be in a position to come out unscathed from these battles in the years to come. This is particularly so given that we are in an era of resource scarcity and that questions are being raised about extraordinarily high tuition costs and faculty effectiveness in teaching—questions to which conservative criticisms are increasingly tied.

Some scholars, such as sociologist Jonathan Cole, argue that conservative attacks on liberal professors and science have reached the point of placing American higher education in immediate jeopardy.[13] This may or may not be so. What is apparent, however, is that if members of the academic community want to be out front setting the terms of the debate over higher education reform, they will need more effective vehicles for responding to criticism, political and otherwise. The petitions, hastily mounted academic conferences, special journal issues, and indignant letters to the editor on academic freedom of the past decade have had their place, but ultimately they are ill-suited for the rough-and-tumble of twenty-first-century American political life. Social science must not be subservient to new, organized political efforts by the professoriate to do better and to defend its good name and the traditions of scholarship for which it stands. But it is possible, as Paul Lazarsfeld saw in his day, that the findings and insights of social science could be drawn on to good effect by all those called to arms to preserve the integrity of the academic enterprise.

Notes

Introduction

1. My convention throughout the book is to give the methodological details of any study or analysis of mine in the endnote to the first reported finding from that study, unless the methodology is discussed explicitly later in the text. The interview with Lorena was one of fifty-seven follow-up interviews that my research assistants and I conducted in late 2006–2007 with respondents to a nationally representative survey of the American professoriate that Solon Simmons and I carried out in 2006 (the Politics of the American Professoriate survey, or PAP, the methodology of which I describe in Chapter 1). As the last question on the survey, PAP respondents were asked if they would agree to a follow-up interview. I targeted sociologists, economists, biologists, engineers, and professors of literature from this list in order to maximize political variation and so that I could compare disciplinary cultures. Potential interviewees were contacted by email. Quota sampling procedures were employed, in which the aim was to secure interviews with approximately ten professors in each discipline, obtain a sufficiently large number of interviewees in each of three institutional strata (community colleges, four-year BA-granting schools, and PhD-granting schools) to allow for meaningful comparisons, and have a sample that was more or less reflective of the gender composition of the five fields. About half of the professors contacted responded to our query. (Sample characteristics are available upon request.) Interviews were conducted by phone over the course of several months and followed a semistructured interview schedule. The average interview length was forty-five minutes. My team also interviewed a select number of survey respondents in other fields, but I do not draw extensively on these in the book. All names from the professor interviews are pseudonyms, and I have changed identifying details where necessary to preserve anonymity. A few of the professors we interviewed were in the targeted disciplines in terms of departmental affiliation, but had degrees in other fields.

2. An analysis of data from the General Social Survey (GSS) for the period 1996–2010 using the 126-category occupational scheme developed by Kim Weeden and David Grusky and defining liberal as a score of 1 or 2 on

the GSS's seven-point liberal-conservative self-identification scale shows that 42% of professors are liberal. (There are 182 professors in the GSS sample in this period, an adequate number for comparative analyses with other occupations, and the 42% number is similar to that reported in Chapter 1 based on specialized surveys. Here and throughout the book I report weighted descriptive statistics unless otherwise indicated.) The next most liberal occupations are authors and journalists (37%), creative artists (34%), librarians/curators (31%), and social scientists working outside academe (29%). A logistic regression with liberal as the outcome variable and occupations as the inputs, with professor as the reference category and controlling for gender, race, age, and survey year, similarly shows that working in all but six other occupations diminishes one's odds of being a liberal (with the cutoff for statistical significance set at .05). If one extends the year range back to 1974, professors tie with authors and journalists as the most liberal occupational group. If one codes liberal as a score of 1, 2, or 3 on the self-identification measure, reducing the size of the moderate category, authors and journalists are the most liberal group in the 1996–2010 period, with professors the next most liberal. See Kim A. Weeden and David B. Grusky, "The Case for a New Class Map," *American Journal of Sociology* 111 (2005): 141–212. Weeden's Stata .do file for recoding various iterations of the Standard Occupational Classification codes is available at http://www.soc.cornell.edu/faculty/weeden/occupations.html (accessed 11/3/11). Alternative occupational coding schemes would undoubtedly yield somewhat different results. Tables and Stata code for this and all the other regressions reported in the endnotes that are not reported in previous papers are available on my website at http://www.soci.ubc.ca/index.php?id=11932.

3. Useful surveys of conservative complaints include Michael Bérubé, *What's Liberal about the Liberal Arts? Classroom Politics and "Bias" in Higher Education* (New York: W. W. Norton, 2006); Bruce L. R. Smith, Jeremy D. Mayer, and A. Lee Fritschler, *Closed Minds? Politics and Ideology in American Universities* (Washington, DC: Brookings Institution Press, 2008); and John K. Wilson, *Patriotic Correctness: Academic Freedom and Its Enemies* (Boulder, CO: Paradigm, 2008).

4. Allan Bloom, *The Closing of the American Mind: How Higher Education Has Failed Democracy and Impoverished the Souls of Today's Students* (New York: Simon and Schuster, 1987); Roger Kimball, *Tenured Radicals: How Politics Has Corrupted Our Higher Education* (Chicago: Ivan R. Dee, 2008); Dinesh D'Souza, *Illiberal Education: The Politics of Race and Sex on Campus* (New York: Free Press, 1991).

5. This finding comes from a telephone poll that Solon Simmons and I conducted for the American Association of University Professors in March 2006. The poll, the Attitudes toward the American Professoriate study (ATAP), was administered by Princeton Survey Research Associates International using random-digit dialing technology. It had a sample size of 1,000 and a response rate of 26%, which is typical for telephone polls without incentives. The data were weighted on gender, race, age, education, Hispanic origin, region, and population density to enhance representativeness for the U.S. adult population. (Sample characteristics are available upon request.) Interviews lasted fifteen minutes on average and covered a range of higher education topics. The item referred to here read, "I'm going to name some issues that some people say are facing colleges and universities today. For each one, please tell me how serious a problem it is for American colleges and universities—very serious, somewhat serious, not too serious, or not at all serious: Political bias in the classroom." Response breakdowns were 37%, 38%, 17%, and 7%, respectively. (Note that here and throughout the book I round, so that percentage totals may not add to 100.) A poll conducted in 2004 by the *Chronicle of Higher Education* found that "half of the respondents said that colleges improperly introduce a liberal bias into what they teach and that professors are liberal in their political views." Jeffrey Selingo, "U.S. Public's Confidence in Colleges Remains High," *Chronicle of Higher Education,* May 5, 2004, A1.

6. Yearly updates on state higher education budgets are compiled by the Grapevine Project at Illinois State University. See http://grapevine.illinoisstate.edu/ (accessed 11/3/11). A study of higher education budgeting at the state level from 1984 to 2004 found that Republican control of the legislature and governorship is associated with diminished state expenditures on higher education. Michael K. McLendon, James C. Hearn, and Christine G. Mokher, "Partisans, Professionals, and Power: The Role of Political Factors in State Higher Education Funding," *Journal of Higher Education* 80 (2009): 686–713.

7. All told, 19% of interviewees contested the claim that liberals predominate in academe.

8. In fact, a survey of college and university presidents conducted in January 2012 found that 65% planned to vote for President Obama in the November elections and that only 10% agreed that "the Republican presidential candidates have articulated a vision that will help American higher education." Republican support was substantially higher among presidents of for-profit institutions. See "The 2012 Inside Higher Ed Survey of College

and University Presidents," http://www.insidehighered.com/download /?file=2012IHEpresidentssurvey.pdf (accessed 5/18/12).

9. The best data on this come from comparative studies of party platforms. See Andrea Volkens, Onawa Lacewell, Pola Lehmann, Sven Regel, Henrike Schultze, and Annika Werner, "The Manifesto Data Collection," Manifesto Project, Social Science Research Center Berlin (2012), https://manifesto -project.wzb.eu/ (accessed 11/3/11). However, John Gerring has noted that although the Democratic Party has never had any truck with socialism, the fact that the Republicans have often been further to the right than mainstream conservative parties in Europe, Scandinavia, and elsewhere means that the political distance between Republicans and Democrats is about the same as that found between major left and right parties in other countries. John Gerring, *Party Ideologies in America, 1828–1996* (New York: Cambridge University Press, 2001), 37–40. I thank Doug Ahler for this point.

10. On business as the most popular major, see "Fast Facts," National Center for Education Statistics, http://nces.ed.gov/fastfacts/display.asp?id=37 (accessed 11/3/11). On the proportion of faculty in applied fields like business, see Jack H. Schuster and Martin J. Finkelstein, *The American Faculty: The Restructuring of Academic Work and Careers* (Baltimore: Johns Hopkins University Press, 2006), 447. The PAP data, which are representative of faculty working in programs that offer undergraduate instruction, show a higher percentage of the faculty working in business (15%).

11. The 51% figure comes from the PAP survey. Updated figures on party affiliation in the general population are reported at Rasmussen Reports, http://www.rasmussenreports.com/public_content/politics/mood_of_amer ica/partisan_trends (accessed 11/3/11).

12. As I explain in Chapter 1, the PAP survey contained a number of questions in which respondents were presented with a term, such as *progressive*, and were asked how well the term described them on a seven-point scale ranging from "not at all" to "extremely well." Fifty-nine percent of Democratic respondents said the term *progressive* described them "quite well" or better.

13. The rationale for the 50%–60% liberal figure, based on a latent class analysis of the PAP data, is presented in Chapter 1. The general population number comes from the 2010 GSS, coding as liberal those who scored 1 or 2 on the political self-identification question.

14. Both claims are made in Stanley Rothman, S. Robert Lichter, and Neil Nevitte, "Politics and Professional Advancement among College Faculty," *The Forum* 3 (2005): article 2. Rothman, Lichter, and Nevitte's claim

that 72% of professors identify themselves as on the left, which resulted from a coding error, is discussed in Chapter 1.

15. An example is Thomas Sowell, *Inside American Education: The Decline, the Deception, the Dogmas* (New York: Free Press, 1993).

16. Ann Coulter, "Radical Loon When Obama Was Only 47," *Human Events*, Oct. 22, 2008, http://www.humanevents.com/article.php?id=29164 (accessed 4/9/12).

17. See the estimates in Chapter 1.

18. I discuss this finding at greater length in Chapter 1. Eight percent of respondents in the PAP survey stated that the term *radical* described them at least "quite" well. The percentage of professors on the "radical" left, as identified by the latent class analysis I report there using this question as well as a host of attitudinal variables, is slightly higher.

19. Satoshi Kanazawa, "Why Liberals and Atheists Are More Intelligent," *Social Psychology Quarterly* 73 (2010): 33–57. I discuss additional studies on this topic in Chapter 2.

20. Over the years the GSS has asked a subset of respondents how important "high income" is to them in a job relative to other characteristics, such as job security and doing meaningful work. Twenty-three percent of liberals (defined as those scoring 1–2 on the political self-identification measure) rank high income as the most important feature of a job, as compared to 20% of conservatives (those scoring 6–7). In an ordered logistic regression predicting how highly respondents rank high income as a desired job characteristic, and controlling for gender, race, age, education, and survey year, moderate or conservative self-identification (relative to liberal) are not statistically significant input variables. Results are not substantively different when the model is run as a multinomial logistic regression.

21. One GSS question asks respondents their level of confidence in the "scientific community." Pooling across years, 48% of liberals report having a "great deal" of confidence, as compared to 41% of conservatives. In an ordered logistic regression using data from 2000 (for the sake of comparability with the model reported in the note following) predicting whether respondents will have a great deal of confidence, only some confidence, or hardly any confidence in the scientific community, political self-identification is a statistically significant input variable when gender, race, age, and education are held constant. A similar result—one that also shows an erosion of conservative confidence over time—is reported in Gordon Gauchat, "Politicization of Science in the Public Sphere: A Study of Public Trust in the United States, 1974 to 2010," *American Sociological Review* 77 (2012): 167–187.

22. Although it is not the variable that all sociologists of religion prefer to use, the GSS contains a measure of how fundamentalist a respondent's religious denomination is. Pooling data across the period 1974–2010, 44% of self-identified political conservatives (defined by a score of 6–7 on the political self-identification question) belonged to a fundamentalist denomination. As part of a recurring "science module," in 2000 GSS interviewers also asked respondents a series of science knowledge questions, including how true they believed the following statement to be: "Human beings developed from earlier species of animals." Seventy-seven percent of fundamentalists said the statement was either "probably not true" or "definitely not true." When the variable measuring belief in evolution was introduced into the regression model described in the previous note, liberal political orientation ceased to be a statistically significant predictor of confidence in the scientific community. For discussion of these issues, see Andrew Greeley and Michael Hout, *The Truth about Conservative Christians: What They Think and What They Believe* (Chicago: University of Chicago Press, 2006), esp. 32–37.

23. Aaron M. McCright and Riley E. Dunlap, "Cool Dudes: The Denial of Climate Change among Conservative White Males in the United States," *Global Environmental Change* 21 (2011): 1163–1172.

24. A useful breakdown of science knowledge questions in the GSS by political orientation can be found at *Discover Magazine*, http://blogs.discovermagazine.com/gnxp/2011/03/the-republican-fluency-with-science/ (accessed 11/12/11). I return to this issue in Chapter 2.

25. These points about evangelicals are made in John H. Evans, "Epistemological and Moral Conflict between Religion and Science," *Journal for the Scientific Study of Religion* 50 (2011): 707–727.

26. See Charles Kurzman and Lynn Owens, "The Sociology of Intellectuals," *Annual Review of Sociology* 28 (2002): 63–90.

27. Pierre Bourdieu, *Distinction: A Social Critique of the Judgment of Taste,* trans. Richard Nice (Cambridge, MA: Harvard University Press, 1984); Pierre Bourdieu, *Homo Academicus,* trans. Peter Collier (Stanford, CA: Stanford University Press, 1988). The best summary of Bourdieu's theory of intellectuals and politics is David Swartz, *Culture and Power: The Sociology of Pierre Bourdieu* (Chicago: University of Chicago Press, 1997).

28. I discuss this literature in more detail in Chapter 2, but particularly relevant here is the debate between Steven Brint and Michèle Lamont. See Steven Brint, "'New Class' and Cumulative Trend Explanations of the Liberal Political Attitudes of Professionals," *American Journal of Sociology* 90 (1984): 30–71; Michèle Lamont, "Cultural Capital and the Liberal Political

Attitudes of Professionals: Comment on Brint," *American Journal of Sociology* 92 (1987): 1501–1506. Also see Michèle Lamont, *Money, Morals, and Manners: The Culture of the French and American Upper-Middle Class* (Chicago: University of Chicago Press, 1992).

29. I explain the finding about the limited explanatory power of Bourdieu's theory, which comes from an analysis of pooled GSS data, in Chapter 2.

30. The relevant findings from the ATAP poll are described in Chapter 3.

31. For a review of some of this literature, see Neil Gross, Thomas Medvetz, and Rupert Russell, "The Contemporary American Conservative Movement," *Annual Review of Sociology* 37 (2011): 325–354.

32. On higher education as a taken-for-granted good, see Evan Schofer and John W. Meyer, "The Worldwide Expansion of Higher Education in the Twentieth Century," *American Sociological Review* 70 (2005): 898–920.

33. Max Weber, "The Meaning of Ethical Neutrality," in *Methodology of Social Sciences,* trans. and ed. Edward A. Shils and Henry A. Finch (New Brunswick, NJ: Transaction, 2011), 1–49, 11.

1. The Politics of American Professors

1. "Number of Degree-granting Institutions and Enrollment in These Institutions, by Size, Type, and Control of Institution: Fall 2009," National Center for Education Statistics, Apr. 2011, http://nces.ed.gov/programs/digest/d10/tables/dt10_244.asp?referrer=list (accessed 11/26/11); "Total Undergraduate Fall Enrollment in Degree-granting Institutions, by Attendance Status, Sex of Student, and Control of Institution: 1967 through 2009," National Center for Education Statistics, Apr. 2011, http://nces.ed.gov/programs/digest/d10/tables/dt10_213.asp?referrer=list (accessed 11/26/11).

2. "Recent High School Completers and Their Enrollment in College, by Sex: 1960 through 2009," National Center for Education Statistics, Apr. 2011, http://nces.ed.gov/programs/digest/d10/tables/dt10_208.asp?referrer=list (accessed 11/26/11). On degree completion, see U.S. Census, Table 229, "Educational Attainment by Race and Hispanic Origin," http://www.census.gov/compendia/statab/cats/education/educational_attainment.html (accessed 11/26/11).

3. Economists debate alternative ways of measuring the macroeconomic effects of higher education. A useful discussion is Kenneth H. Brown and Michael T. Heaney, "A Note on Measuring the Economic Impact of Institutions of Higher Education," *Research in Higher Education* 38 (1997): 229–240.

4. On knowledge as a basis for economic growth, see Richard L. Florida, *The Rise of the Creative Class and How It's Transforming Work, Leisure, Community, and Everyday Life* (New York: Basic Books, 2002); Walter W. Powell and Kaisa Snellman, "The Knowledge Economy," *Annual Review of Sociology* 30 (2004): 199–220.

5. For discussion, see Mitchell L. Stevens, Elizabeth A. Armstrong, and Richard Arum, "Sieve, Incubator, Temple, Hub: Empirical and Theoretical Advances in the Sociology of Higher Education," *Annual Review of Sociology* 34 (2008): 127–151.

6. On professoriate size, see U.S. Department of Education, National Center for Education Statistics, "Digest of Education Statistics 2010," Table 255, http://nces.ed.gov/pubs2011/2011015.pdf (accessed 11/26/11). On labor force size, see U.S. Census Bureau, *Statistical Abstract of the United States: 2012,* "Civilian Population—Employment Status: 1970 to 2010," table 586, http://www.census.gov/compendia/statab/2012/tables/12s0587.pdf (accessed 9/12/12). For a detailed breakdown by field, see U.S. Department of Labor, Bureau of Labor Statistics, "Occupational Employment and Wages—May 2011," http://www.bls.gov/news.release/archives/ocwage_03272012.pdf (accessed 9/12/12).

7. The discussion in Jack H. Schuster and Martin J. Finkelstein, *The American Faculty: The Restructuring of Academic Work and Careers* (Baltimore: Johns Hopkins University Press, 2006), is particularly thorough. Also see Joseph C. Hermanowicz, ed., *The American Academic Profession: Transformation in Contemporary Higher Education* (Baltimore: Johns Hopkins University Press, 2011).

8. Paul F. Lazarsfeld and Wagner Thielens Jr., *The Academic Mind: Social Scientists in a Time of Crisis* (Glencoe, IL: Free Press, 1958).

9. Ellen W. Schrecker, *No Ivory Tower: McCarthyism and The Universities* (New York: Oxford University Press, 1986), 10.

10. Lazarsfeld and Thielens, *The Academic Mind,* 3.

11. Ibid., 378.

12. Ibid., 387.

13. Ibid., 36.

14. Ibid., 95.

15. Ibid., 401. The social meanings of Republican and Democratic Party affiliation, and of liberalism and conservatism, have certainly changed over the years. I discuss some of the changes around conservatism in Chapter 7. For an overview of changes in liberalism, see Paul Starr, *Freedom's Power: The True Force of Liberalism* (New York: Basic Books, 2007). When I draw historical comparisons, I assume only that there are broad

family resemblances between the American left and right of today and their predecessors.

16. Lazarsfeld and Thielens, *The Academic Mind,* 402.

17. Ibid., 133.

18. Ibid., 117.

19. William F. Buckley Jr., *God and Man at Yale* (Chicago: Regnery, 1951).

20. A succinct survey of the period is Roger L. Geiger, "American Universities and Student Protest in the 1968 Era: Causes and Consequences," unpublished manuscript, Pennsylvania State University, 2011.

21. Everett Carll Ladd Jr. and Seymour Martin Lipset, *The Divided Academy: Professors and Politics* (New York: W. W. Norton, 1975).

22. A. H. Halsey and Martin A. Trow, *The British Academics* (Cambridge, MA: Harvard University Press, 1971).

23. Ladd and Lipset, *The Divided Academy,* 26.

24. Ibid., 29–31.

25. Ibid., 60.

26. Ibid., 212–213.

27. Ibid., 14.

28. Richard F. Hamilton and Lowell L. Hargens, "The Politics of the Professors: Self-Identifications, 1969–1984," *Social Forces* 71 (1993): 603–627; Schuster and Finkelstein, *The American Faculty,* 506.

29. Seymour Martin Lipset, "The Academic Mind at the Top: The Political Behavior and Values of Faculty Elites," *Public Opinion Quarterly* 46 (1982): 143–168.

30. The HERI faculty survey formerly included a few social/political attitudes questions, such as those measuring abortion and death penalty attitudes.

31. Linda J. Sax, Alexander W. Astin, William S. Korn, and Shannon K. Gilmartin, *The American College Teacher: National Norms for the 1998–1999 HERI Faculty Survey* (Los Angeles: Higher Education Research Institute, 1999), 37; Alexander W. Astin, William S. Korn, and Eric L. Dey, *The American College Teacher: National Norms for the 1989–1990 HERI Faculty Survey* (Los Angeles: Higher Education Research Institute, 1990), 44.

32. Max Weber, " 'Objectivity' in Social Science and Social Policy," in *Methodology of the Social Sciences,* trans. and ed. E. A. Shils and H. A. Finch (New Brunswick, NJ: Transaction, 2011), 50–112.

33. Daniel B. Klein and Andrew Western, "Voter Registration of Berkeley and Stanford Faculty," *Academic Questions* 18 (2005): 53–65.

34. Ibid., 53, 56.

35. Ibid., 58–59.

36. Ethan Cohen-Cole and Steven Durlauf, "Evaluating Claims of Bias in Academia: A Comment on Klein and Western's 'How Many Democrats per Republican at UC-Berkeley and Stanford,'" unpublished manuscript, University of Wisconsin–Madison, 2005, 4; Klein and Western, "Voter Registration of Berkeley and Stanford Faculty," 64.

37. For details on the PAP sampling strategy, see Neil Gross and Solon Simmons, "The Social and Political Attitudes of American Professors," unpublished manuscript, Harvard University, 2007. In brief, however, the PAP study focused on professors teaching in fields where undergraduate degrees are awarded. We began by drawing up a list of every institution in the country where bachelor's or associate's degrees were offered in 2004 in the twenty largest disciplinary fields, which we oversampled for the sake of generating larger cell sizes, and a list of institutions offering degrees in any other field. We then randomly sampled field-school pairings from both lists, stratifying to ensure adequate representation of community colleges, four-year colleges and universities, nonelite PhD-granting institutions, and elite PhD-granting institutions (defined as those in the top fifty in the most recent *U.S. News and World Report* ranking). Program websites were next consulted, and one apparently full-time faculty member from each was randomly selected. Precontact and study invitation letters were sent to 2,958 targeted respondents by the Center for Survey Research at Indiana University, with the chance to win a $100 gift certificate the incentive. Professors participated in the study by filling out a questionnaire online between April 6 and June 6, 2006. Our final response rate was 51%, with 1,471 valid cases. (In the analyses I report in this book I restrict the sample to professors who in fact had full-time appointments, which reduces the sample size to 1,416.) Extensive analyses of response bias, including short interviews with a sample of nonrespondents, revealed nothing of significance. The final sample is an approximate representation of the population of professors teaching full-time in U.S. colleges and universities, with the important caveat that, as noted earlier, professors were eligible to be sampled only if they taught in departments or programs offering undergraduate degrees. Our smaller study of part-time faculty ran in parallel.

38. Gross and Simmons, "The Social and Political Attitudes of American Professors."

39. A classic argument to this effect is Anthony Downs, *An Economic Theory of Democracy* (New York: Harper, 1957). A variation on it—one that recognizes that "public opinion" may exist as an "emergent" phenomenon not reducible to the preferences of individuals—can be found in Benjamin I.

Page and Robert Y. Shapiro, *The Rational Public: Fifty Years of Trends in Americans' Policy Preferences* (Chicago: University of Chicago Press, 1992).

40. For discussion of relevant conceptual issues, see Ronald Inglehart and Hans Klingemann, "Party Identification, Ideological Preference and the Left-Right Dimension among Western Mass Publics," in *Party Identification and Beyond: Representations of Voting and Party Competition,* ed. Ian Budge, Ivor Crewe, and Dennis Farlie (London: Wiley, 1976), 243–273; Pamela Johnston Conover and Stanley Feldman, "The Origins and Meaning of Liberal/Conservative Self-Identifications," *American Journal of Political Science* 25 (1981): 617–645; John T. Jost, "The End of the End of Ideology," *American Psychologist* 61 (2006): 651–670.

41. Marc J. Hetherington and Jonathan D. Weiler, *Authoritarianism and Polarization in American Politics* (New York: Cambridge University Press, 2009).

42. Shalom H. Schwartz, "Are There Universal Aspects in the Structure and Contents of Human Values?," *Journal of Social Issues* 50 (1994): 19–45.

43. Yuval Piurko, Shalom H. Schwartz, and Eldad Davidov, "Basic Personal Values and the Meaning of Left-Right Political Orientation in 20 Countries," *Political Psychology* 32 (2011): 537–561. Another foundational study here is Milton Rokeach, *The Nature of Human Values* (New York: Free Press, 1973).

44. See also Jesse Graham, Jonathan Haidt, and Brian A. Nosek, "Liberals and Conservatives Rely on Different Sets of Moral Foundations," *Journal of Personality and Social Psychology* 96 (2009): 1029–1046; Jonathan Haidt, *The Righteous Mind: Why Good People Are Divided by Politics and Religion* (New York: Pantheon Books, 2012).

45. Alan Wolfe, *The Future of Liberalism* (New York: Knopf, 2009).

46. George H. Nash, *The Conservative Intellectual Movement in America Since 1945* (New York: Basic Books, 1976).

47. Wolfe, *The Future of Liberalism*, 19.

48. Wolfe has written on "identity politics"; I mean to flag something different.

49. Angus Campbell, Philip E. Converse, Warren E. Miller, and Donald E. Stokes's *The American Voter* (New York: Wiley, 1960) was one of the first books to argue these claims systematically. Also see John Zaller, *The Nature and Origins of Mass Opinion* (Cambridge, UK: Cambridge University Press, 1992). For a review of other relevant findings, see Donald R. Kinder and David O. Sears, "Public Opinion and Political Action," in *The Handbook of Social Psychology,* ed. Gardner Lindzey and Elliot Aronson (New York: Random House, 1985), 2:659–741; Michael X. Delli Carpini and Scott

Keeter, *What Americans Know about Politics and Why It Matters* (New Haven, CT: Yale University Press, 1996); Samuel L. Popkin and Michael A. Dimock, "Citizen Competence and Political Knowledge," in *Citizen Competence and Democratic Institutions,* ed. Stephen L. Elkin and Karol Edward Soltan (University Park, PA: Pennsylvania State University Press, 1999), 117–146. Scholars like Downs were well aware of the information problem; Downs put it front and center in his analysis. For a different line of attack on rational choice approaches to politics see Donald P. Green and Ian Shapiro, *Pathologies of Rational Choice Theory: a Critique of Applications in Political Science* (New Haven, CT: Yale University Press, 1994).

50. A useful introduction to this literature can be found in David O. Sears, Leonie Huddy, and Robert Jervis, eds., *Oxford Handbook of Political Psychology* (New York: Oxford University Press, 2003).

51. Haidt, *The Righteous Mind.*

52. For example, see Clem Brooks and Jeff Manza, *Why Welfare States Persist: The Importance of Public Opinion in Democracies* (Chicago: University of Chicago Press, 2007).

53. Starr's *Freedom's Power* places more emphasis on change than other work in this genre. While in principle the values approach allows for change and historical shifts in meaning, in practice this is often underemphasized. John Gray makes this point in his review of Haidt's *The Righteous Mind,* "The Knowns and the Unknowns," *The New Republic,* Apr. 20, 2012, http://www.tnr.com/article/books-and-arts/magazine/102760/righteous -mind-haidt-morality-politics-scientism (accessed 6/4/12).

54. Haidt, for his part, insists that human beings are inherently "groupish" and that this affects politics as well as religion, ethnicity, and other phenomena. But, despite his endorsement of theories of life narratives, he treats the identity aspects of political group membership—implicit and explicit self-understandings and categorizations—as secondary to the sharing of underlying intuitions and values. Compare to Jan ·E. Stets and Michael J. Carter, "A Theory of the Self for the Sociology of Morality," *American Sociological Review* 77 (2012): 120–140. Thinkers like Wolfe and Starr attend to conflicts between adherents of different political traditions— for example, between liberalism and socialism—but do not highlight the social-psychological dimensions of such conflict, or of tradition adherence more generally.

55. Donald Green, Bradley Palmquist, and Eric Schickler, *Partisan Hearts and Minds: Political Parties and the Social Identities of Voters* (New Haven, CT: Yale University Press, 2002), 213.

56. Ariel Malka and Yphtach Lelkes, "More than Ideology: Conservative-Liberal Identity and Receptivity to Political Cues," *Social Justice Research* 23 (2010): 156–188.

57. One area of political research in which ample attention has been paid to identity is the study of social movements. See Sheldon Stryker, Timothy J. Owens, and Robert W. White, eds., *Self, Identity, and Social Movements* (Minneapolis: University of Minnesota Press, 2000); Francesca Polletta and James M. Jasper, "Collective Identity and Social Movements," *Annual Review of Sociology* 27 (2001): 283–305. An identity focus is also compatible with the "symbolic politics" approach taken by some political scientists. Murray J. Edelman, *The Symbolic Uses of Politics* (Urbana: University of Illinois Press, 1985); David O. Sears, "Symbolic Politics: A Socio-Psychological Theory," in *Explorations in Political Psychology*, ed. Shanto Iyengar and William J. McGuire (Durham, NC: Duke University Press, 1993), 113–149; Conover and Feldman, "The Origins and Meaning of Liberal/Conservative Self-Identifications." In *Partisan Hearts and Minds*, Green, Palmquist, and Schickler explicitly develop an identity-based approach, although one focused on parties rather than ideological groupings. Also see the connection to the political socialization literature in Virginia Sapiro, "Not Your Parents' Political Socialization: Introduction for a New Generation," *Annual Review of Political Science* 7 (2004): 8. On symbolic boundaries, see Michèle Lamont and Virág Molnár, "The Study of Boundaries in the Social Sciences," *Annual Review of Sociology* 28 (2002): 167–195. I consider other work on narrative and identity in Neil Gross, *Richard Rorty: The Making of an American Philosopher* (Chicago: University of Chicago Press, 2008).

58. The latent class analysis my research assistants and I conducted was based on a wide variety of variables that interviews and prior analysis of the PAP data suggested represent meaningful indicators of underlying, categorical political identities among academics. The nineteen indicators in the model measure (1) abortion attitudes, (2) feminist self-identification, (3) views on homosexuality, (4) support for the death penalty, (5) self-identification as a "progressive," (6) self-identification as a "radical," (7) self-identification as a "political activist," (8) self-identification as a "Marxist," (9) party affiliation, (10) self-identification in terms of liberalism or conservatism, (11) views about government regulation of business, (12) views about government assistance for the needy, (13) support for strengthening the military, (14) views of corporate profits, (15) support for environmental regulation, (16) views of censorship of reading materials, (17) belief in the wisdom of fighting terrorism by military means, (18) attitudes toward immigration,

and (19) attitudes toward the war in Iraq. Models were fit using Latent Gold, using weights and Latent Gold's imputation procedure for handling missing values. (As a robustness check, my research assistants also fit the models using the "PROC LCA" procedure in SAS.)

The interviews led me to believe that professors fell into one of six broad classes, so we initially fit a six-class model, along with four-, five-, seven-, and eight-class models so that we could compare fit statistics. Akaike Information Criterion (AIC) and Bayesian Information Criterion (BIC) statistics (based on L^2) showed a slight improvement in model fit with each additional class added (fit statistics are available upon request), but the amount of improvement decreased with every model above a six-class one, while the proportion of variation explained on a key indicator variable—liberal-conservative self-identification—did not increase above six. Closer inspection of the six-class model, however, showed that one of the classes was too small to be substantively meaningful (it included only five cases, based on the modal posterior probabilities); a similar problem plagued the seven- and eight-class models. Since the interviews suggested six major categories in the data, I ended up making a post hoc adjustment to the five-class scheme, dividing into two groups respondents who, according to the latent class model, would be classified by the modal posterior probabilities as left-leaning moderates: academics on the center left and moderates who have some left-leaning but also some right-leaning tendencies. Political self-identification was used to distinguish the two groups. (Means on the variables in the model by latent class are also available upon request. And note that since the latent class model already incorporates the PAP survey weights, the descriptive statistics reported based on the modal probabilities are unweighted.)

Latent class models, like cluster and factor analyses, are quite sensitive to model specification and are thus commonly—and rightly—viewed as more art than science. Readers are warned not to regard the class size numbers and cross-tabulations reported here as anything more than estimates given the methodological and theoretical choices I have made. Also I did not ask my interviewees directly how many distinct political blocs there are in academe; the interpretation that there are six comes from trying to fit interviewees' self-descriptions into as few categories of identity as possible.

59. Jennifer A. Lindholm, Katalin Szelènyi, and William S. Korn, *The American College Teacher: National Norms for the 2004–2005 HERI Faculty Survey* (Los Angeles: Higher Education Research Institute, 2005), 44. In the 2010–2011 HERI survey, which did not include community college faculty, the far left number stood at 12%. Sylvia Hurtado. Kevin Eagen,

John H. Pryor, Hannah Wang, and Serge Tran. *Undergraduate Teaching Faculty: The 2010–2011 HERI Faculty Survey* (Los Angeles: Higher Education Research Institute, 2012), 36.

60. "Radical" is an umbrella term covering people with a range of more specific commitments: "radical democrats," "radical feminists," "radical environmentalists," and so on.

61. The 27% figure differs slightly from that reported elsewhere because I am reporting unweighted tabulations. On professors' religious commitments, see Neil Gross and Solon Simmons, "The Religiosity of American College and University Professors," *Sociology of Religion* 70 (2009): 101–129.

62. Vikingkingq, "Progressive vs. Liberal—What's in a Name?," Daily Kos, Feb. 28, 2008, http://www.dailykos.com/story/2008/02/28/466044 /-Progressive-vs-Liberal-Whats-In-a-Name (accessed 11/29/11). The author of this post is defending the term *progressivism* and responding to the charge that it is "content-less."

63. Radicals have the fewest children, however.

64. Stanley Rothman, S. Robert Lichter, and Neil Nevitte, "Politics and Professional Advancement among College Faculty," *The Forum* 3 (2005) article 2. For correction, see Stanley Rothman and S. Robert Lichter, "The Vanishing Conservative? Is There a Glass Ceiling?," in *The Politically Correct University: Problems, Scope, and Reforms,* ed. Robert Maranto, Richard E. Redding, and Frederick M. Hess (Washington, DC: AEI Press, 2009), 60–78.

65. Gross and Simmons, "The Social and Political Attitudes of American Professors."

66. A Pew study conducted in 2005 using *some* of the same variables found that the American public could be divided into nine political groups: (1) "enterprisers" (9% of the population); (2) "social conservatives" (11%); (3) "pro-government conservatives" (9%); (4) "upbeats," described as strongly supportive of business, government, and the market (11%); (5) "disaffecteds," "deeply cynical" about government (9%); (6) "liberals" (17%); (7) "conservative Democrats" (14%); (8) "disadvantaged Democrats" (10%); and (9) "bystanders," who are not engaged politically (10%). See "Beyond Red vs. Blue," Pew Research Center for the People and the Press, May 10, 2005, http://www.people-press.org/2005/05/10/profiles-of-the-typology -groups/ (accessed 03/30/12). For discussion, see Solon J. Simmons with James R. Simmons, "Latent Classes within the American Electorate: A Reinterpretation of the Pew Center Typology," *Journal of Political Science* 36 (2009): 107–129. The Pew typology has since been updated, but the 2005 numbers are the most directly comparable to PAP.

67. Clem Brooks, "Nations, Classes, and the Politics of Professors: A Comparative Perspective," unpublished manuscript, Indiana University, 2010.

68. John Micklethwait and Adrian Wooldridge, *The Right Nation: Conservative Power in America* (New York: Penguin, 2004). For a different take, see Jacob S. Hacker and Paul Pierson, *Off Center: The Republican Revolution and the Erosion of American Democracy* (New Haven, CT: Yale University Press, 2006).

69. In "The Social and Political Attitudes of American Professors," Simmons and I argued, looking only at data on self-identification, that 44% of professors could be classified as liberal and 9% as conservative. The latent class analysis incorporates a great deal more information, although, as noted earlier, it is more sensitive to model specification and perhaps therefore less suitable as a basis for comparison across studies.

70. According to one estimate, libertarians constitute about 14% of the American population. See David Kirby and David Boaz, "The Libertarian Vote in the Age of Obama," Cato Institute, Jan. 21, 2010, http://www.cato.org/publications/policy-analysis/libertarian-vote-age-obama (accessed 4/23/12).

2. Why Are They Liberal? The Standard Explanations

1. See Scott Jaschik, "(Liberal) Academic Self-Selection," Inside Higher Ed, Mar. 21, 2011, http://www.insidehighered.com/news/2011/03/21/new_studies_back_theory_that_the_professoriate_is_liberal_because_of_self_selection (accessed 11/29/11).

2. For a review of some of the historical literature on May 1968, see Julian Jackson, "The Mystery of May 1968," *French Historical Studies* 33 (2010): 625–653.

3. The classic—though controversial—text on this is Luc Ferry and Alain Renaut, *French Philosophy of the 1960s: An Essay on Antihumanism,* trans. Mary H. S. Cattani (Amherst, MA: University of Massachusetts Press, 1990).

4. Pierre Bourdieu, *Homo Academicus,* trans. Peter Collier (Stanford, CA: Stanford University Press, 1988). Also see Pierre Bourdieu, *Distinction: A Social Critique of the Judgment of Taste,* trans. Richard Nice (Cambridge, MA: Harvard University Press, 1984), 397–465. Followers of Bourdieu will point out that strictly speaking, his is a field-based, not a class-based, theory of academics' politics. Bourdieu sees academics as embedded in nested, structured spaces of social relations; each occupies a position in his or her disciplinary field, in the university field, in the cultural field, and so on,

where positions in fields are a matter of the kinds of capital valued therein and how much occupants hold. Bourdieu argues that there are usually "homologies" between the positions of actors in the various fields they inhabit, although he recognizes that position in any given field may also be determined by individual and collective struggles that play out according to field-specific logics. When he claims that academics typically lean to the left because they possess more cultural than economic capital, this is meant as an argument about where academics as an occupational group stand in a highly general social field encompassing the occupational division of labor. This is all true, but in the end the argument that his approach is field- rather than class-based is a bit of a red herring, for Bourdieu understands class in terms of the structure of this general field. See Elliot B. Weininger, "Foundations of Pierre Bourdieu's Class Analysis," in *Approaches to Class Analysis,* ed. Erik Olin Wright (Cambridge, UK: Cambridge University Press, 2005), 82–118.

5. The literature on intellectuals, class, and politics is in fact quite broad and not exclusively Bourdieusian. In recent years, however, as neo-Marxist accounts of intellectuals' politics have lost favor, Bourdieu's approach has taken center stage.

6. See Michèle Lamont, *Money, Morals, and Manners: The Culture of the French and American Upper-Middle Class* (Chicago: University of Chicago Press, 1992). Bonnie H. Erikson develops this point in the Canadian context in "Culture, Class, and Connections," *American Journal of Sociology* 102 (1996): 217–251.

7. Francie Ostrower, "The Arts as Cultural Capital among Elites: Bourdieu's Theory Reconsidered," *Poetics* 26 (1998): 43–53; Douglas B. Holt, "Does Cultural Capital Structure American Consumption?," *Journal of Consumer Research* 25 (1998): 1–25; Paul DiMaggio and Toqir Mukhtar, "Arts Participation as Cultural Capital in the United States, 1982–2002: Signs of Decline?," *Poetics* 32 (2004): 169–194.

8. Richard A. Peterson and Roger M. Kern, "Changing Highbrow Taste: From Snob to Omnivore," *American Sociological Review* 61 (1996): 900–907.

9. Gindo Tampubolon, "Revisiting Omnivores in America circa 1990s: The Exclusiveness of Omnivores?," *Poetics* 36 (2008): 243–264.

10. Joseph Gerteis, "Political Alignment and the American Middle Class, 1974–1994," *Sociological Forum* 13 (1998): 639–666; Jeff Manza and Clem Brooks, *Social Cleavages and Political Change: Voter Alignments and U.S. Party Coalitions* (Oxford, UK: Oxford University Press, 1999).

11. A penetrating account of class differences in parenting practices is Annette Lareau, *Unequal Childhoods: Class, Race, and Family Life* (Berkeley: University of California Press, 2003).

12. See Ethan Fosse and Neil Gross, "Why Are Professors Liberal?," *Theory & Society* 41 (2012): 127–168. Our strategy in this paper was to divide up the pooled GSS sample (1974–2008) into two groups—professors and nonprofessors—and then use Oaxaca-Blinder regression decomposition to assess how much of the political difference between the two groups, as measured by self-identification (but with alternative models examining attitudes), was a function of different variables. We tested Bourdieu's theory by following the procedure laid out by Keith Hope, "Models of Status Inconsistency and Social Mobility Effects," *American Sociological Review* 40 (1975): 322–343. We first standardized years of education and constant household income, creating a variable that was the sum of the two: a measure of respondents' total level of cultural and economic capital. Then we created a variable that reflected the difference between standardized education and standardized income. We included both variables in our model so that we could examine the effect of a disparity between cultural and economic capital holding constant overall position in the class structure. The 13% finding comes from a model that includes a range of other inputs but not advanced-degree holding (to avoid multicollinearity). In this article we bracketed historical changes in the meanings of liberalism and conservatism as best we could by controlling for survey year. We also conducted a number of sensitivity analyses, examining how results changed under different ways of building our statistical model. Results were essentially the same, although there are no doubt alternative specifications we did not think of that could have yielded different findings. A special thank you is due to Omar Lizardo for pointing us toward the Hope procedure. The Stata .do file we used to conduct our analysis is on my website, as are the tables from the regressions.

13. Stephen Vaisey, "Education and Its Discontents: Overqualification in America, 1972–2002," *Social Forces* 85 (2006): 835–864.

14. One reason the disparity between American professors' levels of cultural and economic capital does not explain more of their liberalism may be that on average they are not *that* poorly compensated relative to other workers with equivalent levels of education. An examination of GSS data from 1974–2010 shows that in all three decades survey respondents who are professors have mean and median family incomes only slightly below those of highly educated Americans in other fields. GSS data are not ideal for measuring income, however, and likely underestimate the incomes of

workers at the top of the distribution. Professorial salaries obviously vary dramatically by type of institution.

15. The mean score on the liberal-conservative self-identification measure for respondents in the PAP part-time sample was 3.7. For full-timers it was 3.1. Our part-time sample was quite small, however, so I also examined data from the HERI Faculty Survey from 1989 to 1998. An ordered logistic regression model controlling for race, gender, age, region, institution type, broad disciplinary area, and survey year confirmed that part-time academic employment is associated with somewhat less liberal political self-identification.

16. Everett Carll Ladd Jr. and Seymour Martin Lipset, *The Divided Academy: Professors and Politics* (New York: W.W. Norton, 1975), 182.

17. See Neil Gross and Catherine Cheng, "Explaining Professors' Politics: Is It a Matter of Self-Selection?," in *Diversity in American Higher Education: Toward a More Comprehensive Approach,* ed. Lisa M. Stulberg and Sharon Lawner Weinberg (New York: Routledge, 2011), 178–194. For this study we analyzed transcripts from professors of business as well, bringing the sample size up to sixty-six.

18. See Ethan Fosse, Jeremy Freese, and Neil Gross, "Political Liberalism and Graduate School Attendance: A Longitudinal Analysis," unpublished manuscript, University of British Columbia, 2011. As mentioned previously, the goal of this paper was to assess whether political liberalism in college is a statistically significant predictor of graduate school attendance, with other variables held constant. As a simple measure of whether attending graduate school shifts people to the left, we compared the political views of two groups of Add Health respondents—those who stopped their education after completing a bachelor's degree and those who enrolled in a graduate program with the intention of completing a PhD—across two waves of the survey, one in which they were enrolled in college (2001–2002) and one in which they were out of college and either attending graduate school or not (2007–2008).

19. Research on this topic is summarized in Donald Green, Bradley Palmquist, and Eric Schickler, *Partisan Hearts and Minds: Political Parties and the Social Identities of Voters* (New Haven, CT: Yale University Press, 2002). Also see M. Kent Jennings and Richard G. Niemi, *The Political Character of Adolescence* (Princeton, NJ: Princeton University Press, 1974); Richard G. Niemi and M. Kent Jennings, "Issues and Inheritance in the Formation of Party Identification," *American Journal of Political Science* 35 (1991): 970–988; Duane Alwin and Ryan McCammon, "Generations, Cohorts, and Social Change," in *Handbook of the Life Course,* ed. Jeylan T. Mortimer and Michael H. Shanahan (New York: Kluwer, 2003), 23–50; Michael S. Lewis-Beck,

Helmut Norpoth, William G. Jacoby, and Herbert F. Weisberg, *The American Voter Revisited* (Ann Arbor, MI: University of Michigan Press, 2008), 138–160.

20. Fosse and Gross, "Why Are Professors Liberal?" On the general relationship between income and voting, with a particular focus on contextual variation, see Andrew Gelman, *Red State, Blue State, Rich State, Poor State: Why Americans Vote the Way They Do* (Princeton, NJ: Princeton University Press, 2008).

21. Among professors in the pooled GSS who answered a question about what kind of work their fathers did when the respondents were sixteen years old, only about 8% stated that their fathers worked in fields associated with high cultural capital like academia, psychology, journalism, or the arts. (This estimate is based on those professors in the sample for whom father's occupation is given in the 1980 Standard Occupational Classification.)

22. Michèle Lamont, "Cultural Capital and the Liberal Political Attitudes of Professionals: Comment on Brint," *American Journal of Sociology* 92 (1987): 1501–1506.

23. In the pooled GSS data, 50% of professors were public-sector workers, compared to 17% of nonprofessors. This variable accounted for just 1% of the politics gap between the two groups. Many American professors teach at private institutions (34%, according to the PAP data), but if the New Class economic interest hypothesis were true, the public sector variable should have nevertheless explained more of the political gap between professors and other Americans.

24. John H. Goldthorpe, *On Sociology,* 2nd ed. (Stanford, CA: Stanford University Press, 2007), 2:173–174.

25. Had there been *no* professors in the GSS sample who listed their work status as self-employed, it would have been impossible to test for the significance of this variable. However, to increase the number of professorial respondents, Fosse and I included all workers who said they were postsecondary teachers, including those working full time and part time, those temporarily laid off, retirees, and others. Three percent gave their work status as self-employed. Almost all who said they were self-employed appeared to be part-time faculty or in some other kind of "nonstandard" employment relationship; they probably meant to indicate that while they received some income from their university employers and identified as academics, the bulk of their income came from another source. (Their responses could also have been errors.) In any event, the self-employment variable accounted for only 2% of the political gap between professors and other Americans.

26. For discussion, see Lawrence Peter King and Iván Szelényi, *Theories of the New Class: Intellectuals and Power* (Minneapolis: University of Minnesota Press, 2004).

27. Steven Brint, " 'New Class' and Cumulative Trend Explanations of the Liberal Political Attitudes of Professionals," *American Journal of Sociology* 90 (1984): 30–71; Steven Brint, "The Political Attitudes of Professionals," *Annual Review of Sociology* 11 (1985): 389–414. Also see his *In an Age of Experts: The Changing Role of Professionals in Politics and Public Life* (Princeton, NJ: Princeton University Press, 1994).

28. Brint did not argue that education was the *only* important factor accounting for liberal attitudes within segments of the white-collar workforce, but he found it to be significant in most of his analyses.

29. In a classic contribution to the sociology of knowledge, *Ideology and Utopia: An Introduction to the Sociology of Knowledge* (London: Routledge, 1991), Karl Mannheim similarly argued that intellectuals compose a relatively "classless" group in the sense that their education and training give them the perspective necessary to transcend the parochial interests associated with their class backgrounds and formulate "objective" knowledge. As he put it, "Participation in a common educational heritage progressively tends to suppress differences of birth, status, profession, and wealth, and to unite the individual educated people on the basis of the education they have received" (138).

30. This research is well reviewed in Ernest T. Pascarella and Patrick T. Terenzini, *How College Affects Students: Findings and Insights from Twenty Years of Research* (San Francisco: Jossey-Bass, 1991); Ernest T. Pascarella and Patrick T. Terenzini, *How College Affects Students: A Third Decade of Research,* vol. 2 (San Francisco: Jossey-Bass, 2005).

31. Theodore M. Newcomb, *Personality and Social Change: Attitude Formation in a Student Community* (New York: Dryden Press, 1943); Duane F. Alwin, Ronald L. Cohen, and Theodore M. Newcomb, *Political Attitudes over the Life Span: The Bennington Women after Fifty Years* (Madison: University of Wisconsin Press, 1991).

32. In the pooled GSS data from 1974 to 2008, 72% of professors indicated that they held a graduate degree. This would seem to reflect an unusually low level of advanced-degree holding for the professoriate: in the PAP full-time data just 2% of respondents do not have an advanced degree. However, among part-time instructors in the HERI faculty sample from 1989 to 1998, only 83% of respondents indicated that they held an advanced degree (i.e., a degree beyond a bachelor's; the 17% of non-degree-holders included a small number of respondents who did not answer the

question). The low level of advanced-degree holding among professors in the GSS thus likely reflects the fact that the subsample includes instructors working in a less than full-time capacity.

33. Ladd and Lipset, *Divided Academy*.

34. Paul F. Lazarsfeld and Wagner Thielens Jr., *The Academic Mind: Social Scientists in a Time of Crisis* (Glencoe, IL: Free Press, 1958).

35. Fosse and I sought to test this hypothesis as well, but it came up short. Six percent of professors in the GSS are Jewish (as compared to 2% of the general U.S. population), but this fact, we found, explained only 4% of the political differences between professors and other Americans. Five percent of respondents to the PAP survey also stated their religious preference as Jewish, although this number may underestimate the number of Jews in academe, since some secular Jews probably indicated that their religious preference was "none." For an analysis of the impact of Jewish overrepresentation on twentieth-century academic life, see David A. Hollinger, *Science, Jews, and Secular Culture: Studies in Mid-Twentieth Century American Intellectual History* (Princeton, NJ: Princeton University Press, 1996). Recent evidence suggests that the number of Jews pursuing PhDs and entering academe may be declining. See Barry R. Chiswick, "The Rise and Fall of the American Jewish PhD," IZA Discussion Paper No. 3384, http://ftp.iza .org/dp3384.pdf (accessed 11/29/11).

36. Louis Menand, *The Marketplace of Ideas: Reform and Resistance in the American University* (New York: Norton, 2010).

37. Two more recent studies on this are Jim Sidanius, Shana Levin, Colette van Laar, and David O. Sears, *The Diversity Challenge: Social Identity and Intergroup Relations on the College Campus* (New York: Russell Sage Foundation, 2008); Jana M. Hanson, Dustin D. Weeden, Ernest T. Pascarella, and Charles Blaich, "Do Liberal Arts Colleges Make Students More Liberal? Some Initial Evidence," *Higher Education* 63 (2012): 1–15.

38. Fosse and Gross, "Why Are Professors Liberal?" To avoid conflating tolerance and liberal political attitudes, we constructed our tolerance measure from questions asking about speech rights for people with whom liberals disagree (e.g., "militarists").

39. Our study examined graduate students in all fields, but we found no greater evidence of liberalization when we looked only at social sciences and humanities students.

40. For example, among young Americans currently enrolled in college, 45% consider themselves liberal, 20% moderate, and 35% conservative. See "Survey of Young Americans' Attitudes toward Politics and Public Service, 19th Edition: February 11–March 2, 2011," http://www

.iop.harvard.edu/sites/default/files_new/IOP_Spring_2011_Topline.pdf (accessed 8/28/12).

41. For review see Kyle Dodson, "The Effect of College on Social and Political Attitudes and Civic Participation," unpublished manuscript, University of California-Merced, 2011. A similar vein of research reexamines the long-standing finding that college attendance diminishes religious belief and participation. See Jeremy E. Uecker, Mark D. Regnerus, and Margaret L. Vaaler, "Losing My Religion: The Social Sources of Religious Decline in Early Adulthood," *Social Forces* 85 (2007): 1667–1692; Damon Mayrl and Jeremy E. Uecker, "Higher Education and Religious Liberalization among Young Adults," *Social Forces* 90 (2011): 181–208.

42. This is an ongoing study that analyzes Add Health data using propensity score matching.

43. Menand, *Marketplace of Ideas*.

44. Richard Arum and Josipa Roksa, *Academically Adrift: Limited Learning on College Campuses* (Chicago: University of Chicago Press, 2011).

45. M. Kent Jennings and Laura Stoker, "Another and Longer Look at the Impact of Higher Education on Political Involvement and Attitudes," paper delivered at the Midwest Political Science Association Meeting, Chicago, 2008.

46. The classic discussion here on activism is Doug McAdam, "Micromobilization Contexts and Recruitment to Activism," *International Social Movement Research* 1 (1988): 125–154. Also see McAdam's "Recruitment to High-Risk Activism: The Case of Freedom Summer," *American Journal of Sociology* 92 (1986): 64–90. For an analysis of colleges and universities as key sites for recruitment into social movements, see Sarah A. Soule, "The Student Divestment Movement in the United States and Tactical Diffusion: The Shantytown Protest," *Social Forces* 75 (1997): 855–882; Ziad W. Munson, *The Making of Pro-Life Activists: How Social Movement Mobilization Works* (Chicago: University of Chicago Press, 2008).

47. James S. Coleman and Thomas Hoffer, *Public and Private High Schools: The Impact of Communities* (New York: Basic Books, 1987).

48. Matthew Woessner and April Kelly-Woessner, "Left Pipeline: Why Conservatives Don't Get Doctorates," in *The Politically Correct University: Problems, Scope, and Reforms,* ed. Robert Maranto, Richard E. Redding, and Frederick M. Hess (Washington, DC: AEI Press, 2009), 38–59.

49. Important sociological work on this topic includes Arne L. Kalleberg, "Work Values and Job Rewards: A Theory of Job Satisfaction," *American Sociological Review* 42 (1977): 124–143; Charles N. Halaby, "Where

Job Values Come from: Family and Schooling Background, Cognitive Ability, and Gender," *American Sociological Review* 68 (2003): 251–278; Margaret Mooney Marini, Pi-Ling Fan, Erica Finley, and Ann M. Beutel, "Gender and Job Values," *Sociology of Education* 69 (1996): 49–65.

50. Ronald Inglehart, *Culture Shift in Advanced Industrial Society* (Princeton, NJ: Princeton University Press, 1990).

51. As in Kazimierz M. Slomczynski, Joanne Miller, and Melvin L. Kohn, "Stratification, Work, and Values: A Polish–United States Comparison," *American Sociological Review* 46 (1981): 720–744.

52. Barbara Schneider and David Stevenson, *The Ambitious Generation: America's Teenagers, Motivated but Directionless* (New Haven, CT: Yale University Press, 1999).

53. One could imagine a process in which most students are unsure about what they want in a career but have a vague sense of it and allow themselves to drift toward occupations that they feel resonate with that sense despite information limits. Their goals and aspirations might then become clarified and solidified over time.

54. David Brooks, *Bobos in Paradise: The New Upper Class and How They Got There* (New York: Simon & Schuster, 2000). In line with Brooks's claim, one study of consumer preferences and politics found that while Republicans are more likely than Democrats to buy luxury sedans (and convertibles), Democrats are more likely to buy luxury station wagons. See "Democrat vs. Republican: Who's Buying What Car?," Strategic Vision, press release, Mar. 29, 2012, http://www.strategicvision.com/press_release.php?pr=42 (accessed 3/30/12).

55. Data from the College Senior Survey show that students on the far left are less interested in making money, while those on the far right are more interested.

56. There are no direct measures of job values in any waves of Add Health, so we measured materialism with a question that asked respondents how important they thought money is to a successful marriage or relationship. In a model predicting PhD-program attendance, and holding constant sociodemographic background, class background, cognitive ability, and academic achievement, this variable was not a significant input, and including it did nothing to moderate the relationship found in prior models between political liberalism in college and graduate school attendance. As a further test of the hypothesis, my research assistants and I analyzed data from the CSS from 1994 to 1999. We found that being moderate or conservative, relative to being liberal, decreased the odds of aspiring to become a professor, with age, race, sex, religion, father's education, father's occupa-

tion, college GPA, SAT scores, and region held constant. Including as an additional input variable how important a life goal it was for the respondent to be "very well-off financially" had only a modest effect on the size of the politics coefficients.

57. This finding comes from an analysis not reported in the published version of our paper, using as a rough measure of autonomy whether GSS respondents report having a supervisor at work. There are significant limitations to this measure, however; it is not at all clear that most respondents interpret the question in the same way.

58. For a nuanced discussion of these issues, see Randall J. Stephens and Karl W. Giberson, *The Anointed: Evangelical Truth in a Secular Age* (Cambridge, MA: Harvard University Press, 2011).

59. John H. Evans, "Epistemological and Moral Conflict between Religion and Science," *Journal for the Scientific Study of Religion* 50 (2011): 707–727. A 2009 Pew survey offers additional evidence on the politics point, finding significant but not massive differences between liberals and conservatives in their appreciation for science. For example, 72% of self-described liberal respondents, as compared to 63% of conservatives, said that scientists contribute "a lot" to our society. Forty percent of liberals versus 31% of conservatives said they enjoyed keeping up with news about science "a lot." Sixty-eight percent of liberals and 67% of conservatives said they regularly watched television programs or channels about science, such as *Nova* or the Discovery Channel. Twenty-three percent of liberals and 20% of conservatives said they regularly read science magazines, such as *Popular Science* and *Scientific American*. At the same time, 43% of conservatives, as compared to 29% of liberals, said that science sometimes conflicts with their religious beliefs. Pew Research Center for the People and the Press, General Public Science Survey, Apr. 2009.

60. The best repeated measure of science attitudes in the GSS is the confidence in science question, which is not very fine-grained. Professors do exhibit greater confidence in science than nonprofessors (62% of professors say they have a "great deal" of confidence, as compared to 43% of nonprofessors), but in a regression decomposition seeking to account for the politics gap between the two groups from 1974–2010, confidence in science explains only 4% in a model that controls for gender, age, race, education, region, and survey year.

61. As I note in Chapter 3, religion could also have had an indirect effect in our models, helping to account for professorial liberalism through our education variable, with the very religious less likely to complete college and pursue an advanced degree.

62. In an ordered logistic regression predicting a respondent's score on the liberal–conservative self-identification variable, identification as a scientist is associated with a more conservative score, with race, sex, age, and institution type held constant. (The variable is significant, however, only at the .10 level.)

63. A 2009 study of members of the American Association for the Advancement of Science found that 52% identified as liberal, compared to just 9% conservative. However, 63% of survey respondents worked in an academic setting. See "Scientific Achievements Less Prominent Than a Decade Ago," Pew Research Center for the People and the Press, news release, July 9, 2009, http://people-press.org/http://people-press.org/files/legacy-pdf/528.pdf (accessed 4/2/12).

64. Helpful surveys of this area can be found in Jeffery J. Mondak, *Personality and the Foundations of Political Behavior* (Cambridge, UK: Cambridge University Press, 2010), and in journalist Chris Mooney's *The Republican Brain: The Science of Why They Deny Science—and Reality* (New York: Wiley, 2012).

65. For example, Ian J. Deary, G. David Batty, and Catherine R. Gale, "Bright Children Become Enlightened Adults," *Psychological Science* 19 (2008): 1–6. A similar result is reported in Gordon Hodson and Michael A. Busseri, "Bright Minds and Dark Attitudes: Lower Cognitive Ability Predicts Greater Prejudice through Right-Wing Ideology and Low Intergroup Contact," *Psychological Science* 23 (2012): 1–9.

66. A useful review of the literature on personality development can be found in Avshalom Caspi, Brent W. Roberts, and Rebecca L. Shiner, "Personality Development: Stability and Change," *Annual Review of Psychology* 56 (2005): 453–484.

67. Three representative pieces of his are John T. Jost and Orsolya Hunyady, "Antecedents and Consequences of System-Justifying Ideologies," *Current Directions in Psychological Science* 14 (2005): 260–265; Dana R. Carney, John T. Jost, Samuel D. Gosling, and Jeff Potter, "The Secret Lives of Liberals and Conservatives: Personality Profiles, Interaction Styles, and the Things They Leave Behind," *Political Psychology* 29 (2008): 807–840; John T. Jost, " 'Elective Affinities': On the Psychological Bases of Left-Right Differences," *Psychological Inquiry* 20 (2009), 129–141.

68. In contrast, a number of political psychologists have argued that openness to new experience and the ability to tolerate cognitive complexity are associated with political centrism. Philip E. Tetlock, "Cognitive Style and Political Belief Systems in the British House of Commons," *Journal of Personality and Social Psychology* 46 (1984): 365–375. This point is made

in response to Jost specifically in Jeff Greenberg and Eva Jonas, "Psychological Motives and Political Orientation: The Left, the Right, and the Rigid," *Psychological Bulletin* 129 (2003): 376–382.

69. John L. Holland, *Making Vocational Choices: A Theory of Vocational Personalities and Work Environments* (New York: Prentice Hall, 1984).

70. See James Sidanius and Felicia Pratto, *Social Dominance: An Intergroup Theory of Social Hierarchy and Oppression* (New York: Cambridge University Press, 2001).

71. Felicia Pratto, Jim Sidanius, Lisa M. Stallworth, and Bertram F. Malle, "Social Dominance Orientation: A Personality Variable Predicting Social and Political Attitudes," *Journal of Personality and Social Psychology* 67 (1994): 742; Theodor W. Adorno, Else Frenkel-Brunswik, Daniel J. Levinson, and R. Nevitt Sanford, *The Authoritarian Personality* (New York: Harper, 1950).

72. Hillary Haley and Jim Sidanius, "Person-Organization Congruence and the Maintenance of Group-Based Social Hierarchy: A Social Dominance Perspective," *Group Processes & Intergroup Relations* 8 (2005): 187–203, 187.

73. See Jim Sidanius, Felicia Pratto, Stacey Sinclair, and Colette Laar, "Mother Teresa Meets Genghis Khan: The Dialectics of Hierarchy-Enhancing and Hierarchy-Attenuating Career Choices," *Social Justice Research* 9 (1996): 145–170.

74. See Jim Sidanius, Felicia Pratto, Michael Martin, and Lisa M. Stallworth, "Consensual Racism and Career Track: Some Implications of Social Dominance Theory," *Political Psychology* 12 (1991): 691–721. For discussion of relevant issues, see Michaël Dambrun, Rodolphe Kamiejski, Nicolas Haddadi, and Sandra Duarte, "Why Does Social Dominance Orientation Decrease with University Exposure to the Social Sciences? The Impact of Institutional Socialization and the Mediating Role of 'Geneticism,'" *European Journal of Social Psychology* 39 (2009): 88–100.

75. See, for example, Peter K. Hatemi, John R. Hibbing, Sarah E. Medland, Matthew C. Keller, John R. Alford, Kevin B. Smith, Nicholas G. Martin, and Lindon J. Eaves, "Not By Twins Alone: Using the Extended Family Design to Investigate Genetic Influence on Political Beliefs," *American Journal of Political Science* 54 (2010): 798–814.

76. The mean score of professors on the vocabulary test was 8 out of 10; for all Americans it was 6. In our final model, which included a range of other input variables including education, the vocabulary variable did not account for any of the political gap between professors and other Americans. An alternative version of the model that excluded education produced

substantively similar results, suggesting that the effect of cognitive ability in the first model was not being masked by its contribution to educational attainment.

77. In a regression decomposition seeking to account for the political gap between professors and others, the effect of low levels of religious affiliation, with sex, age, race, region, and survey year held constant, was little changed when the vocabulary measure was introduced. There was some change when looking at the effect of low levels of fundamentalist Protestant affiliation.

78. The GSS vocabulary test presents respondents with a word and five possible synonyms, asking which synonym comes closest in meaning to the word. This exercise is repeated ten times. The Add Health measure is a "picture" vocabulary test: respondents are asked to choose an image that comes closest in meaning to a word read by the interviewer. Respondents are asked about the meaning of eighty-seven words.

79. Including the vocabulary measure, along with a measure of high school GPA, in a model that also included sociodemographic and class background measures barely changed the extent to which liberalism while in college predicted graduate school attendance versus stopping with a bachelor's degree. In a model excluding the vocabulary measure and GPA, a one-unit difference (toward greater liberalism) on Add Health's five-point political self-identification scale increased the odds of graduate school attendance by 1.9%. In the model inclusive of vocabulary and GPA, the effect was 1.7%.

80. Here liberals are defined as students who gave their political views as far left or liberal, conservative students as those who indicated conservative or far right. The spread on the verbal portion grows to twenty-eight points when comparing students on the far left to those on the far right.

81. This was a logistic regression that controlled for age, race, sex, region, father's education, father's occupation, and type of institution.

82. Another take on this is that there may be differences in the cultural "thought styles" of liberals and conservatives, to recall a concept used by Karl Mannheim in his classic analysis of nineteenth-century German conservatism. It is possible that such differences contribute to the overrepresentation of liberals in academe not in the sense of rendering conservatives uncreative or uninterested in science but by generating tensions between their general patterns of intellectual engagement and those institutionalized in higher education. For a discussion of thought styles, see Rodney D. Nelson, "The Sociology of Styles of Thought," *British Journal of Sociology* 43 (1992): 25–54. As noted earlier, Hetherington and Weiler use the notion of

"cognitive style" in their book on authoritarianism; it appears elsewhere in political psychology as well. I am grateful to Andrew Perrin for this point.

83. Sidanius's paper with Pratto, "Social Dominance Orientation," is typical: many of the questions used to construct their social dominance scale measure preferences for varying levels of equality. See esp. p. 760. A version of this criticism, along with a proposed conceptual remedy, is presented in Chris G. Silbey and John Duckitt, "Personality and Prejudice: A Meta-analysis and Theoretical Review," *Personality and Social Psychology Review* 12 (2008): 248–279.

84. As in Jim Sidanius, Colette van Laar, Shana Levin, and Stacey Sinclair, "Social Hierarchy Maintenance and Assortment into Social Roles: A Social Dominance Perspective," *Group Processes and Intergroup Relations* 6 (2003): 333–352.

85. Classic contributions here are John Van Maanen, "Observations on the Making of Policemen," *Human Organization* 32 (1973): 407–418; Van Maanen, "The Asshole," in *Policing: A View from the Street,* ed. Peter K. Manning and John Van Maanen (New York: Random House, 1978), 221–238.

3. Political Self-Selection and the Academic Profession

1. Matthew Woessner and April Kelly-Woessner, "Left Pipeline: Why Conservatives Don't Get Doctorates," in *The Politically Correct University: Problems, Scope, and Reforms,* ed. Robert Maranto, Richard E. Redding, and Frederick M. Hess (Washington, DC: AEI Press, 2009), 38–59.

2. Ariane Hegewich, Claudia Williams, and Amber Henderson, "The Gender Wage Gap: 2010," Institute for Women's Policy Research, Apr. 2011, http://www.iwpr.org/publications/pubs/the-gender-wage-gap-2010-up dated-march-2011 (accessed 11/30/11). Also see U.S. Department of Labor, Bureau of Labor Statistics, "Highlights of Women's Earnings in 2010," July 2011, Table 1, http://www.bls.gov/cps/cpswom2010.pdf (accessed 11/30/11. There is some disagreement as to how to measure the gap; different methodologies produce different estimates.

3. See Doris Weichselbaumer and Rudolf Winter-Ebmer, "A Meta-analysis of the International Gender Wage Gap," *Journal of Economic Surveys* 19 (2005): 479–511.

4. An entry point into the literature is Maria Charles and David B. Grusky, *Occupational Ghettos: The Worldwide Segregation of Women and Men* (Stanford, CA: Stanford University Press, 2004).

5. See U.S. Department of Labor, Bureau of Labor Statistics, "Highlights of Women's Earnings in 2010," Table 2, http://www.bls.gov/cps/cpswom 2010.pdf.

6. See, for example, Margaret Mooney Marini and Mary Brinton, "Sex Typing in Occupational Socialization," in *Sex Segregation in the Workplace: Trends, Explanations, Remedies,* ed. Barbara F. Reskin (Washington, DC: National Academy Press, 1984), 192–232.

7. Shelley J. Correll, "Gender and the Career Choice Process: The Role of Biased Self-Assessments," *American Journal of Sociology* 106 (2001): 1691–1730.

8. A version of this argument was advanced years ago by Ian D. Currie, Henry C. Finney, Travis Hirschi, and Hanan C. Selvin, "Images of the Professor and Interest in the Academic Profession," *Sociology of Education* 39 (1966): 301–323.

9. This was one of the key insights of the Wisconsin approach to status attainment. See William H. Sewell, Archibald O. Haller, and Alejandro Portes, "The Educational and Early Occupational Attainment Process," *American Sociological Review* 34 (1969): 82–92; William H. Sewell and Robert M. Hauser, "Causes and Consequences of Higher Education: Models of the Status Attainment Process," *American Journal of Agricultural Economics* 54 (1972): 851–861; William H. Sewell and Robert M. Hauser, *Education, Occupation, and Earnings: Achievement in the Early Career* (New York: Academic Press, 1975).

10. "Trends in Educational Equity of Girls and Women: 2004," National Center for Education Statistics, http://nces.ed.gov/pubs2005/equity/Section8.asp (accessed 11/30/11).

11. For example, see Grace Kao and Marta Tienda, "Educational Aspirations of Minority Youth," *American Journal of Education* 106 (1998): 349–384.

12. Jerry Jacobs, *Revolving Doors: Sex Segregation and Women's Careers* (Stanford, CA: Stanford University Press, 1989), 64–87; Xiaoling Shu and Margaret Mooney Marini, "Gender-Related Change in Occupational Aspirations," *Sociology of Education* 71 (1998): 43–67.

13. For a carefully developed social psychological model of self-concept congruence, see Peter J. Burke and Jan E. Stets, *Identity Theory* (Oxford, UK: Oxford University Press, 2009).

14. The classic piece on this is Arthur L. Stinchcombe, "Social Structure and Organizations," in *Handbook of Organizations,* ed. James G. March (Chicago: Rand McNally, 1965), 153–193.

15. Jason Kaufman, "Endogenous Explanation in the Sociology of Culture," *Annual Review of Sociology* 30 (2004): 335–357.

16. This research is reviewed in Martin J. Finkelstein, *The American Academic Profession: A Synthesis of Social Scientific Inquiry Since World War II* (Columbus: Ohio State University Press, 1984). Also see Stephen Cole and

Elinor Barber, *Increasing Faculty Diversity: The Occupational Choices of High-Achieving Minority Students* (Cambridge, MA: Harvard University Press, 2003).

17. Stephen R. Porter and Paul D. Umbach, "College Major Choice: An Analysis of Person-Environment Fit," *Research in Higher Education* 47 (2006): 429–449; Robin L. Bartlett, Marianne A. Ferber, and Carole A. Green, "Political Orientation and the Decision to Major in Economics: Some Preliminary Observations," *International Review of Economic Education* 8 (2009): 13–31. I return to this issue in Chapter 5.

18. Woessner and Kelly-Woessner, "Left Pipeline."

19. There is some evidence to suggest that conservatives are underrepresented at such schools. See Amy Binder and Kate Wood, *Becoming Right: How Campuses Shape Young Conservatives* (Princeton, NJ: Princeton University Press, 2013). I come back to this issue in Chapter 4.

20. Fosse and I presented our theory as an account of the aspiration to become a professor, but the processes involved might be profitably reconsidered in relation to broader labor market sorting and matching dynamics of the kind discussed in Arne L. Kalleberg, *The Mismatched Worker* (New York: W. W. Norton, 2007).

21. Neil Gross and Solon Simmons, "The Religiosity of American College and University Professors," *Sociology of Religion* 70 (2009): 101–129.

22. Steve Balch, " 'Why Professors Are Liberal': Explanation or Apologia?," National Association of Scholars, Apr. 23, 2010, http://www.nas.org /articles/Why_Professors_Are_Liberal_Explanation_or_Apologia (accessed 5/18/12).

23. The term *imprinting* is Stinchcombe's. For a useful discussion, see Victoria Johnson, "What Is Organizational Imprinting? Cultural Entrepreneurship in the Founding of the Paris Opera," *American Journal of Sociology* 113 (2007): 97–127.

24. The theory is thus very much in the vein of historical institutionalism in political science. For discussion, see Kathleen Thelen, "Historical Institutionalism in Comparative Politics," *Annual Review of Political Science* 2 (1999): 369–404.

25. However, these findings may be colored by priming effects. We asked respondents to give us their best guess as to the politics of the average professor rather than asking them, in an open-ended way, to give us their impression of the academic profession, and then looking to see whether liberal politics formed part of their description.

26. See the discussion of early aspirations in Cole and Barber, *Increasing Faculty Diversity,* 81.

27. More recent research finds that Americans on the right are much less likely than those on the left to have a positive view of colleges as social institutions. For example, a 2012 survey found that 69% of liberals, as opposed to 21% of conservatives, had favorable views of professors. See Ryan D. Enos, "The Politicized Value of College," YouGov, Mar. 15, 2012, http://today.yougov.com/news/2012/03/15/politicized-value-college/ (accessed 4/25/12).

28. In our coding of the interview transcripts on these points, we allowed interviewees to volunteer multiple explanations.

29. See Kris Paap, *Working Construction: Why White Working-Class Men Put Themselves—and the Labor Movement—in Harm's Way* (Ithaca, NY: ILR Press, Cornell University Press, 2006).

30. Woessner and Kelly-Woessner, "Left Pipeline"; Stanley Rothman, April Kelly-Woessner, and Matthew Woessner, *The Still Divided Academy: How Competing Visions of Power, Politics, and Diversity Complicate the Mission of Higher Education* (Lanham, MD: Rowman & Littlefield, 2011). A question on job satisfaction is also asked in the HERI Faculty Survey; the results are different from what Rothman, Kelly-Woessner, and Woessner report analyzing the survey done by Rothman, Lichter, and Nevitte. In an ordered logistic regression predicting a respondent's score on a five-category item measuring how much she or he would still want to be a professor if given the chance to start over, and with race, gender, age, institution type, region, and survey year held constant, political liberalism is a significant input.

31. Amy Binder and Kate Wood, " 'Civil' or 'Provocative'? Varieties of Conservative Student Style and Discourse in American Universities," unpublished manuscript, University of California-San Diego, 2011.

32. This was a pared-down version of the Oaxaca-Blinder regression decomposition models discussed in Chapter 2. It sought to determine how much of the political gap between professors and nonprofessors in the GSS was a function of the interaction of advanced degree holding and vocabulary scores, with advanced degree holding and vocabulary scores held constant and with no other input variables. The interaction variable accounted for 59% of the gap.

33. John R. Thelin, *A History of American Higher Education* (Baltimore: Johns Hopkins University Press, 2004), 41.

34. Ibid., 8; Frederick Rudolph, *The American College and University: A History* (Athens: University of Georgia Press, 1990).

35. Rudolph, *The American College and University*, 25.

36. Christian Smith, ed., *The Secular Revolution: Power, Interests, and Conflict in the Secularization of American Public Life* (Berkeley: University of California Press, 2003).

37. The story of the American research university's rise has been frequently told. Noteworthy accounts include Laurence R. Veysey, *The Emergence of the American University* (Chicago: University of Chicago Press, 1965); Christopher Jencks and David Riesman, *The Academic Revolution* (Garden City, NY: Doubleday, 1968); Robert V. Bruce, *The Launching of Modern American Science, 1846–1876* (New York: Knopf, 1987); Julie A. Reuben, *The Making of the Modern University: Intellectual Transformation and the Marginalization of Morality* (Chicago: University of Chicago Press, 1996); Thomas L. Haskell, *The Emergence of Professional Social Science: The American Social Science Association and the Nineteenth-Century Crisis of Authority* (Baltimore: Johns Hopkins University Press, 2000); Roger L. Geiger, *To Advance Knowledge: The Growth of American Research Universities, 1900–1940* (New Brunswick, NJ: Transaction, 2004), 1–57. The role of reformers should not be unduly emphasized. They were important in bringing about change, but so were broader social dynamics like industrialization and the emergence of what Andrew Abbott calls the "system of professions." Andrew Abbott, *The System of Professions: An Essay on the Division of Expert Labor* (Chicago: University of Chicago Press, 1988).

38. Smith, *Secular Revolution,* 36–37.

39. Randall Collins, *The Sociology of Philosophies: A Global Theory of Intellectual Change* (Cambridge, MA: Belknap Press of Harvard University Press, 1998).

40. Daniel Coit Gilman, *University Problems in the United States* (New York: Century, 1898), 178.

41. Smith, *Secular Revolution*.

42. Dorothy Ross, *The Origins of American Social Science* (Cambridge, UK: Cambridge University Press, 1991), 55.

43. Andrew Dickson White, *Report of the Committee on Organization* (Albany, NY: C. Van Benthuysen & Sons, 1867), 18.

44. George M. Marsden, *The Soul of the American University: from Protestant Establishment to Established Nonbelief* (New York: Oxford University Press, 1994), 181. In personal correspondence, Roger Geiger described this quotation from Marsden as misleading: there was also a strong scientific presence at Harvard at midcentury, while the dominance of Unitarian faculty hardly indicated entrenched clericalism.

45. My argument to this effect draws from Shmuel Eisenstadt's work on "multiple modernities" and his earlier accounts of institutional differentiation

processes as multiple, contested, and contingent. See Shmuel Eisenstadt, "Multiple Modernities," *Daedalus* 129 (2000): 1–29; Jeffrey C. Alexander and Paul Colomy, "Toward Neo-Functionalism," *Sociological Theory* 3 (1985): 11–23.

46. For general discussions of the Progressive movement, see James T. Kloppenberg, *Uncertain Victory: Social Democracy and Progressivism in European and American Thought, 1870–1920* (New York: Oxford University Press, 1986); Michael E. McGerr, *A Fierce Discontent: The Rise and Fall of the Progressive Movement in America, 1870–1920* (New York: Free Press, 2003); Maureen A. Flanagan, *America Reformed: Progressives and Progressivisms, 1890s–1920s* (New York: Oxford University Press, 2007).

47. Richard Wightman Fox, "The Culture of Liberal Protestant Progressivism, 1875–1925," *Journal of Interdisciplinary History* 23 (1993): 639–660; Kloppenberg, *Uncertain Victory.*

48. Fox, "The Culture of Liberal Protestant Progressivism," 640.

49. "Stanford Professor Quits," *Washington Post,* May 3, 1901, 1.

50. See Walter P. Metzger, *Academic Freedom in the Age of the University* (New York: Columbia University Press, 1961); Louis Menand, ed., *The Future of Academic Freedom* (Chicago: University of Chicago Press, 1996).

51. I offer two examples of many possible. First, "Academic Freedom of Speech," *Christian Science Monitor,* Mar. 7, 1912, 16, weighed in on Harvard's decision to disallow highly partisan speakers on campus:

> Two of the professors on the faculty of Wellesley College, socialists by creed, having spoken at meetings in Lawrence in ways comforting to the strikers and indicating agreement with some of the extreme claims of the Industrial Workers of the World as to the title of labor to all the increased values of manufacture, it is being hinted that they should be disciplined by the college authorities. No move in this direction by any responsible alumna or trustee has been reported. But discussion of this and similar cases is bound to arise as the ties that bind not a few American intellectuals to "practical" socialists are disclosed during intense agitation or fermenting reconstruction.

Second, "Academic Freedom," *New York Times,* June 20, 1915, 14, was critical of academic freedom: "Academic freedom is subject to . . . misuse. Some young crank gets into a professor's chair, and immediately begins to rewrite the constitution of the universe. Pretending to work against social injustice, these cub professors are too often engaged in teaching the doctrine of laziness."

52. Mary Furner, *Advocacy and Objectivity: A Crisis in the Professionalization of American Social Science, 1865–1905* (Lexington: University Press of Kentucky, 1975); Haskell, *The Emergence of Professional Social Science.*

53. Johnson, "What Is Organizational Imprinting?," 97–98.

54. In some respects, this argument about the endogenous reproduction of academic liberalism overlaps with Ladd and Lipset's intellectualism thesis, which also highlights continuity in the political valence of the intellectual role. Another important take on this can be found in Edward Shils, *The Intellectuals and the Powers and Other Essays* (Chicago: University of Chicago Press, 1972). For a general discussion of continuity in social life, see Orlando Patterson, "Culture and Continuity: Causal Structures in Socio-Cultural Persistence," in *Matters of Culture: Cultural Sociology in Practice,* ed. Roger Friedland and John Mohr (New York: Cambridge University Press, 2004), 71–109.

55. On self-reinforcing institutional processes, see Paul Pierson, "Increasing Returns, Path Dependence, and the Study of Politics," *American Political Science Review* 94 (2000): 251–267.

56. See Ellen W. Schrecker, *No Ivory Tower: McCarthyism and the Universities* (New York: Oxford University Press, 1986).

57. Liberals were not the only ones to oppose America's entry into the war. Some prominent conservatives did too, such as libertarian Albert Jay Nock. A concise summary of the Sacco and Vanzetti case, along with a stinging indictment of the prosecution, is Felix Frankfurter, "The Case of Sacco and Vanzetti," *The Atlantic* (1927), http://www.theatlantic.com/magazine/archive/1927/03/the-case-of-sacco-and-vanzetti/306625/ (accessed 8/28/12).

58. Despite the fact that this was so, most higher education institutions in the 1930s could hardly be said to be committed to left/liberal ideals. For examples of how they were not, see Jerome Karabel, *The Chosen: The Hidden History of Admission and Exclusion at Harvard, Yale, and Princeton* (Boston: Houghton Mifflin, 2005), 139–345; Stephen H. Norwood, *The Third Reich in the Ivory Tower: Complicity and Conflict on American Campuses* (New York: Cambridge University Press, 2009).

59. Philip G. Altbach, *Student Politics in America: A Historical Analysis* (New York: McGraw-Hill, 1974), 57–108. Ladd and Lipset cover this ground as well.

60. Charles J. Hendley, "Unionism in the Educational Field," *Social Frontiers/Frontiers of Democracy* 5 (1939): 238; Berel D. Cohon, "The Religious Educator and Social Responsibility," *Christian Leader* 124 (1942): 269.

61. Gunnar Myrdal, *An American Dilemma: The Negro Problem and Modern Democracy* (New York: Harper & Brothers, 1944), 468.

62. Charles H. Anderson and John D. Murray, eds., *The Professors: Work and Life Styles among Academicians* (Cambridge, MA: Schenkman, 1971), 22.

63. William Wong, "The New Educators: Radical Professors Exert Growing Power on College Campuses," *Wall Street Journal,* Apr. 7, 1971, 1.

64. Neil Gross, "A Pragmatist Theory of Social Mechanisms," *American Sociological Review* 74 (2009): 358–379; Peter Hedström and Peter Bearman, eds., *The Oxford Handbook of Analytical Sociology* (New York: Oxford University Press, 2009).

4. Political Differences among Professors

1. Paul F. Lazarsfeld and Wagner Thielens Jr., *The Academic Mind: Social Scientists in a Time of Crisis* (Glencoe, IL: Free Press, 1958).

2. This is not to deny that there are in fact some long-term continuities in the cognitive habits, knowledge-making practices, and intellectual commitments of members of academic disciplines. What is more, some apparent intellectual change in fields is simply a rehashing of old ideas. For discussion of the latter point see Andrew Abbott, *Chaos of Disciplines* (Chicago: University of Chicago Press, 2001).

3. Here my research assistants and I first fit separate ordered logistic regression models in which we sought to determine whether working in the social sciences, the humanities, or the natural sciences (relative to working in any other field) predicted liberal self-identification with race, gender, and age held constant. These were all significant predictors. For each model we then introduced measures of father's education and family income at age sixteen. In none of the models did we observe any meaningful change in the size of the coefficient for the dummy variable indicating disciplinary area.

4. This claim is developed explicitly in M. Reza Nakhaie and Robert J. Brym, "The Political Attitudes of Canadian Professors," *Canadian Journal of Sociology* 24 (1999): 329–353. Ladd and Lipset made a similar argument with respect to business: "The more closely a discipline is linked to the business world, the more conservative—in the context of academe—it is likely to be." Everett Carll Ladd, Jr. and Seymour Martin Lipset, *The Divided Academy: Professors and Politics* (New York: W. W. Norton, 1975), 71. On disciplines and their external linkages generally, see Stephen Park Turner and Jonathan H. Turner, *The Impossible Science: An Institutional Analysis of American Sociology* (Newbury Park, CA: Sage Publications, 1990); Terence C. Halliday and Morris Janowitz, eds., *Sociology and Its Publics: The Forms and Fates of Disciplinary Organization* (Chicago: University of Chicago Press, 1992); Joachim J. Savelsberg, Lara L. Cleveland, and Ryan D. King, "Institutional Environments and Scholarly Work: American Criminology, 1951–1993," *Social Forces* 82 (2004): 1275–1302; George Steinmetz, ed., *The Politics*

of Method in the Human Sciences: Positivism and Its Epistemological Others (Durham, NC: Duke University Press, 2005); Scott Frickel and Kelly Moore, eds., *The New Political Sociology of Science: Institutions, Networks, and Power* (Madison: University of Wisconsin Press, 2006).

5. Scott Frickel and Neil Gross, "A General Theory of Scientific/ Intellectual Movements," *American Sociological Review* 70 (2005): 204–232.

6. On the notion of political opportunity structures, see Doug McAdam, *Political Process and the Development of Black Insurgency, 1930–1970* (Chicago: University of Chicago Press, 1982); Doug McAdam, "Political Opportunities: Conceptual Origins, Current Problems, Future Directions," in *Comparative Perspectives on Social Movements: Political Opportunities, Mobilizing Structures, and Cultural Framings,* ed. Doug McAdam, John D. McCarthy, and Mayer N. Zald (Cambridge, UK: Cambridge University Press, 1996), 23–40; David S. Meyer and Debra C. Minkoff, "Conceptualizing Political Opportunity," *Social Forces* 82 (2004): 1457–1492.

7. To give Lazarsfeld and Thielens their due, cognitive skills and styles probably matter here as well. Disciplines do not have unchanging intellectual essences, but they exhibit a degree of stability, and what a field looks like intellectually in any period—a function of the scientific/intellectual movements that have occurred within it—determines the skill sets required of those who wish to study the field successfully and then enter it professionally. This may have an independent effect on faculty politics. The cognitive skills and habits necessary to be an outstanding student of literature in an era of high theory, for example, are very different than those required of engineering students in the middle of the nanotechnology revolution, and if these skill-set differences are associated with political views—with people of highly technical minds, say, coming to believe that they and their families would fare better if the leadership of the country favored increases in defense spending and unfettered corporate growth— than this could also help to explain why one observes political differences among faculty members in different fields.

A related possibility, pointed out by one of the anonymous reviewers of this book, is that the political reputations of fields may interact with their demographic characteristics. Fields perceived to be more left-leaning and open in the post-1960s period may have been those entered first by women and people of color. The greater presence of women and people of color in those fields today—in the social sciences, the humanities, and education— may in turn prompt even more people with liberal sensibilities to enter them, since demographics might be a cue for politics.

352

8. The term *audiences* comes from work on the sociology of the professions.

9. Myra Marx Ferree, Shamus Khan, and Shauna Morimoto, "Assessing the Feminist Revolution: The Presence and Absence of Gender Theory and Practice," in *Sociology in America: A History,* ed. Craig Calhoun (Chicago: University of Chicago Press, 2007), 438–479.

10. John David Skrentny, *The Minority Rights Revolution* (Cambridge, MA: Belknap Press of Harvard University Press, 2002).

11. Frank Dobbin, *Inventing Equal Opportunity* (Princeton, NJ: Princeton University Press, 2009).

12. Of course, the NSF dispenses grants through peer review and maintains a strong commitment to basic science, so it is not as though evolving priorities for funding at the federal level would have led to grants being awarded for social scientific work on gender had gender scholars not already gone some way toward establishing the credibility of their intellectual project.

13. Turner and Turner, *Impossible Science.*

14. Daniel Stedman Jones, *Masters of the Universe: The Origins of Neoliberal Politics* (Princeton, NJ: Princeton University Press, 2012).

15. The best account of the links between economics and other sectors of American society is Marion Fourcade, *Economists and Societies: Discipline and Profession in the United States, Britain, and France, 1890s to 1990s* (Princeton, NJ: Princeton University Press, 2009). On the role of economists teaching in business schools in developing and disseminating Chicago school economics, see Marion Fourcade and Rakesh Khurana, "From Social Control to Financial Economics: The Linked Ecologies of Economics and Business in Twentieth Century America," working paper 09-037, Harvard Business School, Organizational Behavior Unit, 2008. In Chapter 7 I discuss some of the conditions that led American business elites to withdraw from the de facto coalition with labor that made the long New Deal era possible—a coalitional membership that also undergirded business tolerance for Keynesian economics.

16. Economists were more conservative than sociologists or anthropologists in the 1950s and 1960s as well, but they appear to have grown more conservative since then. The 1969 Carnegie data show that 19% of economists identified as conservative. According to the PAP data that number is now 30%. (HERI faculty data from 1989 to 1998 indicate that only 10% of economists describe themselves as conservative, but a specialized survey of economists conducted in 2008 found, in line with the PAP data, that 28% percent planned to vote for McCain: http://www.dilbert.com/blog/entry

/dilbert_survey_of_economists/ [accessed 7/5/2012]). For discussion see Ladd and Lipset, *The Divided Academy*, 108–115.

17. See Kelly Moore, *Disrupting Science: Social Movements, American Scientists, and the Politics of the Military, 1945–1975* (Princeton, NJ: Princeton University Press, 2008).

18. For examples of this from different national contexts, see Patrick Carroll-Burke, "Material Designs: Engineering Cultures and Engineering States—Ireland 1650—1900," *Theory & Society* 31 (2002): 75–114; Chandra Mukerji, *Impossible Engineering: Technology and Territoriality on the Canal du Midi* (Princeton, NJ: Princeton University Press, 2009).

19. The dynamics here can be complicated. For example, professional and applied fields sometimes face pressure in the university environment to become more "academic." This can bolster scientific/intellectual movements that borrow heavily from work being done in more traditional liberal arts and science disciplines, including work that has a political orientation at odds with institutional tendencies in the original field. Such a dynamic, alongside generational shifts, might help explain the rise of critical legal studies in law schools in the 1970s and 1980s.

20. Pierre Bourdieu, *The State Nobility: Elite Schools in the Field of Power,* trans. Lauretta C. Clough (Oxford: Polity Press, 1996).

21. Stanley Rothman, S. Robert Lichter, and Neil Nevitte, "Politics and Professional Advancement among College Faculty," *Forum* 3 (2005): article 2; Daniel Klein and Andrew Western, "Voter Registration of Berkeley and Stanford Faculty," *Academic Questions* 18 (2004): 53–65.

22. Daniel B. Klein and Charlotta Stern, "Groupthink in Academia: Majoritarian Departmental Politics and the Professional Pyramid," in *The Politically Correct University: Problems, Scope, and Reforms,* ed. Robert Maranto, Richard E. Redding, and Frederick M. Hess (Washington, DC: AEI Press, 2009), 79–98.

23. Irving L. Janis, *Groupthink: Psychological Studies of Policy Decisions and Fiascoes* (Boston: Houghton Mifflin, 1982).

24. Diane Vaughan, *The Challenger Launch Decision: Risky Technology, Culture, and Deviance at NASA* (Chicago: University of Chicago Press, 1996).

25. This is the "Matthew effect," described in Robert K. Merton, "The Matthew Effect in Science," *Science* 159 (1968): 56–63. For a recent empirical study, see Alexander M. Petersen, Woo-Sung Jung, Jae-Suk Yang, and H. Eugene Stanley, "Quantitative and Empirical Demonstration of the Matthew Effect in a Study of Career Longevity," *Proceedings of the National Academy of Sciences of the United States of America* 108 (2011): 18–23.

26. Neil Gross, Thomas Medvetz, and Rupert Russell, "The Contemporary American Conservative Movement," *Annual Review of Sociology* 37 (2011): 325–354.

27. These claims are based on a tabulation of HERI CSS data, looking at student career aspirations.

28. See the discussion of this in, among other places, Douglas S. Massey, Camille Z. Charles, Garvey F. Lundy, and Mary J. Fischer, *The Source of the River: The Social Origins of Freshmen at America's Selective Colleges and Universities* (Princeton, NJ: Princeton University Press, 2003); Mitchell L. Stevens, *Creating a Class: College Admissions and the Education of Elites* (Cambridge, MA: Harvard University Press, 2007).

29. Forty-four percent of professionals and 39% of managers indicated that in their view the primary goal of higher education is to impart critical thinking skills. Among skilled tradespersons, semiskilled workers, and laborers, the numbers were 16%, 14%, and 19%, respectively.

30. Christine Musselin, *The Market for Academics,* trans. Amy Jacobs (New York: Routledge, 2010); Michèle Lamont, *How Professors Think: Inside the Curious World of Academic Judgment* (Cambridge, MA: Harvard University Press, 2009).

31. Rothman, Lichter, and Nevitte, "Politics and Professional Advancement among College Faculty," 8.

32. Ibid., 13.

33. Jonathan Haidt, "Discrimination Hurts Real People," Your Morals Blog, Feb. 17, 2011, http://www.yourmorals.org/blog/2011/02/discrimination-hurts-real-people/ (accessed 11/13/11).

34. Gary A. Tobin and Aryeh K. Weinberg. *A Profile of American College and University Faculty: Political Beliefs and Behavior* (San Francisco: Institute for Jewish and Community Research, 2006).

35. George A. Yancey, *Compromising Scholarship: Religious and Political Bias in American Higher Education* (Waco, TX: Baylor University Press, 2011).

36. Ibid., 220.

37. Ibid., 57–63. For a similar finding based on a survey of social psychologists, see Yoel Inbar and Joris Lammers, "Political Diversity in Social and Personality Psychology," *Perspectives on Psychological Science* 7 (2012): 496–503.

38. The classic article on this topic is Henri Tajfel, "Social Psychology of Intergroup Relations," *Annual Review of Psychology* 33 (1982): 1–39.

39. For general discussions of this methodology, see Devah Pager, "The Use of Field Experiments for Studies of Employment Discrimination:

Contributions, Critiques, and Directions for the Future," *Annals of the American Academy of Political and Social Sciences* 609 (2007): 104–133.

40. For example, see David Neumark, Roy J. Bank, and Kyle D. Van Nort, "Sex Discrimination in Restaurant Hiring: An Audit Study," *Quarterly Journal of Economics* 11 (1996): 915–941; Marianne Bertrand and Sendhil Mullainathan, "Are Emily and Greg More Employable than Lakisha and Jamal? A Field Experiment on Labor Market Discrimination," *American Economic Review* 94 (2004): 991–1013; Devah Pager, Bruce Western, and Bart Bonikowski, "Discrimination in a Low-Wage Labor Market: A Field Experiment," *American Sociological Review* 74 (2009): 777–799.

41. Devah Pager, *Marked: Race, Crime, and Finding Work in an Era of Mass Incarceration* (Chicago: University of Chicago Press, 2007).

42. The methodological details of this study are discussed in Ethan Fosse, Neil Gross, and Joseph Ma, "Political Bias in the Graduate Admissions Process," unpublished manuscript, University of British Columbia, 2011. I reproduce two sample emails here:

Email 1: Kevin Cook, Sociology, Control Condition

Dear Professor ———,

My name is Kevin Cook. I'm a senior at UC Irvine majoring in sociology, and I'm extremely interested in pursuing graduate work in the field. I'm writing to ask whether you think I'd be a good fit for the ——— program, which I'm considering applying to later this fall. I also have a question I couldn't find the answer to online.

My main interest is the sociology of culture. Several of the papers I've written for my classes have been on the topic and I hope to keep working on it in graduate school. From looking at your department's website it seems there are a number of outstanding professors in the area. Am I right that I would fit in there given my interests?

I want to become a sociologist because I find sociology fascinating, and because, naïve as it might sound, I hope to have an impact on the world. In addition to working hard academically, I've spent a fair amount of time over the last couple of years volunteering for various local organizations.

My other question: I've heard that it's very important to get involved in professors' research projects and coauthor papers with them. Are there opportunities to do that in your program?

Many thanks,

Kevin

Email 2: Jeff Allen, Sociology, McCain Treatment Condition

Professor ———,

Greetings from Santa Barbara. I'm Jeff Allen, and this spring I'll graduate from the sociology department at UCSB.

Over the last couple of years I've come to realize that I want to pursue a career as a sociologist. I'm now wrestling with the question of to which graduate programs I should apply. I've spent a lot of my time as an undergraduate studying the sociology of culture, a topic for which I have a real passion.

As my transcript will show, I'm an extremely serious student. But I've also tried to stay well-rounded during my time in college, doing volunteer work and getting involved with student organizations. When I was a sophomore I also spent a few intense months working for the McCain campaign, which was quite a learning experience.

As I consider various graduate programs, one of my biggest concerns is the availability of funding for research. Are there scholarships students can apply to at ——— that will help fund original research? Also, could you give me some sense for whether the department would be a good home for someone with my interests?

Thank you for your time. I'm sure you must get a lot of emails.

Best,

Jeff

43. Interrater reliability for the information and enthusiasm scales was reasonably high, and somewhat lower—though still within the range of acceptability—for the emotional warmth scale.

44. There is some discussion of the ethical issues involved in audit research in Pager, *Marked*, 76–78.

45. And has for a long time. In 1959 William F. Buckley wrote a letter to Henry Steele Commager asking whether, as Buckley had heard tell, he had changed his middle name to Steele in the 1930s in admiration for Stalin. Commager was incensed and took offense at the question. Buckley replied, "I do not understand the reasons for your excitement. You are a public figure. It strikes me as particularly inappropriate for a professional historian to express dismay at evidence of public curiosity about the background of public figures. . . . I register the hope that those to whom you go for information in the course of your pursuits greet you more cooperatively than you have me." William F. Buckley Jr. to Henry Steele Commager, Oct. 14, 1959, William F. Buckley Jr. Papers, Manuscript Group 576, Box 7, Yale University. This incident is discussed in Neil Jumonville, *Henry Steele Com-*

mager: Midcentury Liberalism and the History of the Present (Chapel Hill: University of North Carolina Press, 1999), 123–126. Jumonville reports that Buckley's accusation was baseless.

46. Many of these can be found in Peter Wood, "Preferred Colleagues," *Chronicle of Higher Education,* Aug. 12, 2012, http://chronicle.com/blogs/innovations/preferred-colleagues/29160 (accessed 12/10/11).

47. Trond Petersen and Ishak Saporta, "The Opportunity Structure for Discrimination," *American Journal of Sociology* 109 (2004): 852–901. However, admissions decisions—unlike the sending of emails—are made in a committee setting in which one might expect some groupthink processes to operate and to magnify whatever individual biases might be present.

48. Stanley Rothman, April Kelly-Woessner, and Matthew Woessner, *The Still Divided Academy: How Competing Visions of Power, Politics, and Diversity Complicate the Mission of Higher Education* (Lanham, MD: Rowman & Littlefield, 2011), 182.

49. See Miller McPherson, Lynn Smith-Lovin, and James M. Cook, "Birds of a Feather: Homophily in Social Networks," *Annual Review of Sociology* 27 (2001): 415–444.

50. Fabio Rojas, *From Black Power to Black Studies: How a Radical Social Movement Became an Academic Discipline* (Baltimore: Johns Hopkins University Press, 2007).

51. Without attending to politics directly, sociologists who study intellectual life have observed that departments and programs often develop idiosyncratic local cultures that form the basis for assessments of academic merit. See Charles Camic, "Three Departments in Search of a Discipline: Localism and Interdisciplinary Interaction in American Sociology, 1890–1940," *Social Research* 62 (1995): 1003–1033. Academic departments are thus an example of what Gary Fine calls "tiny publics." Gary Alan Fine, *Tiny Publics: A Theory of Group Action and Culture* (New York: Russell Sage Foundation, 2012).

52. Quoted in John Tierney, "The Left-Leaning Tower," *New York Times,* July 22, 2011, ED 34.

53. Barry Ames, David C. Barker, Chris W. Bonneau, and Christopher J. Carman, 2005. "Hide the Republicans, the Christians, and the Women: A Response to 'Politics and Professional Advancement among College Faculty,'" *Forum* 2005 (3): article 7.

54. George Yancey, personal communication, Apr. 11, 2011. Another possibility is that in some fields there is political bias in the publications process, restricting the ability of conservatives to rack up prestigious publications and hence be viable candidates for jobs at elite institutions.

55. Friedrich Hayek, "The Intellectuals and Socialism," in *The Intellectuals: A Controversial Portrait,* ed. George Bernard de Huszar (Glencoe, IL: Free Press, 1960), 379.

56. The PAP survey asked respondents to name the institution from which they received their highest degree. We coded schools as top-ranked if they were among the top thirty research institutions listed in the 2010 report prepared by Arizona State University's Center for Measuring University Performance. See Elizabeth D. Capaldi, John V. Lombardi, Craig W. Abbey, and Diane D. Craig, "The Top American Research Universities: 2010 Annual Report," Center for Measuring University Performance, Arizona State University, 2010, 53, http://mup.asu.edu/research2010.pdf (accessed 12/10/11). There are obvious problems with this methodology, but it is not a useless indicator of intellectual capital.

57. This does not appear to be a function of conservatives teaching in more applied fields. In the social sciences, for example, the numbers are 93% versus 79%. Nor is it merely a reflection of the fact that conservatives are more likely to be found in community colleges. Among non–community college professors the numbers are 85% and 71%. A similar difference can be found restricting the sample to professors teaching at non–religiously affiliated colleges or universities. Parallel patterns can be found in the HERI faculty data from 1989 to 1998: 69% of liberal respondents in that data set hold PhDs, as compared to 47% of conservative respondents. And in personal correspondence, Matthew Woessner has relayed that there is a 10 percentage point gap in doctoral degree holding between Democratic and Republican professors in the survey by Rothman, Lichter, and Nevitte. One possible explanation is greater attrition from graduate school for conservatives because of perceptions of a hostile climate, or perhaps because, having gone against type, they feel less "professional role confidence" than liberals. Some might then seek out teaching slots in academe that do not require a doctoral degree. On professional role confidence, see Erin Cech, Brian Rubineau, Susan Silbey, and Caroll Seron, "Professional Role Confidence and Gendered Persistence in Engineering," *American Sociological Review* 76 (2011): 641–666.

58. In this two-step ordered logistic regression, we first sought to determine whether identifying as a liberal instead of as a conservative (thus excluding moderates from the sample) was associated with teaching at a more prestigious type of institution (along a scale running from community college to four-year school to liberal arts college to nonelite PhD program to elite PhD program), holding constant sex, race, age, and disciplinary area. We then in-

troduced the additional variables. The odds ratio for liberal changed from 2.51 to 1.81 (and, again, was rendered not significant at the .10 level) when we did so. Results were substantively similar when we ran the model as a multinomial logistic regression or when we looked at Democrats versus Republicans.

59. Michael T. Hannan and John Freeman, *Organizational Ecology* (Cambridge, MA: Harvard University Press, 1989).

60. Pamela A. Popielarz and Zachary P. Neal, "The Niche as a Theoretical Tool," *Annual Review of Sociology* 33 (2007): 65–84.

61. This idea is compatible with Benjamin Schneider's "attraction-selection-attrition" model for organizational recruitment, which emphasizes the selection of personnel based on perceptions of shared values. See Benjamin Schneider, "The People Make the Place," *Personnel Psychology* 40 (1987): 437–453.

62. In addition, many liberal arts colleges were founded on activist principles.

63. There are clear echoes of Ladd and Lipset in this argument, specifically their claim that insofar as the academic role has come to be associated with critical intellectualism, elite institutions might give a preference in hiring to job candidates who embody that role.

64. Yang Yang, "Bayesian Inference for Hierarchical Age-Period-Cohort Models of Repeated Cross-Section Survey Data," *Sociological Methodology* 36 (2006): 39–74.

65. HERI researchers noted this same trend in their data in 2002. See "UCLA Study Finds Growing Gap in Political Liberalism between Male and Female Faculty," UC Newsroom, Aug. 28, 2002, http://www.universityofcalifornia.edu/news/article/4879 (accessed 11/03/11).

66. An excellent discussion of the gender gap can be found in Pippa Norris, "The Gender Gap: Old Challenges, New Approaches," unpublished manuscript, Harvard University, 2000. On graduate education as a predictor of support for the feminist movement, see Jason Schnittker, Jeremy Freese, and Brian Powell, "Who Are Feminists and What Do They Believe? The Role of Generations," *American Sociological Review* 68 (2003): 607–622. On the institutionalization of academic feminism, see Ellen Messer Davidow, *Disciplining Feminism: From Social Activism to Academic Discourse* (Durham, NC: Duke University Press, 2002).

67. In the CSS data, left or liberal female students who reported having taken at least one women's studies course were more than twice as likely than those left or liberal female students who had not to aspire to become college professors.

68. This explanation does not necessarily hold true for more recent changes in professorial politics. By 2004–2005 HERI data registered a more significant increase in the proportion of professors identifying as far left or liberal, and the increase was fairly evenly apportioned between women and men.

69. For discussion, see Jon A. Krosnick and Duane F. Alwin, "Aging and Susceptibility to Attitude Change," *Journal of Personality and Social Psychology* 57 (1989): 416–425. There are other indicators of the decline of academic radicalism. For example, a Google Books ngram examining the American English corpus shows that after peaking in the 1970s, references to "Marxist sociology" fell off sharply and are now at their lowest levels since the mid-1950s. "Marxist literary criticism" peaked in the 1970s too. From the perspective of social theory anyway this is a loss: radical intellectual traditions have historically been sources of great insight.

70. Abbott, *Chaos of Disciplines*; Karl Mannheim, "The Problem of Generations," in *Essays on the Sociology of Knowledge,* ed. Paul Kecskemeti (London: Routledge and Kegan Paul, 1952), 276–320.

5. The Knowledge-Politics Problem

1. Alvin Ward Gouldner, *The Coming Crisis of Western Sociology* (New York: Basic Books, 1970). Sociologists of scientific knowledge have also explored these issues, though typically their focus is not on conventional politics. For example, see Barry Barnes's classic *Interests and the Growth of Knowledge* (London: Routledge and Kegan Paul, 1977). For more recent discussions, see Scott Frickel, *Chemical Consequences: Environmental Mutagens, Scientist Activism, and the Rise of Genetic Toxicology* (New Brunswick, NJ: Rutgers University Press, 2004); Kelly Moore, *Disrupting Science: Social Movements, American Scientists, and the Politics of the Military, 1945–1975* (Princeton, NJ: Princeton University Press, 2007).

2. Sarah Babb, *Managing Mexico: Economists from Nationalism to Neoliberalism* (Princeton, NJ: Princeton University Press, 2004).

3. John Aubrey Douglass, *The California Idea and American Higher Education: 1850 to the 1960 Master Plan* (Stanford, CA: Stanford University Press, 2000); David Yamane, *Student Movements for Multiculturalism: Challenging the Curricular Color Line in Higher Education* (Baltimore: Johns Hopkins University Press, 2001). Intellectual historians and biographers are the other major exception here, but their work, by its nature, avoids treating the relationship between politics and academic ideas in any kind of general way. A short but instructive account of how politics has shaped work on American history can

be found in E. J. Dionne Jr., *Our Divided Political Heart: The Battle for the American Idea in an Age of Discontent* (New York: Bloomsbury, 2012), 53–68.

4. For an intriguing study on grading and politics at an elite institution, see Talia Bar and Asaf Zussman, "Partisan Grading," *American Economic Journal* 4 (2012): 30–48.

5. The PAP data offer some insight into the frequency of these activities. Fifty-nine percent of respondents told us that during the 2004 presidential campaign they had tried to persuade people to vote for the candidate they preferred; 27% attended a political meeting, rally, or speech; 34% wore a campaign button, put a bumper sticker on their car, or put a campaign sign in front of their house; 43% gave money to one of the candidates; and 11% said that during the prior year they had submitted at least one op-ed piece to a newspaper.

6. The findings reported in this chapter are based on coding of the interview transcripts by two of my research assistants according to an inductively derived, standardized coding scheme. The coders began by coding the same five transcripts. They coded identically 85 percent of the time. Discrepant codings were discussed and corrected, and then three additional transcripts were processed by both coders. This time there was 90% intercoder agreement. The remaining transcripts were subsequently divided up between the two coders. Later, quantitative data were compiled about the distribution of codes and interviewees were placed into broad categories pertaining to teaching based on the codes and my rereading of the transcripts. To reiterate a point made in the notes to the introduction, my research assistants interviewed a small number of scholars whose degrees were in fields different than their departmental appointments. I retained these cases in the analyses conducted for this chapter to reflect the fact that most fields contain some people who work at the intersection of other fields.

7. A useful discussion of this literature is Harold Kincaid, John Dupré, and Alison Wylie, eds., *Value-Free Science? Ideals and Illusions* (New York: Oxford University Press, 2007).

8. Karin Knorr Cetina, *Epistemic Cultures: How the Sciences Make Knowledge* (Cambridge, MA: Harvard University Press, 1999), 3.

9. An engaging account of these developments can be found in François Cusset, *French Theory: How Foucault, Derrida, Deleuze, and Co. Transformed the Intellectual Life of the United States* (Minneapolis: University of Minnesota Press, 2008.) Also see Michèle Lamont, "How to Become a Dominant French Philosopher: The Case of Jacques Derrida," *American Journal of Sociology* 93 (1987): 584–622; Neil Gross, *Richard Rorty: The Making of an American Philosopher* (Chicago: University of Chicago Press, 2008).

10. Edward E. Leamer, "Let's Take the Con out of Econometrics," *American Economic Review* 73 (1983): 31–43.

11. Ben Agger, *Public Sociology: From Social Facts to Literary Acts* (Lanham, MD: Rowman & Littlefield, 2007), 4.

12. While not considering politics per se, classic work in the sociology of science explores the extent of scientists' commitments to notions of objectivity, including the recognition by some that by the books objectivity is neither possible nor desirable. For example, see Ian I. Mitroff, "Norms and Counter-Norms in a Select Group of the Apollo Moon Scientists: A Case Study of the Ambivalence of Scientists," *American Sociological Review* 39 (1974): 579–595.

13. Wolf Lepenies, *Between Literature and Science: the Rise of Sociology,* trans. R. J. Hollingdale (Cambridge, MA: Cambridge University Press, 1988).

14. Bruce L. R. Smith, Jeremy D. Mayer, and A. Lee Fritschler, *Closed Minds? Politics and Ideology in American Universities* (Washington, DC: Brookings Institution Press, 2008), 84.

15. Ibid., 198.

16. Morris P. Fiorina, with Samuel J. Abrams and Jeremy C. Pope, *Culture War? The Myth of a Polarized America* (New York: Pearson Longman, 2005).

17. See Alan I. Abramowitz, *The Disappearing Center: Engaged Citizens, Polarization, and American Democracy* (New Haven, CT: Yale University Press, 2010). On polarization, also see Nolan McCarty, Keith T. Poole, and Howard Rosenthal, *Polarized America: The Dance of Ideology and Unequal Riches* (Cambridge, MA: The MIT Press, 2008); Delia Baldassarri and Andrew Gelman, "Partisans without Constraint: Political Polarization and Trends in American Public Opinion," *American Journal of Sociology* 114 (2008): 408–446.

18. For a revealing discussion of the several varieties of moderates that can be found in American politics, and the relationship between being moderate and political knowledge, see Shawn Treier and D. Sunshine Hillygus, "The Nature of Political Ideology in the Contemporary Electorate," *Public Opinion Quarterly* 73 (2009): 679–703.

19. In fact politics was a major impetus behind the growth of applied fields like business. In the 1970s prominent business elites, fearing that social scientists and humanists were teaching students antibusiness values, pushed hard and donated money for the expansion of undergraduate business programs around the country. See the discussion in Bethany E. Moreton, "Make Payroll, Not War: Business Culture as Youth Culture," in *Rightward Bound: Making America Conservative in the 1970s,* ed. Bruce J.

Schulman and Julian E. Zelizer (Cambridge, MA: Harvard University Press, 2008), 52–70.

20. Javier Arias-Vazquez, "College Majors and Political Attitudes," unpublished manuscript, University of Chicago, 2011, 3.

21. Ibid., 2.

22. A relevant and fascinating literature examines the extent to which economics majors and graduate students are more likely than others to free-ride, and whether this is a result of selection and/or "treatment" (i.e., exposure to economics). The pioneering study in this vein is Gerald Marwell and Ruth E. Ames, "Economists Free Ride, Does Anyone Else? Experiments on the Provision of Public Goods IV," *Journal of Public Economics* 15 (1981): 295–310.

23. Cass R. Sunstein, *Going to Extremes: How Like Minds Unite and Divide* (New York: Oxford University Press, 2009). This point probably applies to the professoriate as well: relative political homogeneity in certain quarters of the academy may push professors' commitments to liberalism further toward the extreme.

24. See "Bachelor's Degrees Conferred by Degree-Granting Institutions, by Field of Study: Selected Years, 1970–71 through 2008–09," National Center for Education Statistics, Apr. 2011, http://nces.ed.gov/programs/digest /d10/tables/dt10_282.asp?referrer=list (accessed 11/31/11).

6. The Campaign against "Liberal Bias"

1. Michael Paul Rogin, *The Intellectuals and McCarthy: The Radical Specter* (Cambridge, MA: The MIT Press, 1967), 232.

2. Robert M. MacIver, *Academic Freedom in Our Time* (New York: Columbia University Press, 1955); Richard Hofstadter and Walter P. Metzger, *The Development of Academic Freedom in the United States* (New York: Columbia University Press, 1955).

3. Sidney Hook, "The Grounds on Which Our Educators Stand," *New York Times,* Oct. 30, 1955, BR6.

4. William F. Buckley Jr., "Columbia's Report on Academic Freedom," *National Review,* Dec. 14, 1955, 23.

5. William F. Buckley Jr., "*National Review* Offers Awards to College Students for Assistance in Research Project," *National Review,* Dec. 28, 1955, 14.

6. And between Buckley and Hook specifically. In the 1960s Hook often appeared on Buckley's television program *Firing Line*. See the discussion in George Cotkin's review of *Sidney Hook Reconsidered, Journal of American History* 92 (2005): 1051–1052. The limited correspondence with Hook that one finds in Buckley's papers is entirely cordial. Buckley recalled Hook fondly

in William F. Buckley Jr., "Sidney Hook, R.I.P.," in *Happy Days Were Here Again: Reflections of a Libertarian Journalist,* ed. Patricia Bozell (New York: Random House, 1973), 379–381.

7. "Ahmadinejad, at Columbia, Parries and Puzzles," *New York Times,* Sept. 25, 2007, A1.

8. "Columbia Unredeemed," *Daily News,* Sept. 25, 2007, 28.

9. For example, see the discussion in Chris Beam, "Is the MEALAC Department Balanced?," *Columbia Spectator,* Apr. 28, 2003, http://www.columbiaspectator.com/2003/04/28/mealac-department-balanced (accessed 12/06/11).

10. "Summers Spoke the Truth," *Boston Globe,* Feb. 28, 2005, 11; "[Summers] Wanted These Intellectuals to Do What They're Supposed to Do—Think," *Chicago Sun-Times,* Apr. 27, 2005, 55.

11. "Academic, Heal Thyself," *New York Times,* Mar. 6, 2006, A21.

12. See "Report on Conclusion of Preliminary Review in the Matter of Professor Ward Churchill," http://archived.wardchurchill.net/12-PreliminaryReview_3_24_05.pdf (accessed 8/28/12).

13. See Norman G. Finkelstein, *Image and Reality of the Israel-Palestine Conflict* (London: Verso, 1995); Norman G. Finkelstein, *The Holocaust Industry: Reflection on the Exploitation of Jewish Suffering* (London: Verso, 2000).

14. David Horowitz, *The Professors: The 101 Most Dangerous Academics in America* (Washington, DC: Regnery, 2006); David Horowitz, *Indoctrination U: The Left's War against Academic Freedom* (New York: Encounter Books, 2007).

15. Students for Academic Freedom, "Academic Bill of Rights," Section II, Paragraph 2, http://www.studentsforacademicfreedom.org/documents/1925/abor.html (accessed 11/03/11).

16. Horowitz does not frame his grievances with academe in terms of bias per se.

17. Massie Ritsch, "Professors Spent Their Summer Vacations Giving to Obama," Open Secrets Blog, Aug. 26, 2008, http://www.opensecrets.org/news/2008/08/professors-spent-their-summer.html (accessed 11/04/11).

18. "Academia on Palin: Liberal Bastions Lack Diversity," *Washington Times,* Oct. 2, 2008, A21.

19. Gary Fine has observed that it is commonplace for political movements to attempt to discredit opposing movements by identifying their "notorious supporters." The implication is that if someone disreputable supports a movement, it must be misguided. No small part of the right's anger toward the academic left takes this form; the attempt to link Obama

with Ayers is but one of many examples. See Gary Alan Fine, "Notorious Support: The America First Committee and the Personalization of Policy," *Mobilization* 11 (2006): 405–426. Neil McLaughlin—who drew my attention to this point—offers an analysis of George Soros that highlights these themes: Neil McLaughlin and Skaidra Trilupaityte, "International Circulation of Attacks and the Reputational Consequences of Local Context: Soros's Difficult Reputation in Russia, Post-Soviet Lithuania, and the United States," *Cultural Sociology,* forthcoming.

20. Scott Jaschik, "Banned in Boston," Inside Higher Ed, Mar. 30, 2009, http://www.insidehighered.com/news/2009/03/30/ayers (accessed 12/05/11); James Risen, "Ex-Spy Alleges Bush White House Sought to Discredit Critic," *New York Times,* June 15, 2011, A1; Steven Greenhouse, "Group Seeks Labor E-Mails by Michigan Professors," *New York Times,* Mar. 30, 2011, A13; Scott Jaschik, "What Freshmen Will Read," Inside Higher Ed, June 4, 2010, http://www.insidehighered.com/news/2010/06/04/books (accessed 12/05/11); "Partners," *New Yorker,* Aug. 29, 2011, 40–51; Peter Dreier, "Glenn Beck's Attack on Frances Fox Piven," *Dissent,* Jan. 24, 2011, http://www.dissentmagazine.org/online.php?id=437 (accessed 03/11/11); Libby A. Nelson, "Santorum and Higher Ed," Inside Higher Ed, Mar. 9, 2012, http://www.insidehighered.com/news/2012/03/09/santorums-views-and-history-higher-education (accessed 4/1/12).

21. For example, Lionel Lewis, "Stifling Academic Freedom: Professors and Colleges Threatened by Accusations of Radicalism," *Buffalo (New York) News*, Apr. 16, 2011, H1.

22. The former resulted in the edited volume of the same name: Beshara Doumani, ed., *Academic Freedom after September 11* (Cambridge, MA: The MIT Press, 2006). The latter yielded two issues worth of papers in the journal *Social Research* (Fall and Summer 2009).

23. "Ad Hoc Committee to Defend the University," https://sites.google.com/site/defenduniversity/home (accessed 11/04/11).

24. The scope of the involvement of the American Federation of Teachers with these issues can be gleaned from Scott Jaschik, "Playing Defense and Offense," Inside Higher Ed, Apr. 18, 2005, http://www.insidehighered.com/news/2005/04/18/aft (accessed 12/10/11).

25. Personal communication with John Curtis, Aug. 15, 2007.

26. "An Exclusive Illinois Academe Interview with AAUP Head (and Illinois AAUP Annual Meeting Keynote Speaker) Roger Bowen," AAUP-IL, Spring 2005, http://www.ilaaup.org/news/IllinoisAcademe/2005_Spring/il_academe_2005sp_Academe_interview.html (accessed 3/21/10).

27. Nelson spells out his views on Horowitz in *No University Is an Island: Saving Academic Freedom* (New York: New York University Press, 2010).

28. A Google Insights for Search analysis similarly shows a spike in web searches for *liberal professors* around 2005–2006, with unusually high volumes of search activity in New York and California.

29. Paul F. Lazarsfeld and Wagner Thielens Jr., *The Academic Mind: Social Scientists in a Time of Crisis* (Glencoe, IL: Free Press, 1958), 378. I do not try to assess in this book any of the consequences for academic life of this perceived level of threat.

30. As indicated in the introduction, I choose Colorado and Wisconsin as interview sites because there had recently been major blowups there: Churchill in Colorado and Kevin Barrett in Wisconsin. Working under contract for me, in the late summer and early fall of 2007 the Center for Survey Research at Indiana University conducted in-depth interviews with thirty-six members of the public in Colorado and thirty-three in Wisconsin. People were recruited for the study through mailings to random household addresses, with $25 offered as an incentive. Interviewees were asked the same questions as on the national poll (along with a few supplements), but for each question were also asked to explain their answers in their own words. Interviews lasted forty-four minutes on average. Sample characteristics are available upon request. Interviewee names mentioned in Chapter 7 are pseudonyms.

31. Richard Hofstadter, *Anti-Intellectualism in American Life* (New York: Knopf, 1963).

32. The Columbia context in which the book was written is discussed in David S. Brown, *Richard Hofstadter: An Intellectual Biography* (Chicago: University of Chicago Press, 2006).

33. Hofstadter, *Anti-Intellectualism,* 7.

34. I draw here on Daniel Rigney, "Three Kinds of Anti-Intellectualism: Rethinking Hofstadter," *Sociological Inquiry* 61 (1991): 434–451.

35. Richard Hofstadter, *The Paranoid Style in American Politics and Other Essays* (New York: Vintage Books, 1967).

36. Seymour Martin Lipset, *The Politics of Unreason: Right Wing Extremism in America, 1790–1970* (New York: Harper & Row, 1970); Theodor W. Adorno, Else Frenkel-Brunswik, Daniel J. Levinson, and R. Nevitt Sanford, *The Authoritarian Personality* (New York: Harper, 1950). On status anxiety accounts of conservatism, see Clarence Lo, "Countermovements and Conservative Movements in the Contemporary U.S.," *Annual Review of Sociology* 8 (1982): 107–134.

37. Richard Hofstadter, "The Pseudo-Conservative Revolt—1954," in *The Paranoid Style in American Politics,* 62.

38. Hofstadter, *The Paranoid Style in American Politics,* 4.

39. Walter W. Powell and Kaisa Snellman, "The Knowledge Economy," *Annual Review of Sociology* 30 (2004): 199–220.

40. For a historical account of the college wage premium, see Claudia Goldin and Lawrence F. Katz, "The Race between Education and Technology," in *The Race between Education and Technology,* ed. Claudia Goldin and Lawrence F. Katz (Cambridge, MA: Belknap Press of Harvard University Press, 2008), 287–323.

41. See the discussion in Enrico Moretti, *The New Geography of Jobs* (New York: Houghton Mifflin Harcourt, 2012).

42. Robert Britt Horwitz, "Utopianism on the Right: Neoconservatism, Religion, and American Foreign Policy," unpublished manuscript, University of California-San Diego, 2011.

43. Most professors are indeed committed to encouraging greater tolerance for diversity. In the 1997 Carnegie faculty survey, 60% of respondents rated this as a "very important goal" for undergraduate education. Jack H. Schuster and Martin J. Finkelstein, *The American Faculty: The Restructuring of Academic Work and Careers* (Baltimore: Johns Hopkins University Press, 2006), 492.

44. The model incorporated measures of to what extent respondents thought (1) liberal bias is a problem; (2) colleges and universities favor liberal professors; (3) the typical professor is radical; (4) professors show respect for students with differing views; and (5) professors are too concerned with issues of race and gender. Model fit statistics are available on request.

45. D. Michael Lindsay, *Faith in the Halls of Power: How Evangelicals Joined the American Elite* (New York: Oxford University Press, 2007), 272, note 12. However, a more recent poll, by Pew, found that 56% of white evangelicals describe college professors as "unfriendly" to religion and that the percentage of Americans holding such a view has grown since 2003. See "More See 'Too Much' Religious Talk by Politicians," Pew Forum on Religion and Public Life, Mar. 21, 2012, http://www.pewforum.org/Politics-and-Elections/more-see-too-much-religious-talk-by-politicians.aspx#reporters (accessed 03/31/12). It is possible that some evangelical support for anti–liberal-professor rhetoric is driven by their perception of academics as irreligious, regardless of the status politics implications: atheists are a reviled outgroup in the United States. Penny Edgell, Joseph Gerteis, and Douglas Hartmann, "Atheists as 'Other': Moral Boundaries and Cultural Membership in American Society," *American Sociological Review* 71 (2006): 211–234.

46. However, the poll was taken when President Bush was still in office, and questions about satisfaction with the direction of the country are sensitive to whether respondents' favored political parties are in power.

47. Rogin, *Intellectuals and McCarthy,* 216.

48. James L. Gibson and Richard D. Bingham, *Civil Liberties and Nazis: The Skokie Free-Speech Controversy* (New York: Praeger, 1985), 604.

49. John Mueller, "Trends in Political Tolerance," *Public Opinion Quarterly* 52 (1988): 1–25; James A. Davis, "On the Seemingly Relentless Progress in Americans' Support for Free Expression, 1972–2006," in ed. Peter V. Marsden, *Social Trends in American Life: Findings from the General Social Survey since 1972* (Princeton, NJ: Princeton University Press, 2012), 19–37.

50. Georg Simmel, *Conflict,* trans. Kurt H. Wolff (New York: Free Press, 1964), 93;

51. Marc L. Hutchison and Douglas M. Gibler, "Political Tolerance and Territorial Threat: A Cross-National Study," *Journal of Politics* 69 (2007): 128–142.

52. Also see Mark Peffley and Robert Rohrschneider, "Democratization and Political Tolerance in Seventeen Countries: A Multi-level Model of Democratic Learning," *Political Research Quarterly* 56 (2003): 243–257.

53. A useful summary of some these findings can be found in John L. Sullivan, James Piereson, and George E. Marcus, *Political Tolerance and American Democracy* (Chicago: University of Chicago Press, 1982).

54. Linda Lyons, "The Gallup Brain: War and Peace Protests," Gallup, Mar. 25, 2003, http://www.gallup.com/poll/8053/Gallup-Brain-War-Peace-Protests.aspx (accessed 11/03/11). Before the invasion, however, there was more such support.

55. Jeffrey M. Jones, "Americans Felt Uneasy toward Arabs Even before Terrorist Attacks," Gallup, Sept. 28, 2001, http://www.gallup.com/poll/4939/Americans-Felt-Uneasy-Toward-Arabs-Even-Before-September.aspx (accessed 12/10/11).

7. Why Conservatives Care

1. Alan Brinkley, "The Problem of American Conservatism," *American Historical Review* 99 (1994): 409.

2. For a review, see Neil Gross, Thomas Medvetz, and Rupert Russell, "The Contemporary American Conservative Movement," *Annual Review of Sociology* 37 (2011): 325–354.

3. See John Gerring, *Party Ideologies in America, 1828–1996* (New York: Cambridge University Press, 2001). For Gerring, neomercantilism refers to

"a general economic philosophy mandating the subordination of economic activity to the interests of the state and nation" (65). Also see Michael Lind, *Land of Promise: An Economic History of the United States* (New York: Harper, 2012).

4. Lionel Trilling, in *The Liberal Imagination: Essays on Literature and Society* (New York: Viking Press, 1950), ix, famously observed, "In the United States at this time . . . there are no conservative or reactionary ideas in general circulation."

5. Nicol C. Rae, *The Decline and Fall of the Liberal Republicans: From 1952 to the Present,* revised ed. (New York: Oxford University Press, 1989); Geoffrey Kabaservice, *Rule and Ruin: The Downfall of Moderation and the Destruction of the Republican Party, from Eisenhower to the Tea Party* (New York: Oxford University Press, 2012). It is not as though conservatives held no power at the national level—many did in their roles as chairs of congressional committees—but they were often conservative Democrats from the South. See Eric Schickler, *Disjointed Pluralism: Institutional Innovation and the Development of the U.S. Congress* (Princeton, NJ: Princeton University Press, 2001). Thanks to Doug Ahler here.

6. Rick Perlstein, *Before the Storm: Barry Goldwater and the Unmaking of the American Consensus* (New York: Hill and Wang, 2001).

7. Thomas Ferguson and Joel Rogers, *Right Turn: the Decline of the Democrats and the Future of American Politics* (New York: Hill and Wang, 1986); David Vogel, *Fluctuating Fortunes: The Political Power of Business in America* (New York: Basic Books, 1989); William C. Berman, *America's Right Turn: From Nixon to Clinton* (Baltimore: Johns Hopkins University Press, 1998); Jacob S. Hacker and Paul Pierson, *Off Center: The Republican Revolution and the Erosion of American Democracy* (New Haven, CT: Yale University Press, 2006).

8. Bruce J. Schulman and Julian E. Zelizer, eds., *Rightward Bound: Making America Conservative in the 1970s* (Cambridge, MA: Harvard University Press, 2008).

9. Jonathan Rieder, "Rise of the 'Silent Majority,'" in *The Rise and Fall of the New Deal Order, 1930–80,* ed. Steve Fraser and Gary Gerstle (Princeton, NJ: Princeton University Press, 1989), 243–268; Thomas Byrne Edsall, *Chain Reaction: The Impact of Race, Rights, and Taxes on American Politics* (New York: Norton, 1992); Thomas J. Sugrue and John D. Skretny, "The White Ethnic Strategy," in Schulman and Zelizer, *Rightward Bound,* 171–192.

10. For alternative takes on the history of race and politics, see Anthony S. Chen, Robert W. Mickey, and Robert P. Van Houweling, "Explaining the Contemporary Alignment of Race and Party: Evidence from California's

1946 Ballot Initiative on Fair Employment," *Studies in American Political Development* 22 (2008): 204–228; Matthew D. Lassiter and Joseph Crespino, eds., *The Myth of Southern Exceptionalism* (New York: Oxford University Press, 2009).

11. Rebecca E. Klatch, *Women of the New Right* (Philadelphia: Temple University Press, 1987); Sara Diamond, *Not by Politics Alone: The Enduring Influence of the Christian Right* (New York: Guilford Press, 1998); Lisa McGirr, *Suburban Warriors: The Origins of the New American Right* (Princeton, NJ: Princeton University Press, 2001); Steven G. Brint and Jean Reith Schroedel, eds., *Evangelicals and Democracy in America,* vol. 2: *Religion and Politics* (New York: Russell Sage Foundation, 2009).

12. John A. Andrew III, *The Other Side of the Sixties: Young Americans for Freedom and the Rise of Conservative Politics* (New Brunswick, NJ: Rutgers University Press, 1997).

13. Steven M. Teles, "Conservative Mobilization against Entrenched Liberalism," in *The Transformation of American Politics: Activist Government and the Rise of Conservatism,* ed. Paul Pierson and Theda Skocpol (Princeton, NJ: Princeton University Press, 2007), 160–188; Steven M. Teles, *The Rise of the Conservative Legal Movement: The Battle for Control of the Law* (Princeton, NJ: Princeton University Press, 2008); Kim Phillips-Fein, *Invisible Hands: The Making of the Conservative Movement from the New Deal to Reagan* (New York: W. W. Norton, 2009); Thomas Medvetz, *Think Tanks in America* (Chicago: University of Chicago Press, 2012).

14. Ellen Schrecker, *The Lost Soul of Higher Education: Corporatization, the Assault on Academic Freedom, and the End of the American University* (New York: New Press, 2010), 101.

15. See Ellen Messer-Davidow, "Manufacturing the Attack on Liberalized Higher Education," *Social Text* 36 (1993): 40–80; Christopher Newfield, *Unmaking the Public University: The Forty-Year Assault on the Middle Class* (Cambridge, MA: Harvard University Press, 2008).

16. "Manufactured Controversy," http://cdn.publicinterestnetwork.org /assets/1VWEvg8YSPXfmG3nZL28TA/Manufactured-Controversy.pdf (accessed 5/18/12).

17. Ibid., 1.

18. Ibid., 11.

19. "Covert Operations," *New Yorker,* Aug. 30, 2010, 44–55; John Zmirak, ed., *Choosing the Right College 2012–13: The Whole Truth about America's Top Schools* (Wilmington, DE: ISI Books, 2011).

20. David Horowitz, *Reforming Our Universities: The Campaign for an Academic Bill of Rights* (Washington, DC: Regnery, 2010), 180–181.

21. Of course, conservative contention around these issues has often entailed a deep concern with education, particularly at the K–12 level. See Mitchell L. Stevens, *Kingdom of Children: Culture and Controversy in the Homeschooling Movement* (Princeton, NJ: Princeton University Press, 2001); Amy J. Binder, *Contentious Curricula: Afrocentrism and Creationism in American Public Schools* (Princeton, NJ: Princeton University Press, 2002); Jonathan Zimmerman, *Whose America? Culture Wars in the Public Schools* (Cambridge, MA: Harvard University Press, 2002).

22. Jesse Walker, "Chilling Effects," *Reason,* Sept. 17, 2003, http://reason.com/archives/2003/09/17/chilling-effects (accessed 1/11/12); "Academic Rights and Wrongs," *Wall Street Journal,* Oct. 7, 2005, W13.

23. It is possible, though, that this reflects disagreements about political tactics and style, as well as personal conflicts with Horowitz, more than disagreement about fundamental interests.

24. There is some independent evidence to confirm this. In 2007 and 2008, for example, the David Horowitz Freedom Center reported revenues of $6.3 and $5.4 million, respectively, on its IRS 990 forms. The website Media Matters reports that major conservative funders gave the organization $656,000 and $730,000 during those years. See http://mediamatters action.org/transparency/organization/David_Horowitz_Freedom_Center /funders?year=2007; http://mediamattersaction.org/transparency/organi zation/David_Horowitz_Freedom_Center/funders?year=2008 (accessed 6/5/12).

25. This is not surprising. A great deal of research by political sociologists points to fractures and divisions among elites, even those who may be on the same side of the political aisle. See Allan H. Barton, "Determinants of Economic Attitudes in the American Business Elite," *American Journal of Sociology* 91 (1985): 54–87; Doug McAdam, "Conceptual Origins, Current Problems, Future Directions," *Comparative Perspectives on Social Movements: Political Opportunities, Mobilizing Structures, and Cultural Framings,* ed. Doug McAdam, John D. McCarthy and Mayer N. Zald (Cambridge, UK: Cambridge University Press, 1996), 23–40; Sidney G. Tarrow, *Power in Movement: Social Movements and Contentious Politics* (Cambridge, UK: Cambridge University Press, 1998); Mark S. Mizruchi, "Power without Efficacy: The Decline of the American Corporate Elite," working paper, University of Michigan, 2007.

26. William F. Buckley Jr., "A Retired Colonel Takes on the Educationalists," *National Review,* July 13, 1957, 64.

27. *National Review,* Oct. 5 1957, 295.

28. Russell Kirk, "Defrauded College Students," *National Review,* Oct. 24, 1959, 428; Russell Kirk, *The Conservative Mind, from Burke to Santayana* (Chicago: Regnery, 1953).

29. Willmoore Kendall, "To Be or Not to be Time-in-Schooled?" *National Review,* Aug. 31, 1957, 63.

30. Allan Ryskind, "The Capture of Pomona College," *National Review,* Nov. 7, 1959, 471.

31. William F. Buckley Jr., "As the Left Goes, So Goes Harvard," *National Review,* Nov. 21, 1959, 487; William F. Buckley Jr., "At Harvard, Sir, We Do Not Fish for Souls, II," *National Review,* Jan. 30, 1960, 75.

32. Russell Kirk, "Little Academic Tyrants," *National Review,* July 14, 1964, 608.

33. Susan Buck, "Life among the Libs," *National Review,* Apr. 7, 1964, 275.

34. Will Herberg, "The New Estate: The Professors and the Teach Ins," *National Review,* July 13, 1965, 590.

35. David A. Horowitz, *America's Political Class under Fire: The Twentieth Century's Great Culture War* (New York: Routledge, 2003), 1.

36. Ibid., 166.

37. Gerard J. DeGroot, "Ronald Reagan and Student Unrest in California, 1966–1970," *Pacific Historical Review* 65 (1996): 107–129.

38. Ronald Reagan, Cow Palace speech, May 12, 1966, quoted in ibid., 111.

39. DeGroot, "Ronald Reagan and Student Unrest in California," 111.

40. Howard S. Becker, *Outsiders: Studies in the Sociology of Deviance* (New York: Free Press, 1991), 147. Contemporary scholars of social movements also emphasize the "passionate" nature of political commitment. Jeff Goodwin, James M. Jasper, and Francesca Polletta, eds., *Passionate Politics: Emotions and Social Movements* (Chicago: University of Chicago Press, 2001).

41. Paul Hollander, *Political Pilgrims: Travels of Western Intellectuals to the Soviet Union, China, and Cuba, 1928–1978* (New York: Oxford University Press, 1981).

42. Raymond Aron, *The Opium of the Intellectuals,* trans. Terence Kilmartin (Westport, CT: Greenwood Press, 1977).

43. The website Right Web, http://www.rightweb.irc-online.org/articles/display/Committee_for_the_Free_World, reports a $10,000 grant from the Smith Richardson Foundation to the organization in 1985, funneled through Dechter's Committee for the Free World (accessed 6/5/12).

44. This is not to deny that philanthropic foundations—liberal, conservative, and otherwise—can and do have programmatic goals and implement them. For a discussion of the "myth" that they do not, see Donald Fisher, "American Philanthropy and the Social Sciences: The Reproduction of a Conservative Ideology," in *Philanthropy and Cultural Imperialism: The Foundations at Home and Abroad,* ed. Robert F. Arnove (Boston: G. K. Hall, 1980), 253. They cannot implement such goals alone, however, and require willing partners.

45. Anne Neal of ACTA, an attorney by training, was the only conservative activist interviewed who did not fit this description.

46. William F. Buckley Jr. and L. Brent Bozell, *McCarthy and His Enemies: The Record and Its Meaning* (Chicago: Regnery, 1954); William S. White, "What the McCarthy Method Seeks to Establish," *New York Times,* Apr. 4, 1954.

47. Russell Kirk, "The Intercollegiate Society of Individualists," *National Review,* Oct. 9, 1962, 271.

48. Steven G. Brint, *In an Age of Experts: The Changing Role of Professionals in Politics and Public Life* (Princeton, NJ: Princeton University Press, 1994).

49. Even in the left-leaning social sciences, Wallace and socialist Norman Thomas together took only 8% of the professorial vote. Paul F. Lazarsfeld and Wagner Thielens Jr., *The Academic Mind: Social Scientists in a Time of Crisis* (Glencoe, IL: Free Press, 1958), 402.

50. My discussion here and in the paragraph that follows is greatly indebted to the work of my research assistant Julian Nemeth and draws on Edward L. Schapsmeier and Frederick H. Schapsmeier, *Prophet in Politics: Henry A. Wallace and the War Years, 1940–1965* (Ames, IA: Iowa State University Press, 1970); Allen Yarnell, *Democrats and Progressives: The 1948 Presidential Election as a Test of Postwar Liberalism* (Berkeley: University of California Press, 1974); Graham J. White and John R. Maze, *Henry A. Wallace: His Search for a New World Order* (Chapel Hill: University of North Carolina Press, 1995); John C. Culver and John Hyde, *American Dreamer: The Life and Times of Henry A. Wallace* (New York: Norton, 2000).

51. For discussion, see Clayborne Carson, *In Struggle: SNCC and the Black Awakening of the 1960s* (Cambridge: Harvard University Press, 1981); John Dittmer, *Local People: The Struggle for Civil Rights in Mississippi* (Urbana: University of Illinois Press, 1994); John P. Jackson Jr., *Social Scientists for Social Justice: Making the Case against Segregation* (New York: New York University Press, 2001); Ted Ownby, ed., The *Role of Ideas in the Civil Rights South: Essays* (Jackson: University Press of Mississippi, 2002).

52. See, for example, Jeffrey Peter Hart, *The Making of the American Conservative Mind: National Review and Its Times* (Wilmington, DE: ISI Books, 2005). There is some analytic danger in focusing too much on Buckley. Intellectuals are important to political movements—and Buckley more so than most—but their importance may also be exaggerated by movement members seeking to produce histories that identify clear ideational turning points. See David S. Meyer and Deana A. Rohlinger, "Big Books and Social Movements: A Myth of Ideas and Social Change," *Social Problems* 59 (2012): 136–153.

53. Jeffrey Alexander and Philip Smith, "The Strong Program in Cultural Theory: Elements of a Structural Hermeneutics," in *Handbook of Sociological Theory,* ed. Jonathan H. Turner (New York: Kluwer Academic/Plenum, 2001), 135–150; Jeffrey C. Alexander, *The Civil Sphere* (New York: Oxford University Press, 2006); Jeffrey C. Alexander, *The Performance of Politics: Obama's Victory and the Democratic Struggle for Power* (New York: Oxford University Press, 2010).

54. Robert S. Jansen, "Populist Mobilization: A New Theoretical Approach to Populism," *Sociological Theory* 29 (2011): 82.

55. The editors of *National Review* were aware of this from the start. For example, in a 1956 letter to Buckley, Frank Chodorov praised the most recent issue of the magazine in the following terms: "I was pleased by your piece on Mexico; you are getting rid of literary sophistication (eggheadism?) and writing in idiomatic English. . . . Willi [Schlamm?] confirmed my suspicion that NR is directed at the elite (which puts a limit on your circulation)." Frank Chodorov to William Buckley Jr., Dec. 21, 1956, William F. Buckley Jr. Papers, Manuscript Group 576, Box 1, Yale University. Laying the groundwork for a mass movement became more important as the 1960s wore on and as *National Review* sought to exert more influence on the Republican Party—for example, by heavily backing (and helping to orchestrate) the nomination of Goldwater.

56. Julian Nemeth makes this point explicitly about *God and Man and Yale:* "Buckley serenely vacillates between elitism and populism, libertarianism and traditionalism, absolutism and relativism. Whether consciously or not, Buckley wrote as if he agreed with Emerson's dictum, 'a foolish consistency is the hobgoblin of small minds.'" See his discussion of academic freedom debates in the 1950s: Julian Tzara Nemeth, "A Central Issue of Our Time: Academic Freedom in Postwar American Thought," MA thesis, Ohio University, 2007, 42. Carl T. Bogus takes a somewhat different view: "Buckley had famously said that he would 'sooner be governed

by the first two thousand people in the Boston telephone directory, than by the two thousand members of the faculty of Harvard University.' This was a clever put-down of what Buckley denounced as the 'intellectual elite.' The problem was that Buckley was not a populist. A good part of him wanted an elite group to govern America; he just wanted it to be a conservative elite rather than the then-dominant liberal elite." See his *Buckley: William F. Buckley Jr. and the Rise of American Conservatism* (New York: Bloomsbury Press, 2011), 3. Michael Kazin takes this position as well, arguing that Buckley, and with him Young Americans for Freedom, "articulated a gentlemanly conservatism" and "us[ed] an elitist idiom to combat the liberal elite." See his *The Populist Persuasion: An American History* (Ithaca, NY: Cornell University Press, 1998), 226. My reading of *National Review* is that, at least in its commentary on the professoriate, anti-elitist rhetoric—though not of the more folksy George Wallace variety, which Buckley rejected—was common and could be even be found, as the passages cited earlier suggest, in the writings of the traditionalist Kirk.

57. In reading through some of Buckley's correspondence in the Yale archives, I found many instances of his being strategic when it came to language use but little discussion of how the magazine's authors should go about characterizing academicians. One example of rhetorical strategy can be found in a 1960 letter from Buckley to Victor Milione, head of the ISI, which was at that point called the Intercollegiate Society of Individualists. Buckley proposed that the ISI change its name, arguing that "individualist" had become a clunky term:

> Although I was the first president of I.S.I., he [Frank Chodorov] was the boss and it is to his credit that the organization flourished. I was then in sympathy with the idea of trying to fashion a word with a meaning more precise than "conservative," although even then some of the solipsistic overtones of the term "individualism" did upset me. In the years that have gone by since then, the term "conservative" has arisen to characterize us, and there is nothing in the world we can do to shake it off, even assuming we should wish to. . . . I am very much persuaded of something, which of course is not new, namely, that in a subtle way college students are extremely status conscious in their relationship with the organizations and institutions to which they pay allegiance. They cannot bear to be laughed at. The tide, I think, is in many respects turning in our favor, but we can certainly move to make easier the way of Damascus in such matters as we can. So long as there is a spontaneous feeling that the term "individualist" is sort of a queer-term, we have a much more difficult time negotiating our

movement. (William F. Buckley Jr. to Victor Milione, Sept. 1, 1960, William F. Buckley Papers, Manuscript Group 576, Box 10, Yale University Library)

58. John Gerring presents evidence that Republican anti-elitist rhetoric actually dates to the 1920s and 1930s. See *Party Ideologies in America, 1828–1996* (New York: Cambridge University Press, 2001), 142–151. As the quotation from Rogin in Chapter 6 illustrates, anti-elitist ideas were clearly part of McCarthy's rhetorical arsenal. On the emergence of a broader anti-elitist rhetoric in the postwar period that targeted New Deal statism, see David A. Horowitz, *Beyond Left and Right: Insurgency and the Establishment* (Urbana: University of Illinois Press, 1996), 214–238. The best source on this, however, is Kazin's *The Populist Persuasion,* which charts the process by which, "in the late 1940s, populism began a migration from Left to Right" (4). Buckley's contribution was to hone and elaborate these themes with special reference to the professoriate, making anti-intellectualism of a sort and attacks on the liberal elite seem more reasonable and less paranoiac than when served up by McCarthy or, later, figures like Wallace. To the extent that this is so, there is more continuity between *National Review's* "responsible" conservatism and the populist conservatism of today than is usually recognized, notwithstanding some issue differences.

59. Robert Jansen, unpublished manuscript, University of Michigan, 2011.

60. A more Machiavellian version of this argument can be found in Geoffrey Nunberg, *Talking Right: How Conservatives Turned Liberalism into a Tax-Raising, Latte-Drinking, Sushi-Eating, Volvo-Driving,* New York Times–*Reading, Body-Piercing, Hollywood-Loving, Left-Wing Freak Show* (New York: Public Affairs, 2006), 85–104. Another factor possibly in the background here is the steeply hierarchical nature of the American higher education system, which was becoming solidified in the postwar period. That it was easy to identify the elite institutions in the system may have made attacks on the intellectual elite more viable. For a comparison of the hierarchical American system to the flatter Canadian one, see Scott Davies and David Zarifa, "The Stratification of Universities: Structural Inequality in Canadian and American Higher Education," *Research in Social Stratification and Mobility* 30 (2012): 143–158. Thanks to Neil McLaughlin for bringing this to my attention.

61. Andrew Jewett, "Naturalizing Liberalism in the 1950s," unpublished manuscript, Harvard University, 2011. For related discussion, see David Paul Haney, *The Americanization of Social Science: Intellectuals and Public Responsibility in the Postwar United States* (Philadelphia: Temple University Press, 2008), 88–121.

62. Criticism of the professoriate also figured prominently in Buckley's second book: William F. Buckley Jr., *Up from Liberalism* (New York: Mc-Dowell, Obolensky, 1959).

63. Charles Tilly, *Popular Contention in Great Britain, 1758–1834* (Cambridge, MA: Harvard University Press, 1995), 5.

64. I draw directly here on a piece I wrote about Tilly, stressing his similarity to scholars influenced by pragmatism who also emphasize the emergence of new habits and routines out of experimentation. Neil Gross, "Charles Tilly and American Pragmatism," *American Sociologist* 41 (2010): 337–357.

65. This may explain why "Kirk's column ['From the Academy'] was to become one of the magazine's most popular features and continue in the same vein for twenty-five years, outlasting every one of the other original columns" (Bogus, *Buckley,* 144).

66. Gregory L. Schneider, *Cadres for Conservatism: Young Americans for Freedom and the Rise of the Contemporary Right* (New York: New York University Press, 1999), 112.

67. Jennifer de Forest, "The Rise of Conservatism on Campus," *Change* 38 (Mar./Apr. 2006): 33.

68. John J. Miller, "Michael S. Joyce, R.I.P.: The Legacy of a Conservative Philanthropist," *National Review,* Feb. 27, 2006, http://old.nationalreview .com/miller/miller200602270759.asp (accessed 01/11/12).

69. For review, see Debra C. Minkoff, "Macro-Organizational Analysis," in *Methods of Social Movement Research,* ed. Bert Klandermans and Suzanne Staggenborg (Minneapolis: University of Minnesota Press, 2002), 260–285.

70. For discussion, see Medvetz, *Think Tanks in America,* esp. 124–129.

71. Paul Pierson and Theda Skocpol, eds., *The Transformation of American Politics: Activist Government and the Rise of Conservatism* (Princeton, NJ: Princeton University Press, 2007).

72. In a piece about North Carolina multimillionaire James Arthur Pope, whose foundations fund the Pope Center for Higher Education Policy, Jane Mayer suggests that Pope, who majored in political science at the University of North Carolina, was influenced by his father, a university trustee who "believed [UNC] had been taken over by radical scholars." Jane Mayer, "State for Sale," *New Yorker,* October 10, 2011, 90.

73. While focusing most of their attention on the professoriate, people like Horowitz and Pipes have also been involved in other strands of conservative activism. For example, both have been vigorous in their defense of Israel and opposition to "Islamo-fascism."

74. One important organization that does not fit this bill is the Foundation for Individual Rights in Education, which focuses on academic freedom

issues and has been particularly concerned to combat campus speech codes. It is primarily a free speech organization; its leadership and staff include liberals and conservatives.

75. A parallel claim about the limits of sociodemographic explanations for Tea Party support is made in Theda Skocpol and Vanessa Williamson, *The Tea Party and the Remaking of Republican Conservatism* (New York: Oxford University Press, 2012).

76. Mark's memory here is faulty. Horowitz did confront angry crowds on campus, but not, he told me, during his speech at Boston College.

77. Some examples: "I've seen some students come out crying because . . . the professor dressed them down and made fools of them in class because they expressed an opinion, a valid opposing opinion or question. They questioned a professor's assertion and that's not right" (82 year old male retiree, Colorado); "To me the professors that I . . . dealt with are set in what they believe and usually they stick with that. They have their views and some of them don't want to listen to somebody else's view" (58 year old female child care worker, Colorado); "I don't know but my experience with professors at an undergraduate level, very often . . . if you challenge something they tend to get slightly defensive like I am the expert and you are the student so just take it for what I say" (33 year old male financial advisor, Colorado); "I've never been able to conduct my own poll but the ones that you see on TV—these guys are bright guys especially in biology, anthropology, and things like that. A lot of them . . . very proudly pronounce that. I wouldn't have any problem with that per se except . . . the attitude that I feel that they're conveying is that if you're not an atheist, you're kind of unwashed and a dolt" (57 year old self-employed male, Colorado); "My one daughter went to the University of Madison and a lot of her professors were very liberal. When it came to certain things they had their way of thinking and they looked down upon anybody who thought differently" (54 year old male tree service worker, Wisconsin).

78. Differences in means on these variables between the two groups ranged from about 0.1 to about 0.3 on a confidence scale ranging from 1 to 3.

79. See "Colleges Viewed Positively, but Conservatives Express Doubts," Pew Research Center for the People and the Press, Mar. 1, 2012, http://www.people-press.org/2012/03/01/colleges-viewed-positively-but-conservatives-express-doubts/ (accessed 5/30/12).

80. My thinking on this point has been influenced by Jonathan Rieder, *Canarsie: The Jews and Italians of Brooklyn against Liberalism* (Cambridge, MA:

Harvard University Press, 1987); Michèle Lamont, *The Dignity of Working Men: Morality and the Boundaries of Race, Class, and Immigration* (Cambridge, MA: Harvard University Press, 2000); and especially by Christian Smith's "subcultural identity theory" of religious change in *American Evangelicalism: Embattled and Thriving* (Chicago: University of Chicago Press, 1998). Subcultural identity theory is pushed in a political direction in Lydia Bean, Marco Gonzalez, and Jason Kaufman, "Why Doesn't Canada Have an American-Style Christian Right? A Comparative Framework for Analyzing the Political Effects of Evangelical Subcultural Identity," *Canadian Journal of Sociology* 33 (2008): 899–943.

81. It is also likely that conservative attacks on the professoriate and science have bolstered the right's reputation for anti-intellectualism, contributing to whatever professorial animosity may exist.

82. Anthony Downs, "Up and down with Ecology—The 'Issue-Attention Cycle,'" *Public Interest* 28 (1972): 39.

83. Also see the analysis of "policy windows" in John W. Kingdon, *Agendas, Alternatives, and Public Policies* (New York: Longman, 2003). Social movement scholars likewise see political opportunities as fleeting.

84. "ASA Officers Respond to Attacks on Frances Fox Piven," American Sociological Association, Jan. 24, 2011, http://www.asanet.org/press/asa_presidents_respond_to_attacks_on_piven.cfm (accessed 11/04/11).

Conclusion

1. Mitchell L. Stevens, Elizabeth A. Armstrong, and Richard Arum, "Sieve, Incubator, Temple, Hub: Empirical and Theoretical Advances in the Sociology of Higher Education," *Annual Review of Sociology* 34 (2008): 127–151.

2. Douglas S. Massey, *Categorically Unequal: The American Stratification System* (New York: Russell Sage Foundation, 2007).

3. An intriguing effort along these lines is Christopher P. Loss, *Between Citizens and the State: The Politics of American Higher Education in the 20th Century* (Princeton, NJ: Princeton University Press, 2011).

4. Erik Wright, "Intellectuals and the Class Structure of Capitalist Societies," in *Between Labor and Capital,* ed. Pat Walker (Boston: South End Press, 1979), 191–212; Robert J. Brym, *Intellectuals and Politics* (London: Allen & Unwin, 1980); Jerome Karabel, "Towards a Theory of Intellectuals and Politics," *Theory & Society* 25 (1996): 205–233.

5. Ronald Inglehart as well as Kim Weeden and David Grusky do consider processes of political self-selection, but not with reference to political

typing specifically. See Ronald Inglehart, *Culture Shift in Advanced Industrial Society* (Princeton, NJ: Princeton University Press, 1990); Kim A. Weeden and David B. Grusky, "The Case for a New Class Map," *American Journal of Sociology* 111 (2005): 141–212. There is also a small body of work on how political activism shapes subsequent career choices. See, for example, Darren E. Sherkat and T. Jean Blocker, "Explaining the Political and Personal Consequences of Protest," *Social Forces* 75 (1997): 1049–1070.

6. Survey data from other sources suggest that officers are more conservative than enlisted personnel, likely reflecting differences in class and racial background as well in the salience of political identity in driving the decision to pursue a military career. Jason K. Dempsey, *Our Army: Soldiers, Politics, and American Civil-Military Relations* (Princeton, NJ: Princeton University Press, 2010).

7. Lipset was led, partly by his studies of professors, to conclude that in the post–World War II period voting was no longer as tied to class as it once had been. But it does not necessarily follow that class voting is in decline generally simply because there is evidence that select occupational groups are not voting in line with their apparent class interests. Indeed the theory of political typing offers one way to make sense of such anomalous tendencies. See Terry Nichols Clark and Seymour Martin Lipset, "Are Social Classes Dying?," *International Sociology* 6 (1991): 397–410.

8. See Mario Luis Small, David J. Harding, and Michèle Lamont, "Reconsidering Culture and Poverty," *Annals of the American Academy of Political and Social Science* 629 (2010): 6–27.

9. See, for example, the essays in Alan Sica and Stephen Turner, eds., *The Disobedient Generation: Social Theorists in the Sixties* (Chicago: University of Chicago Press, 2005).

10. One major exception to this claim is Steven M. Teles, *The Rise of the Conservative Legal Movement: The Battle for Control of the Law* (Princeton, NJ: Princeton University Press, 2008). The dominant trend in the sociology of knowledge recently has been to argue that politics has only an indirect effect on knowledge production, shaping the contours of intellectual fields in which thinkers make moves according to a strictly intellectual logic, doing so mostly to enhance their own social standing relative to other intellectuals. For a critique of this trend on the grounds that it ignores the political see Patrick Baert, "Introduction to the Special Section on Intellectuals and Politics," *European Journal of Social Theory* 14 (2011): 409–413.

11. An interesting way into this issue, as the culture and poverty example suggests, is to consider how academics' political commitments may affect

their willingness to abandon cherished theories or interpretations given disconfirming data. The psychological literature on motivated reasoning is relevant. See Ziva Kunda, "The Case for Motivated Reasoning," *Psychological Bulletin* 108 (1990): 480–498.

12. Some of these findings are discussed in Bill Bishop, *The Big Sort: Why the Clustering of Like-Minded America Is Tearing Us Apart* (Boston: Houghton Mifflin, 2008).

13. Jonathan R. Cole, *The Great American University: Its Rise to Preeminence, Its Indispensable National Role, Why It Must Be Protected* (New York: Public Affairs, 2009).

Acknowledgments

Some of my favorite sociology books have been artisanal efforts undertaken by lone researchers ensconced for years in the archives or living day in and day out among the people and groups they profile, a few tattered ethnographies brought with them into the field their only sociological companions. This is not such a book. It would have been impossible to make headway with the questions I take up without the cooperation of a small army of collaborators and research assistants.

My collaborators on the studies and papers from which I draw include some of the smartest young sociologists that I know: Catherine Cheng, Ethan Fosse, Jeremy Freese, Scott Frickel, Joseph Ma, Tom Medvetz, Rupert Russell, Solon Simmons, and Jeremy Uecker. At every turn their thinking has informed mine, and I have been the beneficiary of their theoretical and methodological savvy, erudition, and good sense.

For outstanding research assistance on various phases of the project, I thank Doug Ahler, Colin Campbell, Anujit Chakrabarti, Chris Chiego, Frederic Clark, Jeff Denis, Jake Fisher, Stephen Goggin, Dana Grayson, Patrick Hamm, Xiaoshuo Hou, Ce Huang, Tamara Ibrahim, Andrew Le, Emily Levy, Laura MacDonald, Julian Nemeth, Alina Shepherd, Michelle Steward, Helen Sung, Nicholas Tabor, and Joanne Wong. I owe a special debt to Rebecca Dickson, who has worked with me since my arrival in Vancouver and whose analytical skills and keen eye for detail have been invaluable.

Large-scale social science also requires resources. For their financial support I wish to acknowledge the Richard Lounsbery Foundation, the Spencer Foundation, Harvard University, and the University of British Columbia. Jesse Ausubel, Roger Bowen, Neil Guppy, Darrin Lehman, Louis Menand, and Maxmillian Angerholzer III facilitated grant getting. Thank you.

John Kennedy and his team at the Center for Survey Research at Indiana University did a first-rate job administering the Politics of the American Professoriate survey and conducting interviews with members of the public in Colorado and Wisconsin. For their help with the Attitudes toward the American Professoriate poll, thanks are due to Kristen Purcell and her colleagues at Princeton Survey Research Associates International, and to the staff at the American Association of University Professors, especially John Curtis.

Too many people offered suggestions for improving the empirical studies discussed in the book for me to list them all. They know who they are and that the studies—and the book—are better for their good ideas. Peter Baehr, Christopher Bail, David Bills, Amy Binder, Charles Camic, Gary Fine, Roger Geiger, Julian Go, Jonathan Imber, Robert Jansen, Andrew Jewett, Michèle Lamont, Neil McLaughlin, Andrew Perrin, Ellen Schrecker, Bruce Schulman, Solon Simmons, Mitchell Stevens, David Swartz, and Christopher Winship took the time to read and comment on the manuscript. Their insightful suggestions strengthened it and helped me avoid missteps. Thanks are due as well to the many individuals who participated in the project as research subjects.

At Harvard University Press, Elizabeth Knoll helped me see what was wrong with previous drafts of the manuscript and pushed me line by line to make it better, more readable, less pedantic. She cannot be blamed for any academese that remains. Three anonymous reviewers provided very useful feedback.

Finally, I would like to express my profound appreciation (and love!) for my wife, Jessica Berger Gross. Without her writerly know-how, passion for politics, patience, and inspiration—and without the countless hours she put in caring so amazingly well for our son, Lucien—this book would never have come together.

Table 4.1 is from Jack H. Schuster and Martin J. Finkelstein, *The American Faculty: The Restructuring of Academic Work and Careers* (Baltimore: Johns Hopkins University Press, 2006), 505, Table A-5.17. © 2006 The

Johns Hopkins University Press. Reprinted with permission of The Johns Hopkins University Press.

A significant portion of Chapter 5 appeared previously in Neil Gross, "American Academe and the Knowledge-Politics Problem," in *The American Academic Profession: Transformation in Higher Education,* ed. Joseph C. Hermanowicz (Baltimore: Johns Hopkins University Press, 2011), 111–130. © 2011 The Johns Hopkins University Press. Revised with permission of The Johns Hopkins University Press.

Index